A NEW
DYNAMIC 2
EFFECTIVE
SYSTEMS IN
A CIRCULAR
ECONOMY

D1291941

Edited by
Ellen MacArthur Foundation

Ellen MacArthur Foundation
The Sail Loft
42 Medina Road
Cowes
Isle of Wight
PO31 7BX
United Kingdom

www.ellenmacarthurfoundation.org

Copyright

First edition
Ellen MacArthur Foundation Publishing

A catalogue record for this book is
available from the British Library.

Edited by Ken Webster, Craig Johnson,
Joss Blériot and Lena Gravis

Designed by Graham Pritchard.
Copy editing by Caroline Walker and Ruth Sheppard

Total pages: 210 excluding cover

FOREWORD
COMPLEX SYSTEMS AND CIRCULAR ECONOMY

The world in which we live can be characterised by its extreme complexity and the exponential rate at which it evolves.

Politicians and industrialists are confronted with the necessity to act on complex systems to enable society, or their companies, to make progress in the right direction. But their decision-making process is based on an antiquated method. It uses a linear, analytical, and Cartesian approach, through which they try to simplify complexity into separate elements in order to control the relationship between cause and effect.

The evolving world is composed of interrelated networks, creating a dynamic interdependence between elements integrated into a whole. New properties emerge from the system's constitutive elements that cannot be predicted.

The analytic method's primary disadvantage is its incapacity to evaluate the impact of interconnections between different fields or disciplines, and therefore the particularities of the emerging properties.

While it was essential to the foundation of science, the analytic approach is no longer appropriate to explain the dynamics and evolution of complex systems, feedback, equilibrium, increasing diversity, or self-organisation.

Similarly, governments have traditionally approached developmental and environmental issues in a sectorial and compartmentalised way. The concept of sustainability is much broader than the word itself implies. For me, it means *re-investment in the eco-capital*, through money, time, energy, and knowledge. Because the industrial system is an ecosystem, like natural ecosystems, it can be described as a flow of materials, energy, and information through nodes, links, and networks. Furthermore, the entire industrial system relies on the biosphere's resources and services, from which it cannot be disconnected.

As Suren Erkman expresses it: 'industrial ecology aims at looking at the industrial system as a whole. It does not address just issues of pollution and environment, but considers as equally important, technologies, process economics, inter-relationships of businesses, financing, overall government policy and the entire spectrum of issues that are involved in the management of commercial enterprises'. Besides the conceptual framework of scientific ecology, industrial ecology can also be seen as a practical approach to sustainability and has a role to play in the building of a regenerative economy.

What we need is a new culture of complexity, employing systems thinking rather than the traditional analytical and sequential extrapolation. The authors of *A New Dynamic: Effective Systems in a Circular Economy* emphasise this fundamental culture.

This important book, a typical product of the values advocated by the Ellen MacArthur Foundation, underlines the complementary approach of a group of specialists in architecture, agriculture, business models, social engineering, energy analysis, and city planning, to help understand complex systems and make decisions about the best way to transform them to evolve in the right direction.

The circular economy represents a path that could provide concrete solutions for the future governance of complex systems, as shown and demonstrated in this book. It explores practically important concepts including 'regenerative design', remanufacturing, designing ecosystem models, energy efficiency in buildings or in the food system, chaotic self-organising systems, and the millennials' generation culture for the sharing economy.

This universal systems approach makes us understand that humanity is now participating in the creation of a huge living organism the size of the planet. We are its cells and it has a global metabolism and a neuron-like communication network – the digital ecosystem.

The Copernican revolution allowed humanity to step out of its confining *geocentrism*. This was the birth of the first paradigm. The Cartesian revolution made the universe accessible through reason. This constituted the second paradigm. The Darwinian revolution put human beings fully back into nature, freeing them from *anthropocentrism*. This was the basis of the third paradigm. Today's systemic revolution has reintegrated knowledge into a coherent whole and given humanity back its role in the universe. It characterises the fourth paradigm.

The fifth paradigm is in the process of coming into existence. The sciences of complexity give rise to a unified approach of organisations and time, leading to individual and collective human action. Technology and art, the artificial and the natural, culture and civilisation, are now joined together in a coherent whole. The future belongs to human societies living in symbiosis with their ecosystems, both natural and digital.

The design and planning of a global macro-organism for the benefit of humanity, through improved knowledge of natural laws, will be the new horizon for humanity in the new millennium. This book provides an eloquent and clever path to hope.

Joël de Rosnay
Ph.D - Special Advisor to the President of Universcience,
CEO of Biotics International

INTRODUCTION

Somewhere between *Strategy for an ever-changing landscape* and *Making sense of complexity* lies the perfect title for a definitive textbook of the world in the 21st century - should anyone ever bother to write it. Caught in the crossfire of emerging economic forces, reality-defying technologies and an increasingly maladapted interpretative framework, society is gradually coming to terms with the idea of its own metamorphosis.

This transformation can be difficult to reconcile with everyday perception. How can a tipping point that seems to stretch over years be construed as anything more than a gradual change? In a media-saturated world that uses terms such as revolution of paradigm shift as purely conversational artefacts, keeping a balanced sense of scale is somewhat challenging. Yet it seems that, intuitively at least, the notion of something huge happening is becoming part of our collective consciousness.

With this comes the need to understand its nature. The first edition of our *New Dynamic* series focused on the economic applications of a more metabolic - as opposed to mechanistic – worldview. This new volume goes beyond business models to hint at further-reaching implications of applying the circular mindset - because therein resides the real enabler. Profound transformation is only marginally technology-related: most of it has to do with the way we look at the world, which in turn shapes what we wish to make of it. By revealing the sophistication and hyper-connectivity of the systems we encounter on a daily basis, the following chapters all acknowledge the necessity of adopting big picture thinking as the default position.

Granted, Dirk Helbing's article on self-regulating traffic light management might not have a lot to do with circularity per se, but challenging our own tendency to make quick and reductive associations is useful in itself. Highlighting the complex dynamics of flows does in fact help us picture the economy as a perpetual movement of people, capital, energy and materials – a concept less than evident in classical economic theory, where levers are pulled and predictable things happen. And on the subject of misconception, isn't it strange that Hunter Lovins's *Circular economy of soil* comes across as radical, when in fact it states basic biological facts? We have somehow internalised a very recent notion – that of industrial agriculture – and seem unable to look beyond it. Lovins' chapter finds a pragmatic echo in Stuchtey & Rossé's *Towards a regenerative food system,* and both texts join forces to challenge a skewed yet widely accepted view.

Changing the lens through which we observe systems also has important implications when we consider the much-discussed and crucial topic of cities: though appearing to epitomise modernity, they in fact owe their basic conception to the Neolithic revolution. By highlighting the discrepancy between cities' relative structural immobility and the image of fast-paced progress we associate them with, Michael Batty opens a window on their potential future and highlights the possibility of an opportune rethink. An approach complemented, at a more granular level, by Michael Pawlyn's vision of a biomimetic architecture, relying on insights from living systems.

Such examples abound in all eleven chapters of *Effective systems in a circular economy,* which aims to provide a new and enticing perspective on a world whose dominant operating system can be reinvented. The impending tidal wave of transformation requires a cognitive guide as much as it does a technical one

Joss Blériot.
Executive Officer
Ellen MacArthur Foundation

CIRCULAR BUSINESS OPPORTUNITIES FOR THE BUILT ENVIRONMENT

Ellen Franconi, Brett Bridgeland and Marissa Yao

1

Buildings serve as homes and workplaces, providing us with shelter and protecting us from external environment, and as a result we spend the majority of our time in them. But our behaviours regarding the way we use buildings, or more importantly, the way we design them often fails to take a whole-systems approach. There are now however, numerous examples in the building sector of companies taking an innovative approach and designing in material and energy productivity solutions. Using some of the most emblematic international case studies, this chapter illustrates how circular economy thinking faces multiple challenges but makes good business sense and that alternative solution concepts in the building sector are increasingly possible.

Ellen Franconi
Ellen Franconi, PhD Building Systems Engineering, is a Manager at Rocky Mountain Institute (RMI) in Boulder, Colorado. Her work embraces integrated design principles and utilises building performance modeling and meter-based savings verification to demonstrate the business case for efficiency investment.

Brett Bridgeland
Brett is a registered Architect and Senior Associate at RMI. His work on energy efficient, smart buildings ranges from energy modeling of individual buildings, to district and city-scale energy strategy, to macro-scale analysis of energy savings by the entire Chinese building sector.

Marissa Yao
At SunPower, Marissa Yao works on various programmes ranging from Circular Economy to Life Cycle Assessments to social enterprise. Marissa is part of a team focused on obtaining Zero Waste to Landfill, Cradle to Cradle and LEED certifications for all of Sunpower's panel assembly sites around the world.

Buildings represent an important energy end-use sector worldwide. Buildings use more primary energy than any other sector in the world and account for nearly 40 percent of primary energy consumption.[1] Buildings serve as our homes, work places, and community centres. Buildings shield us from the elements and shape our lives. We spend the majority of our time inside them – turning on lights, powering up electronics, and maintaining thermal comfort. But too frequently, our behaviour regarding buildings includes tearing down relatively new ones, quickly constructing others, and failing to take a whole-systems approach in their design, products, and services. This creates some of the very things we use buildings to protect ourselves against: namely air pollution, environmental degradation, and extreme weather events.

The consultants McKinsey and Company identified building operational efficiency as the number one global resource savings opportunity, placing its value at USD 696 billion (US 2010 dollars), assuming only cost-effective technologies installed.[2] This enormous savings potential does not even take into account natural resource savings associated with efficient use of materials in building construction, fitting out the interior, IT systems and equipment. Eliminating waste from buildings by minimising material use and operational energy consumption to the maximum extent possible promises cost savings and reduced risk from fossil-fuel cost volatility. Entrepreneurs have much to gain from capitalising on this opportunity to reduce resource waste associated with the built environment. Those that embrace an innovative, circular approach can further benefit from increasing material productivity and its economic value creation.

Buildings encompass a wide scope of potential business offerings involving their design, construction, equipment, products, supplies, operation, and maintenance. A simple framework is proposed to assess the circularity of business models for their products and services. Illustrated in Figure 1, the framework is rooted in several fundamental principles associated with a circular economy, which are listed below.[3]

1. The fossil fuel and natural resources expended to handle logistics, manufacturing/maintenance/refurbishment/reuse/recycling, and operation are justified based on the economic value that the business produces.
2. The business model accounts for and benefits from valuing the fossil fuel and other natural resources consumed.
3. The model includes a feedback loop to evaluate and improve this benefit.

Figure 1 **Circular business models take into account resource use and service value over lifetime**

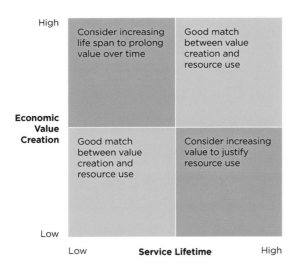

Notes: 1) 2x2 chart assumes fossil and natural resources use increases with increased lifetime or value
2) Chart content inspired by *Products That Last – product design for circular business models*

Three key factors for circular business models are indicated in the chart, namely: resource use, service lifetime, and economic value creation. The chart indicates a 'good match' between service life and value creation for products that fall within the two yellow diagonal squares. For example, it makes good business sense to produce consumables using biological solutions since the materials utilised serve a short-lived function. It also makes good business sense to create durable products using technical solutions to serve long-term needs. And it makes even better business sense for durable products to be adaptable or easily refurbished so they can provide ongoing, high economic value over their lifespan.

In the chapter sections that follow, the framework is applied to compare variations in business models that address the needs of buildings across different phases of their life cycle, namely: 1) design, 2) construction, and 3) fit-out with equipment and products. Through a progression of steps, shifts in needs that support alternative business models are suggested to improve circularity. Case studies illustrate the successes and challenges of real-world applications.

Energy-efficient building design

As revealed through the 2010 McKinsey study,[4] we routinely waste vast amounts of fossil fuels in powering and conditioning our buildings. While addressing worldwide building efficiency issues is a challenge, it also presents a business opportunity. Proven by experience, we know that engineers and architects can achieve radical resource efficiency and save their clients money by leveraging whole-system design principles – like Rocky Mountain Institute's Factor Ten Engineering Design (10xE) initiative.[5] The 10xE methods are pertinent across a wide range of applications. While a 10-fold reduction in energy consumption might not be achieved in every case, 2- to 3-fold reductions are not uncommon. Key concepts for achieving radical efficiency improvements for buildings are encapsulated in the following principles, extracted from the 17 comprising 10xE.

1. Reward desired outcomes – Smart reward structures encourage risk-taking in design, creativity, and teamwork, as well as practical well-managed solutions produced on schedule and on budget. New 'integrated project delivery' techniques and 'managed energy service agreements' directly align incentives with beneficiaries to lower fuel use, operating costs, construction times, and risks.

2. Define the end use – Understand what you are really trying to accomplish and why. The practice reveals how to do the right steps in the right order. For buildings, this means critically examining comfort criteria and light-level requirements, minimising building loads through a high-performance envelope and passive strategies, and right-sizing energy-using systems and equipment.

3. Tunnel through the cost barrier – Conventional designs produce incremental efficiency solutions, until the gains no longer repay the costs. Much larger savings can often be justified through an integrative design approach – potentially making very large savings cost less than small savings by eliminating, simplifying, or downsizing systems.

4. Include feedback in the design – Transform dumb systems into intelligent ones by incorporating feedback loops to inform current and ongoing performance. Monitor and possibly graphically display data, trigger timely maintenance and replacements, and incorporate lessons learned to improve future operation.

Figure 2 illustrates the application of these principles and their potential for improving the circularity of building operational efficiency. Step one involves reducing fossil fuel use by operating an existing building as efficiently as possible. This can be accomplished by maintaining building systems, automating equipment on/off scheduling, and developing an energy management plan. Step two involves retrofitting the building and incorporating efficiency upgrades into capital improvement projects. The building retrofit follows an integrative design process, which reduces loads and downsizes systems to save in operating expenses, and possibly capital costs. Incorporating passive strategies and upgrading equipment expends additional natural resources but it adds economic value and saves fossil fuels use over time. In step three, the retrofit cost is offset by operational savings through a managed energy service agreement (ESA). With this approach, incentives are aligned with desired outcomes. The investor/developer is motivated to follow a whole-systems thinking process to drive design innovations and maximise profit. In addition, an attentive vigilance to its operation will follow – further ensuring the ongoing operational efficiency of the building.

Figure 2 **Building design and operation: steps towards increasing resource productivity**

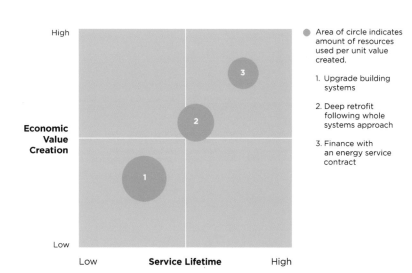

Case study: Empire State Building Deep Retrofit
The retrofit of the New York City historic skyscraper, the Empire State Building (ESB), in 2010 was an innovative undertaking. It included the on-site remanufacturing of its 6,514 windows into super-windows. Cutting winter heat loss by at least two-thirds and summer heat gain by half, the advanced glazing, along with improved lighting and office equipment will cut the building's peak cooling load by one-third. The load reduction allowed the renovation of the old chiller plant, which was slated for replacement and expansion – saving more than USD 17 million in budgeted capital expenditure. The savings help pay for other efficiency improvements and cut the overall incremental simple payback for energy retrofit to three years. The achieved 38% energy savings are several times the savings commonly achieved from a typical retrofit. Additional details about the project are provided below.[6]

Table 1 **ESB Deep Retrofit Project Overview**

Project Overview	Project Highlights
• Building size 2,700,000 sq. ft • Total retrofit cost of USD 550 million • Energy related cost USD 106 million • Incremental capital cost USD 13.2 million • Annual energy use 88 kBtu/sq ft pre-retrofit; 60 kBtu/sq ft projected • Estimated energy savings of 38% or USD 4.4 million annually • Three-year simple payback	• Deep retrofit eliminated need to expand chiller plant, saving USD 17 million • 6,514 windows remanufactured on site • Partially financed with an energy service performance contract (ESPC) • 2014 savings based on partial implementation verified at USD 2.8 million – exceeding performance guarantee by 16%

The project

The project prompted cascading energy savings from several efficiency measures, including: rebuilding the windows with improved solar heat gain coefficient and insulation R-value, radiant heat-loss barriers on exterior-wall heating units, improved daylighting from plenum height reductions that exposed full window area, constant-volume air distribution system replaced with more efficient variable-volume system, demand control ventilation that reduces outdoor ventilation rate but tying it to measured indoor air quality, and energy controls system upgrade.

The above measures, along with rebuilding the chiller, were implemented as of November 2010. Additional measures are being installed in tenant spaces on an ongoing basis as leased spaces turn over. These involve reducing lighting power density, installing dimmable ballasts and photosensors for perimeter spaces and providing occupants with a plug load occupancy sensor for their personal workstation. The tenant space improvements formed the basis for tenant fit-out design guidelines and are a component of a tenant engagement programme.

The approach

A collaborative team was formed to develop the optimal energy efficiency retrofit solution through a rigorous and iterative process that involved energy and financial modelling. An Energy Service Company (ESCO), the ESB, and the tenants were each responsible for delivering some of the project savings (61%, 22%, and 17%, respectively). As part of the service contract, ESB paid USD 20 million for capital improvements to the ESCO, which guaranteed ~20% energy cost reduction for 15 years. To engage tenants to reduce energy use, ESB developed tenant design guidelines and built out pre-finished green spaces to showcase their benefit and value.

Figure 3 **ESB efficiency improvement capital costs and estimated operating savings**

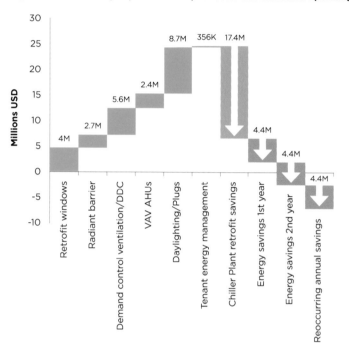

Note: Efficiency measures costs (shown in gold), chiller replacement savings, (shown in blue), and annual energy savings (shown in green); net costs of USD 13.2 million with less than a 3-year simple payback

The Empire State Building approach illustrates the leveraged savings potential of a deep retrofit. The project followed the key principles outlined in 10xE and 'tunneled through the cost barrier,' as indicated in Figure 3. Taking advantage of an already planned renovation enabled the building owners to make energy improvements an incremental cost. The project showed that it makes good business sense to make large and significant energy efficiency improvements.

Project highlight – on-site window manufacturing

The 6,500 existing insulated glass units were remanufactured into super-windows on site within ESB in a dedicated processing space created on the fifth floor. Each double-hung window was removed, delivered to the processing space, dismantled and rebuilt to include a suspended coated film and gas fill. The upgrade more than tripled the insulating value. Remanufacturing allowed 96% of the original glass and window frame to be reused in the project, greatly reducing construction waste and disposal fees. Doing it on site eliminated the need to transport the windows to another facility. Care was taken to avoid disrupting tenants during business hours by choosing a space with easy contractor access away from occupied floors and adding soundproof drywall around the work area.

Figure 4 **The ESB super-windows were remanufactured onsite in a temporary processing space[7]**

The total capital cost for the measure was USD 4.5 million, USD 15.5 million less than the projected cost of new windows, and the annual energy savings are projected to be USD 410,000. Additional benefits to tenants include: increased comfort in summer and winter, lower heating and cooling energy use, ultraviolet-light blocking to protect furnishings, and non-existent glass-surface condensation.

Building construction

Circular end-of-life solutions are increasingly possible but still limited in applications for building structural materials. Wood structures can return to the biosphere; structural steel can be remanufactured, and in fact already is almost entirely recycled, according to the American Institute of Steel Construction;[8] and engineered steel kit-of-parts solutions, such as proprietary systems ConXtech[9] or BONE Structure,[10] can be disassembled and reassembled without remanufacture. But these systems have constraints. Lightweight wood framing is limited to low-rise structures, and large-scale timber structures have size limitations and/or reliance on supplemental steel or reinforced concrete elements, as is the case in Skidmore, Owings and Merrill's Timber Tower Research Project.[11] Given a sufficient supply of steel scrap stock, steel remanufacturing could theoretically run on renewable electricity in electric arc furnaces, but it is still very energy intensive. In 2006, the steel industry used 5% of all US industrial energy, mostly in the form of fossil fuel combustion.[12] Disassembly and reassembly of steel kit-of-parts solutions requires an after-use market for structural components, likely decades after initial construction. This can be facilitated by increasing adherence to design-

Figure 5 **ConXtech's ConXR 200™ System for high-density residential structures**[9]

Credit: Dr. Robert B. Fleischman

and construction-industry standard structural sizing.[13] And aside from end-of-life issues, site work and heavy construction rely on heavy machinery, which today runs almost entirely on fossil fuels. To varying degrees the systems above may rely on substructures of concrete, though innovations are underway to reduce that reliance. This is important because the cement industry is the most energy intensive of all US manufacturing industries[13], and today concrete down-cycles material at end-of-life."

Due to the end-of-life challenges and inherent energy intensiveness of construction, the conversation of circularity for building structures involves matching the embodied energy of the structure with the building's potential to provide economic value. For iconic buildings, a structure with high embodied energy can be justified due to its extended useful lifetime. By greatly extending building lifetimes, resource leakage per product service can be substantially reduced. For more temporary structures, more biological construction solutions involving materials with low embodied energy and requiring less resource-intensive fabrication are most desirable. As with other aspects of circular economy thinking, the selection of building construction materials represents an economic opportunity for maximising the financial return per manufacturing expenditure – as indicated in the illustrative example depicted in Figure 6.

Case study: Puukuokka Housing Block[16]

Located in a suburb near Kuokkala, Finland, Puukuokka comprises 150 apartments within a set of three timber-framed, energy-efficient housing blocks that are six to eight storeys high. OOPEAA in conjunction with the local Jyväskylä city planning department designed the 10,000 m² development, which utilised prefabricated modular cubical structural elements and Stora's Enso cross-laminated timber (CLT), which provide an affordable, eco-efficient housing solution that is adaptable, lightweight and ready-to-install. The frame is load-bearing, provides a stiffening element, and includes a vapour barrier and partial heat insulation. Its prefabricated modular design results in fewer joints, fewer installation flaws, and less material needed than in conventional timber buildings. In addition, Puukuokka provides homeowners with a low-cost, low-risk funding option. Before moving in, the future owner pays a modest down payment (7% of the home's value). The remaining pre-negotiated sum is covered by a state-guaranteed 20-year bank loan, which the occupant pays off as rent over the loan period.

Figure 6 **Building construction: steps towards increasing resource productivity**

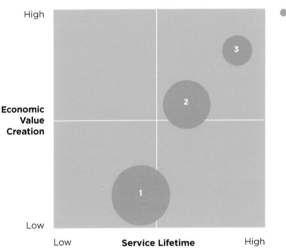

● Area of circle indicates amount of resources used per unit value created.

1. Durable building design

2. Adaptable for increased property value over time

3. Owner with long-term view of building investment

Building construction

Durable buildings tend to have high embodied energy (see step 1 in Figure 6). More sustainable solutions are emerging, which result from a combination of construction quality and material technological advances. Hycrete concrete admixture, for example, is a Cradle-to-Cradle (C2C) Gold certified material designed to reduce water permeability of concrete, protecting steel rebar, enhancing structural durability and extending a building's useful life.[17] Thoma Holz100, is a 100% wood structural system with no glues or metals.

Rather, connections are made with dowels that swell as they soak up moisture and increase the solidity and durability of the whole assembly.[15] Physical durability is important for long-lasting buildings. What is often overlooked, though, is that buildings must also be economically durable.

Economic durability

Circular economy concepts should be applied not only to the materials and methods used in constructing buildings, but also to space planning and real estate value propositions during the initial decision to build. With the correct foresight, a structure can be designed to nimbly endure many cycles of programmed space usage, maximising the return on initial infrastructure investment (step 2 in Figure 6). At the end of one programme life, another programme life can begin, with very high effectiveness and no down-cycling of spatial quality or building functionality.

Case Study: Boston Convention and Exhibition Center[19]

A new parking garage in Boston exemplifies this approach to value planning. Since the completion of the Boston Convention & Exhibition Center (BCEC) in 2004, the South Boston waterfront area has exploded with economic growth, and Massachusetts Convention Center Authority (MCCA), the public authority in charge of developing the area, expects decades of continued economic development in this so-called 'Innovation District'. Though convention venues themselves are typically not profitable, MCCA expects to generate regional revenue from the multiplier effect of high-value functions such as hotels, restaurants, retail and tourism, not to mention potential offices, laboratories or entertainment. But, today, they need a parking garage. So when the MCCA identified that need for a new 1,500-vehicle parking structure to accommodate an expansion to the convention center, they designed it with a universal structural system, capable of accommodating the variety of future uses noted above.

Boston Convention and Exhibition Centre

As an institutional developer with long-term ownership, they are incentivised to plan for full economic life-cycle costs and benefits of the structure being built today (step 3 in Figure 6). Thus, they optimise their use of scarce public funds and stand ready to capitalise on the higher-value, higher-return real estate functions expected to move into the area in the future, without costly and time-consuming demolition and reconstruction. This development model contrasts with other typical models, which often involve flipping property for high, short-term gain. In such a model, operation is subsequently delegated to a second party whose focus is on maximising return on rental income. The business model for neither of those parties – builder or operator – typically includes scoping long-term, programmatically flexible building life. While this lack of long-term planning may be partially attributed to the discounting of future cash flows, it is also attributed to reacting only to an immediate, certain real estate market, rather than hedging against future market evolution.

In this example, universal structural design involved a variety of advance-planning items normally not considered in parking design: universal concrete structural bay dimensions; a steel vehicle ramp at the building perimeter, designed for the possibility of disassembly; higher ceiling heights; and pre-emptive mechanical, electrical, plumbing, elevator, stairway and facade accommodations for future retrofits. These items amount to small compromises in spatial and structural efficiency from a normal garage layout, but allow for higher returns in the future when the building function transitions.[20]

Case study: China buildings sector

These concepts are particularly important in China, where more cement was used in three years than was used in the United States in the entire 20th century.[21] Globally, cement represents around 5% of all anthropogenic carbon dioxide emissions, and around half of that occurs in China.[22] Strategies to reduce cement-related emissions tend to focus on the supply side, including plant efficiency, alternative fuels, limestone substitutes or carbon capture and sequestration (CCS),[23] but often neglect the resource savings potential on the demand side.

It is reported that Chinese buildings currently last only thirty years,[24] serving a single function before being torn down to accommodate the next, higher-value function. This is in part due to poor construction quality that forces a premature structural end of life. Worker training and high-quality construction management practices are part of the solution to this problem. The growth of the nascent Chinese prefabricated construction industry will also be important, by which structural elements could be manufactured in a factory setting, under an automated, streamlined process with better quality controls and less material waste, then shipped to the site for rapid assembly. Prefabrication enables rapid, streamlined construction that reduces construction waste and improves building quality and durability. Cases of prefabrication in China and elsewhere have resulted in lifetimes lengthened by 10–15 years, reductions in construction material loss by 60%, and reductions in overall building waste by 80%. While prefabrication is still relatively new in China, its promotion will accelerate its adoption across industry. The Broad Sustainable Building, a prefab construction firm, is claiming to be the world's fastest builder after erecting the 57-story Mini Sky City building in the Hunan provincial capital of Changsha. The project involved assembling three floors a day using a modular pre-fabrication method.[25] The building is 80% more efficient than a standard building made of steel and concrete.[26]

Short building life in China results from long-term land-use planning being conducted with short-sighted or speculative single-use zoning, rather than allowing for evolving and adapting land-use patterns. A land-use planning policy that encourages building adaptability and rewards longer building lifetimes can provide both economic and environmental benefits. This careful planning is particularly pressing during China's period of rapid urbanisation, ongoing housing reform and emerging, affluent lifestyles. And the forthcoming transition to a more service-based economy demands an adaptable building stock that can accommodate ever-evolving 21st-century office concepts, laboratories, data centres, etc. The building and land-use policy decisions made now will impact China's real estate cost effectiveness for many decades. As with the case of the South Boston waterfront, forward-looking universal structures can maximise full life-cycle returns on building and infrastructure investment.

Building products

As with building structures, products used in buildings that have a long functional lifespan are a cornerstone for circularity. The impact of product material waste is minimised through the design of durable products with economic value over a long lifetime. For products with functionality or aesthetics that require frequent updates, designing for refurbishment or upgradeability presents a promising opportunity.

To date, the return, collection, reuse or recycling of a product has often been driven by regulatory requirements related to extended producer responsibility. However, several CE100 companies working with the Ellen MacArthur Foundation have shown alternative business models can also facilitate this cycle. One example is leasing which enables manufacturers to a) track and manage their assets and b) transition towards being service providers. Examples of building products and services include Philips and their shift from lighting to lumens or HP's shift from selling equipment to office-based services.

Performance or output-based business models and fee structures encourage purchasers to prioritise features that are more financially or environmentally preferable such as product lifetime and reliability. Unlike consumables, which are often discarded and 'lost' in the waste management system, durable building products are often permanent or semi-permanent fixtures. When combined with performance monitoring software, these types of building products have the potential to be tracked and collected since the manufacturer or vendor knows where the products are, how are they performing and when they should be replaced or repaired. While not a guarantee that these products will be recycled or upcycled, asset tracking should encourage manufacturers to explore ways in which they can collect and reuse their assets and materials. Benefits would include reduced waste and also potential financial savings stemming from reduced raw material purchases.

Figure 8 illustrates the application of these principles and their potential for improving the circularity of building products. Step 1 involves increasing product life. Step 2 incorporates ease of repair. Step 3 promotes asset tracking and collection through a performance service contract. Step 4 reduces resource waste through cradle-to-cradle certification.

Figure 8 **Building products: steps towards increasing resource productivity**

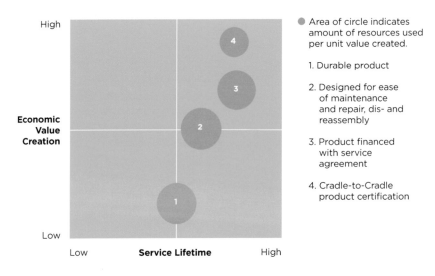

Area of circle indicates amount of resources used per unit value created.

1. Durable product

2. Designed for ease of maintenance and repair, dis- and reassembly

3. Product financed with service agreement

4. Cradle-to-Cradle product certification

Case study: SunPower Corporation
One of the tenets of the circular economy is that systems should ultimately aim to run on renewable energy, which include wind, solar and geothermal sources. Renewable energy is environmentally friendlier than fossil fuels,

produces no greenhouse gas emissions, provides price stability, and enables energy independence. According to two roadmaps published by the International Energy Agency (IEA), solar photovoltaic has the potential to become the world's largest source of electricity by the year 2050.[27] As IEA points out, the last decade has seen exponential growth in total installed capacity for solar photovoltaic (PV) systems. Compared to 2008, there is at least 10 times more solar PV installed around the world today. By the end of 2014, total installed capacity worldwide increased nearly 26% from 140 gigawatts in 2013 to approximately 177 gigawatts according to the IEA's Photovoltaic Power Systems Program.

The solar technology company, SunPower, sees itself as a contributor to a circular economy through the role it plays in driving toward a sustainable industrial system powered by renewable energy. The company is also exploring various forms of circular business models through innovative product design, certifications, and service offerings. Their efforts – including designing for durability, cradle-to-cradle (C2C) certification, and power purchase-agreement business models – are described below.

Designing for durability and recyclability

For electricity-producing photovoltaic solar modules, designing for durability and reliability are essential customer requirements. Consequently, SunPower's modules have a long expected useful life of more than 40 years (defined as 99% of modules producing at least 70% of their power). SunPower has expanded its modules' lifespan through fundamental design changes, including the use of n-type silicon and a tin-coated copper foundation, which provide protection against real-world physical and environmental stresses such as thermal cycling and repeated snow and wind loading. By designing for durability, the goal is to move away from the concept of a 'disposable' product and to minimise resource consumption and waste generation.

While the ultimate goal is to design out as much material waste as possible, the fact remains that products will reach an end to their useful life or will undergo replacement by the customer. Ideally, products can be disassembled so that components can be reused, refurbished or recycled into higher-value products (often referred to as upcycling). For SunPower modules, a Reuse and Recycle Program has been created to allow functional products to be reused at SunPower facilities or recycled at certified facilities. Currently, over 95% (by weight) of a module can be recycled but efforts continue to identify more circular practices including using recycled content material and upcycling waste material into higher-value products.

Cradle-to-Cradle certification

Circular product design and financial models can each be overly complex for the company just beginning its circular economy journey. So, how and where can a company begin? C2C product certification provides a framework to help companies develop a comprehensive corporate sustainability strategy. Since 'C2C certified' is one of the most rigorous eco-labels and certified products are eligible for additional points under the latest version of the Leadership in Energy and Environment Design (LEED) green building rating programme, building product manufacturers can ensure customers gain the most economic, environmental and social value from their products. For SunPower, C2C certification provides not only a scorecard by which progress to their sustainability goals can be tracked but also a roadmap for future innovation in their products, operations and supply chain.

The five categories of C2C certification are: Material Health, Material Reutilisation, Water Stewardship, Carbon Management and Renewable Energy, and Social Fairness. The first two categories focus on the material composition of a product and demonstrate how manufacturers can retain or even increase material value of their products through the reduction of material toxicity and improving reusability and recyclability. The reduction and eventual elimination of hazardous materials is key to certification as is the confirmation that no harmful waste by-products enter the biosphere at the product's end of life. Benefits of non-toxicity include brand differentiation, customer preference, reduced risk and waste disposal costs. To meet these requirements, SunPower set internal goals and collaborated with suppliers to ensure materials and services (e.g. recycling) supplied met regulatory and sustainability requirements. Water Stewardship and Carbon Management & Renewable Energy focus on manufacturing resource consumption. With goals related to water management (use, recycling) and energy use, these two categories provide specific operational goals to help internal teams (Facilities, Environmental, Health and Safety, Manufacturing) integrate circular considerations and systems thinking into manufacturing processes and building facilities. It facilitates the reduction of a product's manufacturing footprint by requiring the use of renewable energy and water recycling to move beyond basic certification. The final category, Social Fairness, focuses on responsible employment practices and community relations. The human element cannot be overlooked in a circular system because it is vital to have people engaged and aware to reap the full benefits of C2C certification and circular thinking. Taken together, C2C and circular economy principles enable companies to think systematically and work towards the goal of not just minimising harm ('less bad') but maximising value and benefit ('more good') to customers, employees and communities.

Alternative business models

Innovative business models that offer solar-generated electricity as a service are becoming increasingly popular. Two forms of these business models

The Solar Star Projects are a 579- megawatt solar installation in Kern and Los Angeles Counties in California. SunPower Corporation was the developer of the project.

© Sunpower

include: the Power Purchase Agreement (PPA) and the Yieldco. In a PPA financial agreement, a developer provides the design, permitting, financing and installation of a solar energy system on a customer's property – at little or no cost to the customer. The developer sells the power generated to the host customer at an agreed-upon fixed rate for a fixed period. Typically, contract periods range from 10 to 25 years. Over this time, the developer is responsible for operation and maintenance of the system. The owner's electric costs are offset by the purchase of the solar-generated electricity, which provides price stability. The developer receives the income from the sale of electricity, as well as any tax credits and other incentives generated from the system. At the end of the PPA contract term, a customer may be able to extend the PPA, have the developer remove the system or choose to buy the solar energy system from the developer. Very similar to a PPA is a solar lease, which does not involve the sale of electric power. The system is owned by a third party but the customer leases the system as they would an automobile. The host customer receives the benefits of solar with little or no up-front costs.

Another mechanism for financing renewable energy projects is through a Yieldco. A Yieldco is a publicly traded company that bundles long-term contracted operating assets in order to generate predictable cash flows.

The 41-acre, 8 MW Exelon City Solar installation in Chicago, Illinois utilises the SunPower® T0 Tracker photovoltaic system

©Sunpower

Yieldcos allocate cash distribution each year or quarter to shareholders in the form of dividends. This investment can be attractive to shareholders because they can expect low-risk returns that are projected to increase over time. Renewable energy projects face some uncertainty during the development stage but generally produce low-risk cash flows once they are operating. Applying Yieldcos to renewable assets have the potential to raise financing for projects and attract new investors who might otherwise avoid renewable projects due to perceived unacceptable risk or lack of appropriate channels for investing. Yieldco investors typically receive 3–5% returns and long-term dividend growth targets of 8–15%. Currently, six renewable energy Yieldcos operate in the US market, including: NRG Yield, Pattern Energy Group, Inc., TransAlta Renewables, Abengoa Yield, Next Era Energy Partners, and TerraForm Power.[28]

These alternative business models provide new sources of capital for developing on-site and commercial renewable energy projects. They also provide another opportunity for companies, such as SunPower, to retain and monitor assets to facilitate the tracking, repair, refurbishment, upgrade or upcycling of materials.

Circular framework application

New business models prompted by concerns of wastefulness and its implications for climate change are emerging as it becomes increasingly apparent that our growth-oriented economic system is not sustainable. Globally, there exists an enormous resource savings potential in the built environment, which can be tapped across the building life cycle – during design, construction, fit-out, and operation. We hope that the framework depicted in the 2x2 chart introduced in this chapter provides the reader with an easy-to-understand structure for considering three key factors effecting circularity – 1) natural resource consumption, 2) useful lifespan, and 3) economic value. While the framework has been applied cross the wide range of products and services associated with the built environment, it is generic. Its underlying key factors are basic to circular concepts and the approach can be applied to other opportunity areas. Similarly, the reader can apply the illustrated, step-wise process for assessing the level of circularity relative to business-as-usual in order to progress circular activities.

Some questions to consider in applying the approach:

1. Are long product life and circularity synonymous?
2. How effective is the proposed simple framework for distinguishing between shades of circularity?
3. What other attributes of circularity are important for circular business models targeting the built environment? For other applications?

Notes

1 International Energy Agency website, https://www.iea.org/aboutus/faqs/energyefficiency/

2 R. Dobbs, J. Oppenheim, F. Thompson, M. Brinkman and M. Zornes, *Resource Revolution: Meeting the world's energy, materials, food, and water needs* (London: McKinsey & Company, 2011; http://www.mckinsey.com/Insights/Energy_Resources_Materials/Resource_revolution).

3 C. Baker, M. den Hollander, E. von Hinte, and Y. Zljlstra, *Products that Last: Product Design for Circular Business Models* (Delft: TU Delft Library, 2014) and P. Hawken, A. Lovins, and H. Lovins, *Natural Capitalism: The Next Industrial Revolution* (New York: Little, Brown & Company, 1999),

4 R. Dobbs et al., *Resource Revolution: Meeting the world's energy, materials, food, and water needs* (London: McKinsey & Company, 2011)

5 Rocky Mountain Institute website, *10xE Principles* (Snowmass, CO: Rocky Mountain Institute, 2010; http://www.rmi.org/rmi/10xe%20principles).

6 E. Harrington and C. Carmichael, *Project Case Study: Empire State Building* (Boulder, CO: Rocky Mountain Institute 2009; http://www.rmi.org/Content/Files/ESBCaseStudy.pdf).

7 NRDC website, *Smarter Business: Case Studies – Empire State Realty Trust: Empire State Building Window Retrofit* (April 2014; http://www.nrdc.org/greenbusiness/empire-state-building-windows.asp).

8 AISC website, *How 'green' is structural steel* (https://www.aisc.org/content.aspx?id=3788).

9 http://www.c2ccertified.org/products/scorecard/conxl_and_conxr

10 BONE Structure website, *Technology* (http://bonestructure.ca/en/solutions/technology/).

11 http://www.som.com/ideas/research/timbertowerresearchproject

12 US Energy Information Administration website, Steel Industry Analysis Brief (http://www.eia.gov/consumption/manufacturing/briefs/steel/).

13 US Energy Information Administration webiste, The cement industry is the most energy intensive of all manufacturing industries (http://www.eia.gov/todayinenergy/detail.cfm?id=11911).

14 BONE Structure website, *Technology* (http://bonestructure.ca/en/solutions/technology/).

15 http://www.c2ccertified.org/products/scorecard/thomaholz100

16 OOPEAA website, *Puukuokka Housing Block* (http://oopeaa.com/project/puukuokka-housing-block/).

17 http://www.c2ccertified.org/products/scorecard/hycrete_admixtures

18 OOPEAA website, *Puukuokka Housing Block* (http://oopeaa.com/project/puukuokka-housing-block/).

19 Will Macht, *Universal Structures as Long-Term Sustainable Assets* (Urban Land magazine, 23 January 2015; http://urbanland.uli.org/planning-design/universal-structures-long-term-sustainable-assets/).

20 Ibid.

21 Ana Swanson, *How China used more cement in 3 years than the U.S. did in the entire 20th Century* (The Washington Post, 24 March 2015; http://www.washingtonpost.com/blogs/wonkblog/wp/2015/03/24/how-china-used-more-cement-in-3-years-than-the-u-s-did-in-the-entire-20th-century/).

22 International Energy Agency, Technology Roadmap: Cement (2009; http://www.iea.org/publications/freepublications/publication/technology-roadmap-cement.html); Ke et al., Estimation of CO2 Emissions from China's Cement Production: Methodologies and Uncertainties, http://eetd.lbl.gov/publications/estimation-of-co2-emissions-from-ch-0

23 Madeleine Rubenstein, *Emissions from the Cement Industry State of the Planet* (Earth Institute, Columbia University, 9 May 2012; http://blogs.ei.columbia.edu/2012/05/09/emissions-from-the-cement-industry/).

24 L. Hong, N. Zhou, N. Fridley, W. Feng and N. Khanna, *Modeling China's Building Floor-Area Growth and the Implications for Building Materials and Energy Demand*, conference proceedings from ACEEE Summer Study Conference (Pacific Grove, CA, 2014; http://aceee.org/files/proceedings/2014/data/papers/10-230.pdf).

25 *Chinese construction firm erects 57-storey skyscraper in 19 days* (The Guardian, 30 April 2015; http://www.theguardian.com/world/2015/apr/30/chinese-construction-firm-erects-57-storey-skyscraper-in-19-days).

26 http://usa.chinadaily.com.cn/epaper/2015-05/05/content20626039.htm

27 International Energy Agency press release, *How solar energy could be the largest source of electricity by mid-century* (29 September 2014; http://www.iea.org/newsroomandevents/pressreleases/2014/september/how-solar-energy-could-be-the-largest-source-of-electricity-by-mid-century.html).

28 Marley Urdanick, *A Deeper Look into Yieldco Structuring* (National Renewable Energy Laboratory, 9 March 2014; https://financere.nrel.gov/finance/content/deeper-look-yieldco-structuring).

References

Baker, C., den Hollander, M., von Hinte, E., and Zljlstra, Y., *Products that Last: Product Design for Circular Business Models* (Delft: TU Delft Library, 2014)

Harrington E. and Carmichael, C., *Project Case Study: Empire State Building* (Boulder, CO: Rocky Mountain Institute 2009; http://www.rmi.org/Content/Files/ESBCaseStudy.pdf)

Hawkins, P., Lovins, A., and Lovins, H., *Natural Capitalism: The Next Industrial Revolution* (New York: Little, Brown & Company, 1999)

Hong, L., Zhou, N., Fridley, N., Feng W. and Khanna, N., *Modeling China's Building Floor-Area Growth and the Implications for Building Materials and Energy Demand*, conference proceedings from ACEEE Summer Study Conference (Pacific Grove, CA, 2014; http://aceee.org/files/proceedings/2014/data/papers/10-230.pdf)

McKinsey & Company. *Resource Revolution: Meeting the world's energy, materials, food, and water needs* (London: McKinsey & Company, 2011; http://www.mckinsey.com/insights/energyresourcesmaterials/resourcerevolution)

Rocky Mountain Institute website, *10xE Principles* (Snowmass, CO: Rocky Mountain Institute, 2010; http://www.rmi.org/rmi/10xe%20principles).

THE RENEWABLE ENERGY TRANSITION – INSIGHTS FROM GERMANY'S *ENERGIEWENDE*

Patrick Graichen and Markus Steigenberger

Germany's *Energiewende* (energy transition) is an attempt to transform the nation's energy sector from a nuclear-fossil based system to an almost entirely renewable one. Because of the limited resource availability of biomass and hydropower, and major cost degressions in wind and solar technologies, it can be assumed that wind power and solar photovoltaics will provide the largest share of electricity generation in Germany's future power mix. As wind power and solar are variable sources, this development brings about a paradigm shift: the main feature of Germany's future power system will be flexibility. This chapter provides an overview of the current state of play on how this paradigm shift impacts the system and the main challenges deriving from this change.

Patrick Graichen
Patrick is Executive Director, Agora Energiewende. From 2001 to 2012, Patrick worked in Germany's Federal Ministry of Environment: from 2004 to 2006 he was Personal Assistant to the Secretary of State, and from 2007 was Head of the Unit for Energy and Climate Change Policy.

Markus Steigenberger
Markus is Deputy Executive Director of Agora Energiewende. Before working with Agora, Markus led the Germany programme of the European Climate Foundation (ECF).

Introduction

When it comes to Germany's energy transition ('Energiewende'), it seems that there are only two opinions: either it is considered a curse – or a blessing. Some praise it for creating jobs, producing clean and distributed energy, reducing import dependency and minimising climate and nuclear risks. Others blame it for escalating costs and increased grid instability. Why does Germany's energy transition provoke such heated debate? The answer is simple: because it is real. Germany has taken decisions that can not be seen as temporary political phenomena any more. They were taken by three-quarter-majorities in the Parliament; and citizens firmly support the energy transition as surveys regularly prove. These decisions are quite radical: Germany has decided to decarbonise its energy sector on the basis of new renewable energy. No other decarbonisation technology, neither nuclear nor carbon capture and sequestration is considered feasible in the domestic context. As no comparable country – Germany is still the fifth biggest economy of the world with a strong industrial basis – has ever attempted to do this, no blueprint exists. So far, there is no master plan for how to implement the energy transition. It is rather a stepwise exploration of new territory for Germany. Naturally, decision-makers discover pitfalls, difficulties and challenges. And, again naturally, a transition as fundamental as the one Germany is envisaging – from a fossil-nuclear to an almost entirely renewable energy supply – is creating uncertainty. Market participants, consumers and decision-makers feel threatened by the dimensions of this renewable energy transition.

Starting from this observation, this chapter aims to give clarity on what Germany's energy transition is all about, where it stands and where it is heading. The focus of this article is the power sector, because it is the key sector for decarbonising the economy: in order to reach the European Union's goal to reduce greenhouse gases by 2050 to 80–95% below 1990 levels, it is necessary to nearly fully decarbonise the energy sector – which implies that the transport and heat sector will have to shift their energy base to a very large degree from fossil fuels to clean electricity. The European Commission, for instance, in its Energy Roadmap 2050 calls for 93–99% emissions reduction in the power sector as key to reaching Europe's climate targets. In this article we first describe the most important developments and the state of play. Secondly, we identify the key characteristics of the transition in the power sector deriving from high shares of variable renewable sources in Germany's future energy mix. We conclude by briefly discussing the key challenges and taking a look at future developments.

Goals and current status of the transition

With the energy concept of 2010 and the legislative package of 2011, Germany has decided on a set of concrete goals in different energy sectors. The track record of the energy transition can best be judged against these targets. Although officially no hierarchy exists, four main goals can be identified:

• reducing greenhouse gas emissions by 40% in 2020 and 80–95% in 2050 (against 1990)
• phasing out nuclear energy by end of 2022
In order to achieve these two main goals, a set of additional targets, policies and instruments has been established over the years. Among these, two stand out:
• increasing the share of renewable energy
• using energy more efficiently.

The following table summarises the main targets.

Table 1 **Status quo and official targets of Germany's energy transition[3]**

	Status Quo	2020	2025	2030	2035	2040	2050
Greenhouse gas emissions (against 1990)	-27,7% (2014)	-40%	-	-55%	-	-70%	-80 to -95%
Nuclear phase-out	11 power plants shut down since 2000	Stepwise phase-out of the remaining 8 power plants until end of 2022					
Overall renewable energy (share in consumption)	13,7% (2014)	18%	-	30%	-	45%	≥60%
Electric renewable energy (share in electricity consumption)	32,5% (2015)	-	40–45%	-	55–60%	-	≥80%
Primary energy efficiency (primary energy use, against 2008)	-8.9% (2014)	-20%	-	-	-	-	-50%
Electric energy efficiency (electricity demand, against 2008)	-3,4% (2015)	-10%	-	-	-	-	-25%

Progress towards achieving these targets has been significant in recent years in Germany. By the end of 2014, greenhouse gas emissions have been reduced by roughly 26% since 1990. More than a third of these reductions occurred between 1990 and 1995 and can thus be attributed both to the industrial breakdown in Eastern Germany after 1990 and the modernisation of the inefficient power plants of the former GDR.

Regarding the nuclear phase-out, since 2000 11 GW of nuclear capacity have been shut down. According to the phase-out law decided by a 90% majority in parliament in 2011, the remaining roughly 11 GW nuclear power plants will be shut down in a stepwise approach (2017, 2019, 2021) by end of 2022 at the latest.

In the field of energy efficiency, the target translates into an annual increase in energy productivity by 2.1%. Between 1990 and 2013, overall efficiency of the German economy has been increased by 1.7% per year – thus falling short of the target. Moreover, progress has slowed down in recent years. While overall efficiency increased by 2.2% between 1990 and 2000, the rate was down to 1.3% between 2000 and 2013.[4] Finally renewable energy has grown significantly. In 1990, renewables counted for approximately 3% of Germany's electricity consumption and 2% of overall energy consumption. Today, gross consumption from renewable sources across all sectors is at 12%, with the electricity sector reaching 27%.[5] This development was not only a change in market structures: triggered by the feed-in tariff, almost 50% of today's renewable generation is owned by citizens – a fact that is considered one of the reasons why the energy transition remains highly popular in Germany as shown in Figure 1.[6]

Entering the second phase of transition

Breaking the 25% threshold of renewable electricity consumption in 2013 symbolically illustrates the change to the second phase of the energy transition in the key sector of the energy system, the electricity sector. While the first phase was characterised by innovation and technology development of a variety of renewable technologies, the current debate is about renewable technologies becoming the dominant generation source. This brings about fundamental changes and challenges to the system described in the following section.

Figure 1 **One secret of success – renewables are largely being owned by the citizens themselves**

Ownership structure of installed renewables 2012

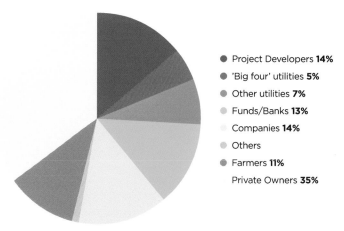

- Project Developers **14%**
- 'Big four' utilities **5%**
- Other utilities **7%**
- Funds/Banks **13%**
- Companies **14%**
- Others
- Farmers **11%**
  Private Owners **35%**

Source: Trend research

Accumulated number of citizens' energy cooperatives 2006–14

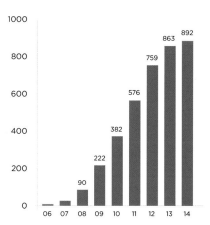

Source: Leuphana

It is all about wind power and solar PV

Two renewable technologies will provide the biggest share among all
generation technologies in the future in Germany: wind power and solar
photovoltaics (solar PV). The reason for this prediction is simple: wind and sun
do not face major resource constraints and are comparatively cheap. All other
renewable technologies are either significantly more expensive or have limited
potential in central Europe. Figure 2 shows the development of renewable
expansion in Germany since 2000 and the anticipated scenario until 2035
according to the German transmission system operators.

Figure 2 **The key insight for the Energiewende: 'It's all about the wind and solar!'**

Gross electricity generation of renewable energies 1990–2035

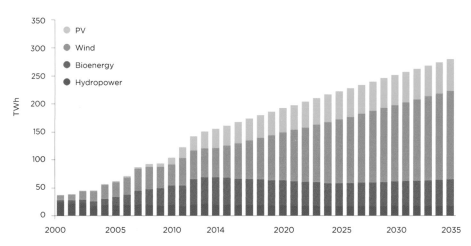

Source: AG Energiebilanzen (2000–14); BNetzA, own calculations (2015–35)

In fact, the technology development of wind power and solar PV has been rapid in recent years (see Figure 3). Wind turbines of today are 20 times more powerful than those 20 years ago (average: 2.6 MW instead of 170 kW), and costs for solar PV have fallen by up to 90% in the last 25 years. Furthermore, there is no reason to believe that the end of the learning curve has already been reached.[8] The potential for both technologies is significant. Even in densely populated Germany, 1,200 GW of wind power onshore could theoretically be installed.[9] The technical and ecologically sound potential of PV is estimated at about 275 GW.[10]

Figure 3 **Wind energy has become a mature technology, with windmills of 2–3 MW being standard**

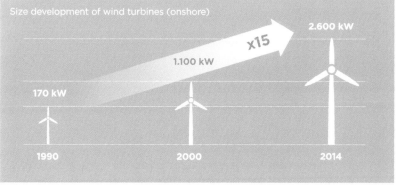

Source: Fraunhofer IWES

In contrast to these figures, other renewable technologies will not be able to increase their share in the power mix significantly. Bioenergy today already counts for 7.5% of Germany's electricity generation. However, projections expect it to remain below 10% in the long run. The reason is resource constraints – as acreage is limited, the use of wood and energy crops directly competes with other needs, especially growing food crops or raw materials for industry – in Germany and other countries. The quantity of low-cost biomass is more or less exhausted, and remuneration rates for biomass plants in the German support scheme are rising rather than falling.[11] Hydropower is currently contributing approximately 4% to Germany's electricity mix – and will remain at this level, as the potential for expanding hydropower capacity is very limited in Germany. The situation with geothermal is similar: limited potential and high costs suggest that this technology will not increase its share significantly. Other technologies such as wave power or osmosis are still in the development stage. Whether they will ever be able to play a significant role is unclear.

©Jason-CC Flickr

Interestingly, comparing the cost of wind power and solar PV with conventional generation technologies, (Figure 4) one finds that these two renewable sources can already produce electricity at the same cost level as new coal and gas plants. Current remuneration rates for wind power lie between 7 and 10 ct/kWh, for solar PV between 8 and 11 ct/kWh – depending on size and location.[12] In 2016, both wind power onshore and large-scale solar PV are expected to be able to produce electricity at a cost range between 7 and 10 ct/kWh (levelised costs of electricity).[13] This is in general at the same level as new coal and gas plants.[14]

Variable renewables will fundamentally change the system
Thus, the more Germany pursues the path of a decarbonised energy system, wind power and solar PV will form the basis of Germany's future power supply. By the time renewable sources provide around 50% of total German electricity supply – quite likely around the year 2030 at the latest – wind power and solar PV will already have a share of 35% of total electricity supply.

As both technologies have some very specific characteristics, this development implies a paradigm shift in how the power system works. While the 'old' system was based on large centralised power plants that provided electricity in very stable and predictable conditions, the new system will be quite the opposite.

Figure 4 **Today, wind and solar are already cost competitive to all other newly built energy sources – and cheaper than nuclear and Carbon Capture and Storage**

Upper and lower range of levelised cost of electricity of different technologies in 2015

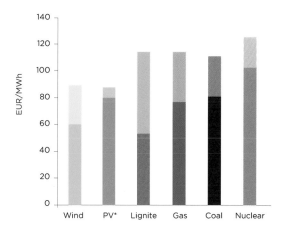

Source: Agora Energiewende

Three features have to be taken into account:

• By definition, wind power and solar PV produce electricity dependent on weather conditions. Strong winds and sunny days bring about plenty of kilowatt hours, while reduced wind and daylight naturally limit the output. Thus, power generation by wind and solar PV cannot be adjusted to demand or price signals at the market.

• Wind power and solar PV installations are almost entirely determined by capital expenditures. As costs for operation and maintenance are very low and fuel costs are non-existent, wind power and solar PV have a marginal cost close to zero. Thus, the initial capital investment pays for almost the entire electricity production for the next 20 to 30 years.

• Although some wind power and solar PV parks can be as large as several hundred megawatt, by nature wind power and solar PV are decentralised technologies. Millions of installations – roof-top solar PV and individual wind-power turbines – are scattered all over the land and produce electricity that is mainly fed into the distribution grid.[15]

These characteristics will fundamentally challenge the old system.

First, conventional power plants face a shrinking market: as more and more renewables enter the system, fossil fuel plants will gradually be pushed out. Second, and even more important in the short term: the old concept of 'base load power plants' is no longer valid. While in the old system, especially nuclear and lignite plants were designed to run 24/7, in the new system, renewables will, in times of high wind and/or sun availability, cover large shares of the load for more and more hours, thus reducing the load factor of conventional plants.

All in all, the growing dominance of wind power and solar PV will require the rest of the system to become very flexible. Flexible resources both on the supply and the demand side will have to be able to cope with two key challenges: firstly, they must cover weeks of very little wind and solar PV production, typically occuring in Germany in November. Secondly, they need to respond very quickly to immediate weather changes. Already at a share of 50% renewable sources in the German power system, radical changes in net load (i.e. load minus wind power and solar PV production) are expected. If, for example, the wind calms down at times of sunset and at the same time people come home from work and turn on their heaters and televisions, an increase of net load of up to 6 GW within 15 minutes might happen.[16] Thus, back-up resources have to be able to ramp up and down very flexibly.

A lot of flexibility options exist
The increasing flexibility challenge has two dimensions: Firstly, the technical system has to be able to provide highly flexible back-up resources, and secondly, the power market design needs to be of such a kind that it rewards deployment of flexible resources and incentivises investments in new (flexible) installations. From a technical perspective, the following flexibility options exist:
• expansion of the transmission and distribution grids
• improving the flexibility controllable capacity of – both conventional and renewable
• forcing demand to become flexible
• curtailment of renewable generation
• different kinds of energy storage
These are described in more detail in Agora Energiewende's report (2013).[17]

Considering system costs
Levelised costs of wind power and solar PV are as of today comparatively cheap – in Germany between 7 and 10 ct/kwh. However, from a system perspective, a wider concept of costs is required, as variable renewables need backup technologies to run a secure power system. Thus, in order to understand the cost of a renewable-based system, it is in fact necessary to look not only into the technology costs of wind power and solar PV, but to

take into account the entire system costs. More concretely, a power system based on decentralised variable renewable capacity will produce additional costs for grid expansion, back-up capacity and curtailment of renewable supply.[18] These extra costs can however be significantly reduced by rendering demand more flexible.

Recent studies indicate that these 'integration costs' of wind power and solar PV are not rendering a wind and solar based electricity system unaffordable. The International Energy Agency calculated the system cost of an electricity system the size of Germany with 45% variable renewables to be 13% to 25% higher than a system without variable renewables, depending on the flexibility of the power generation fleet and the demand side.[19] Furthermore, there are indications that a system based on wind and solar might be the cheapest way to decarbonise the electricity sector. Calculations by Prognos compared two greenfield electricity systems given today's installation cost: a power system with a generation mix of 50% wind/PV plus 50% gas back-up on one side with an electricity system of 50% new nuclear baseload and 50% gas peakload on the other side.[20] The results show that not only wind and PV are a lot cheaper than new nuclear in terms of levelised cost of electricity, but also that the renewable-based system is 20% cheaper than the nuclear-based system. Since this analysis does not take into consideration additional costs for grid expansion, these are not overall system cost comparisons and further research is needed. However, future cost developments were not taken into account, and here further cost reductions with wind and solar PV are to be expected.[21]

Next challenges

As shown above, entering the second phase of the energy transition will require some fundamental shifts. The key question is: How to realise the transition in a cost-efficient way without risking system reliability? If Germany is serious about the transition, in the upcoming second phase it needs to address challenges such as:

Focusing on the cheapest renewable technologies

As discussed, wind power and solar PV will provide cheap low carbon electricity. The paradigm of cost efficiency therefore requires that the focus be mainly on these two technologies in future renewables deployment. In fact, this step has currently been taken in Germany.

Reducing the overall burden through energy efficiency

The German government considers energy efficiency to be one of the key strategies to successfully implement the energy transition. Energy efficiency may reduce total consumption and thus the overall burden of transformation – and it may significantly reduce overall costs of the power system.[22]

Making the system more flexible

As discussed above, an energy system based on high shares of variable renewable generation needs flexibility. Different flexibility options exist and would need to be further exploited in the future. Germany has already started to address this challenge: the need to expand the grid has led to a very comprehensive grid planning process; industrial load shifts are at least considered for emergency situations; and research on new storage technologies is supported by the government.

Decarbonising the system

Germany is currently facing a paradox: despite growing renewable energy deployment quickly, greenhouse gas emissions were rising between 2011 and 2013 (See Figure 5). While overall emissions in Germany were down 26% to 929 million tonnes in 2011 (from 1,250 million tonnes in 1990), they rose again to 951 million tonnes by the end of 2013.[23] The situation in the power sector is even more distinct: since 2010, emissions rose from 305 mt to 322 mt in 2013. The development in the power sector was caused by a fuel switch from gas to coal that can be explained by low coal and CO_2 prices in recent years. In 2014 emissions were down again to 307 million tonnes because increasing shares of renewables and less demand is now starting to replace coal use.

Figure 5 **During 2010–13 coal power plants reduced gas, leading to higher emissions. But as of 2014, renewables are replacing coal**

Greenhouse gas emissions of the power sector 1990–2014

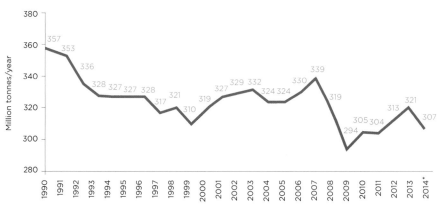

Source: UBA (2014), own calculations   *prognosis

However, in order to achieve the German greenhouse gas emissions targets, the share of coal and lignite in the power mix will have to decrease radically from approximately 45% today to only 19% in 2030. Output of hard coal and lignite plants would have to decrease by 80% and 62% respectively, while gas would need to double its share in electricity generation.[24] Thus, Germany will have to address the issue of coal in a substantial manner in order to reach its climate targets.

Integrating the energy transition across Germany and into Europe
It will be important over the coming years to build new grids to better connect North and South Germany. Cooperation among European neighbours could make the energy transition easier and less costly. Significant gains could be expected if the optimisation of the power market design were realised on the pan-European level. Studies have estimated annual net benefits of a pan-European power system integration in the range of EUR 12.5–42.6 billion.[25] As a first step, it is more probable that a regional approach will evolve, starting at the level of few already well-integrated countries and scaling up to the European level at a later stage. From a German perspective, closer cooperation with the Nordic countries as well as the Alpine region could be interesting as the hydro capacity in these countries could match quite well with increasing variable renewable generation in Germany. Another example of regional integration is the so-called Pentalateral Energy Forum that was established to integrate energy-only markets in France, Germany, The Netherlands, Belgium and Luxembourg in the context of the market coupling process. The Penta countries were the first to achieve the target of full coupling of their day-ahead markets in 2010, with deeper integration steps to follow in later years.[26] In 2013, the governments of the Penta countries – now expanded to Austria and Switzerland as an observer – decided to take the next steps and address joint resource adequacy issues.

Market design requirements
The most difficult challenge is to develop an advanced market design for the future power system. The current market design – consisting of the energy-only market and ancillary services markets – will not deliver the results needed in a power system dominated by variable renewable generation sources. However, while it does ensure an efficient dispatch of generation units, it does not sufficiently incentivise flexibility options, nor does it guarantee system reliability; and wind power and solar PV cannot generate sufficient revenues to cover their costs.

• Although there are lots of flexibility options provided by the technical system, they are not sufficiently rewarded in the current market design. Existing options – be it in the ancillary services markets or through the regulation for interruptible loads[27] – are incoherent.

• There is a long debate among energy economists whether the energy-only market guarantees system reliability. While from a classical point of view a perfectly designed energy-only market with a high price elasticity of demand would theoretically ensure sufficient revenues for market participants in order to guarantee the capacity to cover peak load, there are serious doubts regarding the reality test, especially concerning the underlying assumptions on price elasticity of demand and the behaviour of investors. Furthermore, there are policy risks: it seems rather unlikely that politicians will accept on a regular basis very high price spikes up to e.g. 10,000 EUR/MWh in hours of shortage.[28]

• Finally, there are serious doubts whether the current market design will ever be able to finance variable renewables, even when they are cheaper than conventional generation technologies. Wind power and solar PV enter the market with marginal costs of (almost) zero. Thus, whenever the sun is shining and the wind is blowing, they produce plenty of electricity, therefore pushing other technologies with higher marginal costs out of the merit order and thus effectively driving down wholesale market prices. In times without wind and sun, prices increase again – but, obviously, they do not produce electricity and thus cannot generate the revenues to cover their costs. In other words: in the current marginal costs based market, wind power and solar PV cannibalise their own price and thus are generally unable to survive without additional support.[29]

It is thus necessary to think about adapting the market design to future needs. A lot of different design options exist which should be analysed carefully. One option would be to develop an investment market which optimally incentivises the needed installations while positively interacting with the energy-only market and the market for ancillary services. The German government is suggesting to stick to the energy-only market approach, but to complement it by a capacity reserve. As for the financing of renewables, auctions for the supporting market premiums are envisaged. The parliament is to decide on these two reforms in 2016.

Figure 6 **An advanced market design for the energy transition is necessary which delivers new investments at lowest cost**

Illustrative structure of a future market design

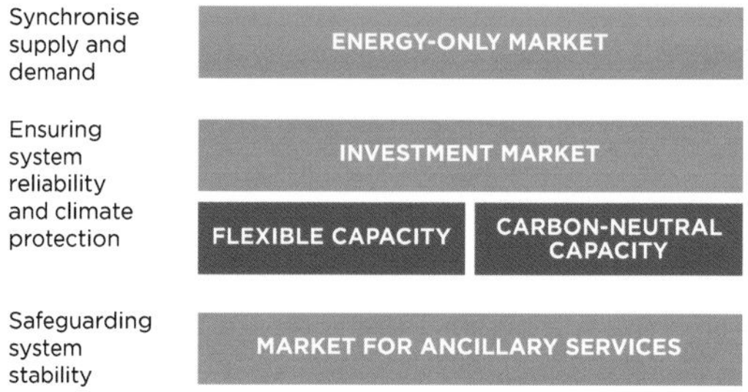

Source: Agora Energiewende

Conclusion

Germany's future energy system will be based on wind power and solar photovoltaics. Consequently, the flexibility challenge has been identified as the main paradigm shift in Germany's energy policy: smart grids, renewable assets, fossil power plants, electricity demand and storage facilities will have to be highly flexible, adapting to the continuously changing electricity production by wind power and solar PV. There are a lot of technological solutions already available to solve this issue at comparable low cost, so that the key task to be solved by German energy politics is to develop a market design to ensure resource adequacy, the necessary build-up of renewables and a fair competition between the different flexibility options.

The remaining key question is therefore: is what we have described as the *Energy transition*, in fact the German way to do it, a kind of German *Sonderweg*? Or, is Germany a first mover, i.e. the first major industrialised country to pursue this path?

There are good reasons to believe that the latter is true and other countries will follow – or even overtake the developments in Germany. If one compares solar radiation in Germany with the rest of the world, one will find very few countries with less sun. In other words, now that solar PV is cheap in Germany, its deployment in sunny industrialised countries such as Australia or parts of the United States (e.g. Hawaii or California) will increase rapidly. 2015 trends in the world solar PV market show that Germany is already no longer the leading market, by a large margin. The highest shares of new solar PV installations are found in China, Japan and the USA. Similarly, in many countries of the world, conditions for wind power energy are much better than in Germany. And, again, it is China and the USA that are leading in new wind and solar power energy deployment in 2013/2014.

More and more international institutions and financial investors are discovering that the future of energy systems lies in wind power and solar PV. The scenarios calculated for the European Commission in the context of the EU's Energy Roadmap 2050 found that in 2050 wind power and solar PV will provide 25–67% of Europe's energy supply – based on outdated data from the European Commission regarding technology costs.[30] It is thus fair to believe that Germany is just the testing case for what is going to happen in many places and countries in the years to come. Researchers are therefore well advised to have a closer look at the technology and market design challenges in the context of power systems with high shares of variable renewable energies.

Figure 7a **Average wind speed at 80m above ground level**
There is wind available all over the world...

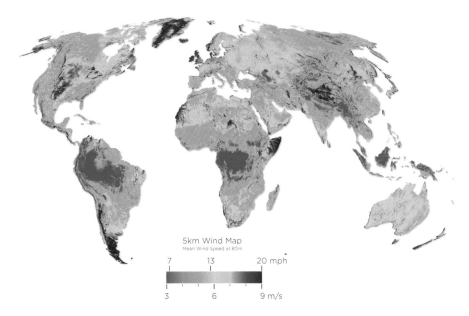

Figure 7b **Annual solar radiation in W/m²**
... and almost everywhere there is more sunshine than in Germany!

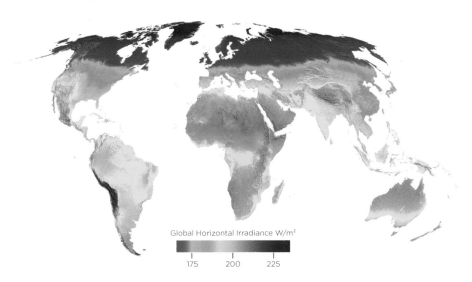

Notes

1 See e.g. European Climate Foundation (ECF), *Energy Roadmap 2050 – a practical guide to a prosperous, low carbon Europe and European Commission* (2010); *Energy Roadmap 2050* (2011).

2 This classification in goals of first and second order was first developed by the independent expert group for monitoring of the energy transition; see http://bmwi.de/DE/Themen/Energie/Energiewende/monitoring-prozess.html

3 Targets according to energy concept of 2010, except for the nuclear target (taken from the Nuclear Phase-Out Act of 2011) and share of renewable energy in electricity (taken from the Renewable Energy Act of 2014).

4 J. Blazejczak et al., *Improved energy efficiency: vital for energy transition and stimulus for economic growth* (DIW Economic Bulletin 4, 2014) and AG Energiebilanzen (2013) Ausgewählte Effizienzindikatoren zur Energiebilanz Deutschland. Daten für die Jahre von 1990 bis 2012).

5 AG Energiebilanzen 2015.

6 Trend Research, *Definition und Marktanalyse von Bürgerenergie in Deutschland* (2014).

7 The dominating technology is wind onshore. While the installed capacity of wind offshore was less than 1 GW in 2013, the government is planning to increase it to 6.5 GW in 2020.

8 For projections of future cost developments of renewable technologies see e.g. Fraunhofer ISE, *Levelized Costs of Electricity – Renewable Energy Technologies* (2013). M. Ragwitz, Fraunhofer ISI et al., *RE-Shaping – Shaping an effective and efficient European renewable energy market*, study undertaken on behalf of the Executive Agency for Competitiveness and Innovation (EACI) of the European Commission (2012). C. von Hirschhausen et al., *European Electricity Generation Post-2020: Renewable Energy not to be underestimated* (DIW Economic Bulletin, 3/9, 2013).

9 UBA, *Potenzial der Windenergie an Land. Studie zur Ermittlung des bundesweiten Flächen und Landnutzungspotenzials der Windenergienutzung an Land* (2013).

10 UBA, *Stromerzeugung aus erneuerbaren Energien* (2011).

11 In 2002, basic remuneration for small biomass plants was 10.1 ct/kWh, while in 2012 it was at 14.3 ct/kWh.

12 Details are noted in the German Renewable Energy Act (EEG) itself.

13 While wind power onshore is already at this level, further cost decreases for solar PV are expected. In 2015, a large solar PV plant will produce below 10 ct/kWh, e.g. under the following conditions: installation costs 1,000,-/kWp, electricity yield 1,000h/year, 25 years working life, operating costs of 1% of installation costs, interest costs for capital investment of 5% annually.

14 EWI, *Untersuchungen zu einem zukunftsfähigen Strommarktdesign*, report for the German Federal Ministry for Economy (2012), 27ff; and DLR/Fraunhofer IWES/IfnE, *Langfristszenarien und Strategien für den Ausbau der erneuerbaren Energien in Deutschland bei Berücksichtigung der Entwicklung in Europa und global*, study undertaken on behalf of the German Federal Environmental Ministry (2012), 217. For the system's perspective on technology cost, see section 'Considering system costs' of this chapter.

15 This is the case for solar PV and onshore wind power. Offshore wind power is different as it is usually built in large parks and feeds directly into the transmission grid. Still, even offshore wind power parks are significantly smaller than modern conventional power plants that easily are of the size of 1 Gigawatt.

16 VDE, *Erneuerbare Energie braucht flexible Kraftwerke – Szenarien bis 2020*, ETG Task Force for the Flexibilisation of Power Plants (2012).

17 Agora Energiewende, *12 Insights on Germany's Energy transition* (2013).

18 For a discussion see e.g. L. Hirth, *The Market Value of Variable Renewables* (Energy Economics 38, 2013), 218–236.

19 IEA, *The Power of Transformation – Wind, Sun and the Economics of Flexible Power Systems* (2014).

20 Agora Energiewende, *Comparing the Cost of Low-Carbon Technologies: What is the cheapest option?* (2014).

21 Regarding future cost developments, the general trend shows further cost reductions for wind power and solar PV, while nuclear installations are expected to be more expensive than today; see e.g. Hirschhausen et al., *European Electricity Generation Post-2020: Renewable Energy not to be underestimated.*

22 See the Renewable Energy Act of 2014.

23 Data for 2013 preliminary, see http://www.umweltbundesamt.de/en/press, no. 10/2014.

24 Prognos/EWI/GWS, *Energieszenarien 2011* (2011).

25 Booz & Co., *Benefits of an Integrated European Energy Market?* (2013).

26 It should be noted that Nordic countries – Norway, Sweden, Finland and Denmark – integrated their markets in the 1990s (Nordpool) and thus served as the blueprint for the market coupling process in Europe.

27 Verordnung über Vereinbarungen zu abschaltbaren Lasten.

28 For an overview of this discussion see e.g. P. Cramton & A. Ockenfels, *Economics and design of capacity markets for the power sector* (Zeitschrift für Energiewirtschaft 36/2, 2011), 113–134.

29 O. Kopp et al., *Können sich erneuerbare Energien langfristig auf wettbewerblich organisierten Strommärkten finanzieren?* (Zeitschrift für Energiewirtschaft online, 2012).

30 European Commission, *Energy Roadmap 2050* (2011).

See also

Agora/ECF/RAP, *Positive Effects of Energy Efficiency on the German Power Sector* (2014)

TOWARDS A REGENERATIVE FOOD SYSTEM

Martin Stuchtey and Morten Rossé

This chapter explores the potential benefits of the transition to a more regenerative food system. Based on numerous concrete examples, the authors describe how the circular economy approach could be applied to a global agriculture system in retaining and restoring natural capital, in regenerating soil through the recovery of nutrients by 'closing the loop', optimising peri-urban and urban food production and reducing food waste by creating digital supply chains. This systemic approach, combined with the best of traditional agriculture, would both improve soil and food quality, whilst using significantly less synthetic fertiliser, pesticides, energy, land and water.

Martin Stuchtey
Martin is the Director of the McKinsey Center for Business and Environment and leads the firm's work on strategic resources. He is based in McKinsey's Munich office.

Morten Rossé
Morten is an Expert Associate Principal with McKinsey's Sustainability & Resource Productivity practice, he is also based in Munich. Alongside the Ellen MacArthur Foundation, they are co-authors of the report *Growth Within: A Circular Economy Vision for a Competitive Europe.*

The agricultural story of the 20th century was one of unprecedented success: due to more intensive and specialised cultivation, farmers markedly improved productivity and kept food prices low. However, this industrialisation has created problems of its own, and may – unaltered – be running out of steam. In 2010, for the first time in a century, the growth of global grain yields fell below that of the global population growth.

That is why we believe it is time to move away from what has become a 'linear food system.' By that, we mean a take, make, dispose system in which too often synthetic inputs go into the land; the land gets overused; and a huge proportion of the food produced is wasted and ends up in landfill. In addition, many nutrients never make it back to the field, stacking up in contaminated sludge. The goal should be to move toward a regenerative system in which land is restored as it is used and in which nutrient and material loops provide much-needed inputs, resulting in a healthier food supply.

A modern, circular agricultural system would bring the field closer to consumers and consumers closer to the food they eat. They would also be more knowledgeable, as apps and other innovations inform them about their food options and offer on-demand ways to shop intelligently. Improved use of data squeezes out waste all along the value chain.

This article explores how this can be done. Our focus is on developed countries, with a particular emphasis on Europe, because these economies are in a position to figure out what works and how. That said, many problems, such as soil erosion, nutrient runoff, and water management, are in evidence around the world. We believe, then, that our recommendations could be relevant globally. Moreover, Europe and other developed countries are highly skilled and productive; if they can make these principles work in practice, the demonstration effect will be powerful. That matters: an estimated 9.6 billion people will need to be fed by 2050, so the time to start rethinking the food system is now.

Introduction

Agriculture uses almost 40% of the land on the planet;[1] in addition to filling the world's dinner plates, it can provide essential ecosystem services, such as water retention and treatment, pollination, and energy. It also continues to be the largest single source of global employment, particularly in poorer countries and rural areas.

But there are three looming issues. The global food system is wasteful. It causes undue environmental harm. And it is not as healthy as it could and should be.

There is a common underpinning to these problems – the limits and side-effects of the post-war industrial model of agriculture. The great advantage of this approach, which emphasised ever-greater inputs and scale, was that the higher productivity associated with it did feed the world. But now that approach is faltering. Global productivity grew 2.2% a year in the 1960s, but only in 0.9% in 2010, according to the Food and Agriculture Organization. With the global population expected to reach 9.6 billion by 2050 and increasing wealth encouraging people to consume more protein, the world's farmers will need to produce 70% more food calories in 2050 than they did in 2000 to meet demand.

This chapter plants some preliminary thoughts on what a more restorative and regenerative food system would look like and what opportunities it could create. Organic, sustainable or conservation farming has a long history, of course; we seek to enrich the discussion by applying the concept of a circular, regenerative economy to agriculture. The findings are based in large part on the recent report, *Growth Within: A Circular Economy Vision for a Competitive Europe*. This was the result of a nine-month study by the Ellen MacArthur Foundation, Stiftungsfonds für Umweltökonomie und Nachhaltigkeit (SUN), and the McKinsey Center for Business and Environment.[2]

Three problems
The global food system has three major shortcomings:

The system is wasteful. About one-third of all food produced in the world is lost or wasted before people consume it.[3] For fruits and vegetables, this number may approach 50%. Consumers in developed countries waste almost as much food (222 million tonnes) as sub-Saharan Africa produces (230 million tonnes). These numbers represent all types of waste along the supply chain, from farmer to shop, as well as food wasted by consumers. The problem exists in both developing and developed countries, though for different reasons. In developing countries, more than 40% of the food losses occur at the post-harvest and processing stages, often due to lack of refrigeration or storage. In developed countries, more than 40% of the food losses occur at the retail and consumer stages.

Too often, agricultural production also wastes water and fertiliser. Agricultural activities account for 70% of global water withdrawals. In mature economies like Europe, 25% of water is lost in conveyance[4] and crops absorb less than 35% of the water applied to the field. When food losses are added to the equation, the bottom line is that in Europe, people consume only 20% of the water withdrawn for agriculture. Meanwhile, 23% of the European surface area is water-scarce during the summer (11% year-round); that number is expected to increase to 45% (30% year-round) by 2030.[5] Globally, the 2030 Water Resources Group estimates that there will be supply-demand water gap of 40% by 2030.[6]

©Chafer Machinery-CC Flickr

The same pattern holds for fertilisers. In Europe, crops absorb only 30–50% of applied fertiliser[7] and use almost 25% of that amount to create the non-edible parts of crops; these are mostly discarded and not used to fertilise the land. Taking into account food waste and the fact that the human body does not absorb all the nutrients consumed, this means that 95% of the fertiliser used does not end up providing nutrients to people.

Finally, most nutrients in food waste, sewage, and waste water are not recovered. They are incinerated or landfilled, or they leak into the biosphere. In the EU-27, 70% of the phosphorus in sewage sludge and biodegradable solid waste is not recovered.[8] This is an example of why we consider the system linear in design. A circular, or regenerative, system would put these by-products to work.

The system contributes to natural capital degradation.[9] Specialisation and the greater use of inputs such as nitrogen, phosphorus and potassium fertiliser, pesticides, and fuel have clearly helped to increase productivity. But there are serious downsides to these practices.

Consider nitrogen, which is a required building block for plants to grow. The nitrogen in the air gets 'fixed' in the ground, nurturing the plants above ground. An alternative way is to do this is to use synthetic nitrogen. Today, more nitrogen is fixed synthetically in fertilisers than is fixed naturally[10] – an indication of the astonishing amount of fertiliser that is being used. Phosphorus flows into the ocean at twice the safe operating limits of global

Figure 1 Looking down on earth from space the scale of destruction is astonishing

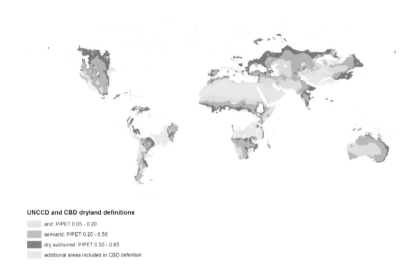

UNCCD and CBD dryland definitions

arid: P/PET 0.05 - 0.20

semiarid: P/PET 0.20 - 0.50

dry subhumid: P/PET 0.50 - 0.65

additional areas included in CBD definition

ecosystems.[11] The run-off of fertiliser into rivers, lakes, and oceans creates a breeding ground for algae that cause eutrophication, depleting stocks of fish and other species. This has created more than 400 dead zones or low-oxygen zones in oceans and lakes around the world.[12]

The wasteful use of fertilisers, irrigation, and machinery can also damage bio-diversity and exhaust topsoil. Globally, 5–10 million hectares of arable land are lost each year.[13] One quarter of the planet's land is highly degraded (Figure 1); at current rates of degradation, all of the world's topsoil could be lost within 60 years.[14]

Degraded soil does not absorb as much carbon; better land-use practices and restoring degraded land, then, could be a key factor in reducing CO_2 levels.[15] Intensification, specialisation, and agriculture-related deforestation are principally responsible for the 25% of the global greenhouse gas (GHG) emissions that come from agriculture.[16]

The system does not produce healthy outcomes. Food quality should improve over time. During the second half of the 20th century, however, the nutritional content of several vegetables studied fell significantly. Compared with the 1950s, tomatoes in the US provide 55% less potassium, cucumbers 78% less iron, and salad 63% less vitamin B2.

In addition, today's food often contains traces of toxic chemicals or plastics. Fish, for example, accumulate plastics and toxic pollutants by eating small fragments of debris floating in the ocean and by absorbing heavy metal contamination and other pollutants.[17] While these issues are alarming, they also create compelling reasons to think differently. They point to the need for a new direction – and also what direction that should be. The answer, ironically, is to think in circles.

Five ways to reshape the food system
In terms of how to get started on the circular path, there are a number of promising approaches (Figure 2).

Some of these approaches are already working and are likely to scaled up in the near future; others are nascent and will require companies, policymakers, consumers, and other stakeholders to make decisions for them to take root.

Here are four approaches derived from this framework that are worth considering.

Retain and restore natural capital (Regenerate). Restoration of large, damaged ecosystems is possible. One famous example is the Loess plateau in China, where 1.5 million hectares of degraded land have been restored since the mid-1990s. This project lifted more than 2.5 million people out of poverty, almost tripling their income, by replacing low-value agricultural commodities with high-value products. Per capita grain output rose 60% and the perennial vegetation cover doubled from 17% to 34%. In addition, flood control, water use, employment, biodiversity, and carbon absorption all improved.[18]

The commercial potential of restoration is already proven. The Savory Institute, based in Colorado, US, promotes a process that emulates nature. As the institute describes it, managers control the livestock so that conditions mimic the predator/prey relationships that were in existence when the grasslands evolved. This involves dividing land into smaller paddocks, putting cattle in large herds, and moving them frequently across the property. Depending on the season and other conditions, managers can vary the size of herds and the frequency of herd movements. The land benefits from the cycle of use and rest – the same pattern observed in grazing animals in natural grassland ecosystems. This approach has regenerated more than 2.5 million hectares.

SLM Partners is a British-Australian investment fund that acquires and manages rural land on behalf of institutional investors; it delivers financial returns and environmental benefits by scaling up regenerative, ecological farming systems following the methodology of the Savory Institute. SLM has acquired more than 480,000 hectares of grazing land in Australia to produce grass-fed beef cattle in a fund, which has raised AUD 75 million. The Land Life Company is a Dutch firm that provides a low-cost, biodegradable product, the COCOON, which gathers water more efficiently and thereby can regrow trees with much higher likelihood of survival in dry areas. This improves the ecological and aesthetic value of land as part of large restoration and landscaping projects. It has done so successfully in Spain and Saudi Arabia.

Return recovered resources for use in organic production systems (Regenerate). There is great potential to recover nutrients from various waste streams and either put them to work into new systems or return them to where they came from as inputs. That is what we mean by 'closing the loop' – a cycle of use and reuse. For example, the EU has made progress in recovering phosphorus from sewage sludge, meat and bonemeal, and biodegradable solid waste; this material now accounts for almost 30% of synthetic phosphorus fertiliser use in the region.[19]

There are other examples of closing nutrient loops in pockets of the European economy. In Sweden, two municipalities have mandated that all new toilets must[20] separate urine from faeces; urine makes up only 1% of domestic waste water volume but contains most of the nutrients.[21] Local farmers can collect the urine for use as liquid fertiliser.

In Italy, more than 4,000 municipalities conduct intensive separation of food and garden bio-waste. These efforts affect about 40 million inhabitants;

Figure 2 **Reshaping the food system**

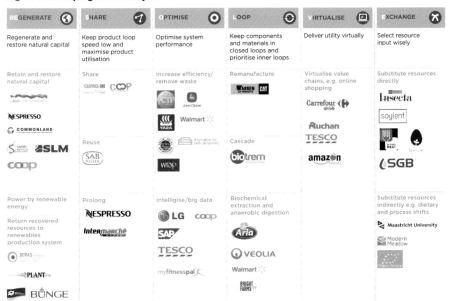

Source: Company interviews; Web search. S. Heck and M. Rogers, Resource revolution:
How to capture the biggest business opportunity in a century, 2014.

4.8 million tonnes of bio-waste are collected for treatment in composting or anaerobic digestion plants.[22] In the UK, two-thirds of sewage sludge is treated in 146 anaerobic digestion plants, and another 175 plants produce bio-energy from solid waste, a number that is growing rapidly.[23]

Several companies have developed systems that use by-products or waste from one process as inputs for other ones further along the value chain. Bunge, a global agribusiness and food company with headquarters in the United States, used its sugarcane refining process to remove the soluble sugars from soybeans, because fish and some other marine organisms are unable to digest soluble sugars. With those removed, soybeans can be used as feed. The by-product can also be fermented to produce ethanol or used to extract more sugars from the soybean.[24]

The Plant, an urban farm in Chicago, uses carefully selected tilapia, vegetables, beer, and kombucha tea production to balance waste and feedstock needs. The waste from one product is used as inputs to support production of others. Other waste is put into an anaerobic digestion chamber and converted into power. This is a fully closed-loop, zero-waste system.[25]

Various sustainable and regenerative agricultural practices return the recovered resources as described above and use them in organic production systems that

The Lufa Farms in Montreal has two rooftop greenhouses totaling 1.75 acres. The production of greens, herbs, peppers and eggplants is delivered to approximately 4,000 local customers each week. ©: Lufa Farms

preserve natural capital and optimise long-term yields. Organically cultivated land area in Europe is expanding 6% a year.[26] Silvopastoral systems combine forestry and grazing of domesticated animals in a mutually beneficial way that enhances soil protection.

The Baltic Ecological Recycling Agriculture and Society (BERAS) promotes 'ecological recycling agriculture'; this integrates organic crop production with the cultivation of leguminous grassland and animal husbandry. Animal manure becomes fertiliser for the land; the result is a high degree of self-sufficiency in fodder and fertilisers.[27]

Promote peri-urban and urban food production (Optimise). The demand for local, fresh, and relatively unprocessed food is growing. Walmart has built greenhouses at or near their stores to produce fresh vegetables. In addition, in 2010, it committed to source at least USD 1 billion of produce from local small farmers. That pledge helped to propel growth in the US local food market, which nearly tripled in value from about USD 4 billion in 2002 to more than USD 11 billion by 2012. American greenhouse operator, Bright Farms, has signed a contract with supermarket chain Giant Foods to supply 450 tonnes of produce annually to 30 Washington, DC area stores from a 100,000+ square foot greenhouse located in the metro area. This is expected to be the largest urban greenhouse operation anywhere in world. In Europe, Barcelona has announced a goal of producing half its food in the metropolitan region.[28]

Establishing shorter supply chains between farms and retailers or consumers reduces the waste associated with transport. Doing so can also help to create local jobs and strengthen rural/urban links.

On a smaller scale, urban farming is also emerging, in the form of vertical, hydroponic, and aquaponic farms. Vertical farms grow produce inside or on top of buildings. Hydroponic agriculture grows plants without soil; instead they are rooted in a watery solution of mineral nutrients. In aquaponic farms, plants absorb fish excretions as nutrients, and clean water returns to the fish basins. All three forms of urban farming typically happen in a controlled environment that enables faster crop cycles, and thus more crop rotations per year. Typically, these farms use 70–90% less water and fertiliser than conventional ones because they keep unabsorbed water and nutrients in the system. Vertical Farm Systems, an agriculture-tech company based in Queensland, Australia, offers equipment that integrates an automated growing system,[29] robotic seeding, and automated harvesting functions; these are controlled from a single computer. PlantLab, a private research facility, in Den Bosch, central Netherlands, grows Fittonia plants in special darkened rooms illuminated by blue and red LEDs. There are many of these examples, where the farm has moved inside, and technology secures the right light, water, and temperature levels.

© Marjo van de Peppel - PlantLab

Of course, not all crops can grow in a controlled environment, and soil-less farming is limited mainly to vegetables and herbs; it needs hardly be said that cities are not going to supplant traditional farms. But given that more than half the world's population now lives in urban areas (a percentage that is growing), the idea that cities have a role to play in food production makes sense. Understanding the full potential of this sector will require further analysis.

Create digital supply chains to reduce food waste (Optimise). Twenty percent of food gets wasted on its way from the farm to the store in developed economies. Big data and IT can help to improve inventory management and thus shrink that figure. Tesco, the British supermarket chain, uses weather forecasts to predict local sales and required stock levels. A rise in the temperature on a summer weekend, for example, can translate into demand for more picnic-type foodstuffs. SAP, the German software giant, offers retailers a dynamic consumer-pricing system that changes item prices in real time, based on availability and expiration date of the product. COOP, a European food retailer, has automated its fresh-food replenishment system to manage one of the largest sources of waste.[30] Digital solutions, such as smart refrigerators, on-demand e-commerce delivery, and wearable monitors can help consumers to buy the right quantity and quality of food at the right times. This will help to cut down the amount of food that people throw away.

Figure 3 **Potential economic and environmental impact of current development scenarios vs circular scenario**

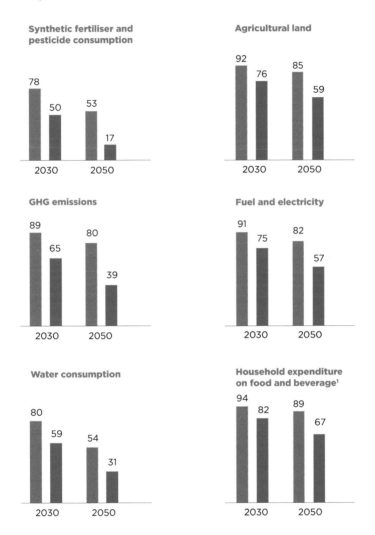

● Current development scenario ● Circular scenario   EU-27, indexed (2012 = 100)

1 Including food and catering services (e.g. restaurants).

Source: Expert interviews; Eurostat household expenditure data; MGI, *Overcoming obesity: An initial economic analysis*, 2014; FAO, *Global food losses and food waste – Extent, Causes and Prevention*, 2011; EEA, *Towards efficient use of water resources in Europe*, 2012; EU Commission, *Official journal of the EU, Commission Agriculture and Rural Development, 2012 budget*, 2012; FAOSTAT; Kimo van Dijk, *Present and future phosphorus use in Europe: food system scenario analyses*, Wageningen University, 2014; Josef Schmidhuber, *The EU Diet – Evolution, Evaluation and Impacts of the CAP*, 2008; Gregor Zupančič and Viktor Grilc, *Anaerobic Treatment and Biogas Production from Organic Waste*, 2012; Joint Research Centre (JRC) of the European Commission et al., *Precision agriculture: an opportunity for EU farmers – potential support with the CAP 2014-2020*, 2014; Ellen MacArthur Foundation, *Delivering the circular economy: a toolkit for policymakers*, 2015.

The EUR 320 billion opportunity
A circular food system would combine all these approaches, while also incorporating the best of traditional agriculture, to improve both the quality of the food produced and the health of the land that produces it.

In terms of consumption, combining lower-calorie intake with a significant reduction in food waste could mean that Europeans could have a diverse and interesting diet while using up to 40% fewer calories in 2050 than today. This could lower average annual household spending on food by almost 25% by 2030 and 40% by 2050, with no sacrifice in quality. In terms of production, a circular system would use significantly less synthetic fertiliser, pesticides, energy, land, and water, while emitting fewer GHGs (Figure 3).

The circular scenario might also produce more jobs than otherwise, because organic farming and waste management are relatively labour-intensive activities. All told, we estimate that if Europe implemented the four approaches described above, the direct and indirect economic benefits could reach **EUR** 320 billion (compared to the current development path).

This will not just happen; it will require new policies and priorities. For example, there needs to be prices for resources, natural capital, and environmental effects and support for restoring degraded lands. There would be mechanisms to collect, separate, and process bio-waste, waste water, and sewage to maximise the recovery and reuse of nutrients and reduce the need for synthetic fertilisers. Better labelling and packaging could reduce consumer food waste. Related efforts would explore new business models to change how people consume food, such as broader use of subscriptions for daily or weekly delivery of recipes that specify the right quantity of the necessary ingredients. Public and private initiatives and IT-based delivery of dietary information, such as health and diet trackers, could reverse the upward trend in daily calorie intake.[31] Public interventions could address portion control, labelling, nutritional education, and healthy diets in schools and public institutions.

Nowhere else is the link between long-term economic viability of our model use and the health of the underlying assets as evident as in agriculture and soil. And nowhere have we departed so visibly from the concept of regeneration, replenishment, and circularity. Building a new food system that puts the long-term productivity of our biological systems at the centre won't be easy, but the time is right to start. Multiple trends in Europe – greater attention to health and diet, the growing awareness of food waste and the need for natural capital conservation and rehabilitation, the better understanding of soil and plant biology, and new digital technology – are creating new possibilities for change.

Notes

1 http://data.worldbank.org/indicator/AG.LND.AGRI.ZS/countries

2 Ellen MacArthur Foundation, SUN, McKinsey Center for Business and Environment, *Growth Within: A Circular Economy Vision for a Competitive Europe* (2015).

3 FAO, *Global food losses and food waste – Extent, causes and prevention* (2011).

4 European Environmental Agency, *Towards efficient use of water resources in Europe* (2012).

5 *Gap Analysis of the Water Scarcity and Droughts Policy in the EU* (2012).

6 2030 Water Resources Group, *Charting Our Water Future* (2009).

7 IFDC, *Eight Reasons FDP is Changing Bangladesh* (22 October 2015; ifdc.org/?s=fdp).

8 Kimo van Dijk et al., *Present and future phosphorus use in Europe: food system scenario analyses (including meat and bone meal)* (2014).

9 See http://www.eea.europa.eu/soer-2015/europe/agriculture, #note5 for more details on the environmental externalities.

10 European Environmental Agency, *The European environment – State and outlook* (2015).

11 J. Rockström et al., *Planetary boundaries: Guiding human development on a changing planet* (Science, 2015).

12 Bob Diaz of the Virginia Institute of Marine Science (VIMS) and Swedish researcher Rutger Rosenberg

13 G. S. Chahal et al., *Principles and Procedures of Plant Breeding: Biotechnological and Plant Breeding* (Alpha Science, 2006).

14 United Nations statement on World Soil Day.

15 New Climate Economy, *Better growth, better climate: The New Climate Economy Report* (2014).

16 IPCC, *Climate Change 2014: Mitigation of climate change* (2014).

17 C. M. Rochman et al., *Ingested plastic transfers hazardous chemicals to fish and induces hepatic stress* (Nature Scientific Reports, 2013).

18 World Bank.

19 Kimo van Dijk et al., *Present and future phosphorus use in Europe: food system scenario analyses* (2014).

20 Dana Cordell et al., *The story of phosphorus* (Global Environmental Change, 19, 2009), 292–305.

21 Approximately 80% of the nitrogen, 55% of the phosphorus, and 60% of the potassium. Caroline Schönning, *Urine diversion – hygienic risks and microbial guidelines for reuse* (Swedish Institute for Infectious Disease Control, 2001).

22 http://www.waste-management-world.com/

23 www.biogas-info.co.uk, update January 2015.

24 Ellen MacArthur Foundation, *Case study: Bunge* (http://www.ellenmacarthurfoundation.org/case_studies/bunge).

25 Plant Chicago website, www.plantchicago.com

26 European Commission, *Facts and figures on organic agriculture in the European Union* (2013), based on Eurostat data, 2002–2011; in 2011, organically cultivated land represented 5.4% of the total utilised agricultural area in Europe.

27 Beras International website, www.beras.eu

28 Interview with Vicente Guallart, chief architect of Barcelona City Council.

29 Association for Vertical Farming website, http://vertical-farming.net/

30 PlanetRetail, *The Challenge of Food Waste: Retailers step up to the next level of inventory management* (2011).

31 McKinsey Global Institute, *Overcoming obesity: An initial economic analysis* (2014).

ECOSYSTEMS AS A UNIFYING MODEL FOR CITIES AND INDUSTRY

Michael Pawlyn

This chapter argues that if waste is seen as a nutrient or an underutilised resource then a new economic paradigm emerges and wealth can be created by consuming fewer resources. Two case studies show how ecosystem models can be applied to, firstly a factory and, secondly, a project that combines agriculture and technologies to produce a regenerative system. These examples illustrate that the characteristics of ecosystems can be used as a unifying model for cities and business. It is possible to develop solutions that are cyclical, resilient, run on current solar income and, crucially, go beyond the sustainability paradigm to deliver regenerative benefits to the human and natural capital on which they depend.

Michael Pawlyn
Michael is the Director of the architectural practice Exploration which delivers innovative solutions for commercial clients. He is also a Founding Partner of The Sahara Forest Project and the author of *Biomimicry in Architecture* (RIBA Publications, 2011).

Sustainability has been known to be a problematic word for some time now. Amory Lovins captures this well when he says "If you were to ask one of your friends how their relationship is with their partner and they were to say 'It's sustainable, you would probably say, 'I'm sorry to hear that'".[1] The word implies a situation that is just about bearable but a long way short of enjoyable. All too often 'sustainability' has involved mitigating negatives rather than optimising positives. It is time we moved beyond this to develop approaches to 'regenerative design'. Although this idea has been around for some time, it is satisfying to see it advanced in Naomi Klein's book *This changes everything,* in which she stresses the urgency of moving from an 'extractivist' mindset to a regenerative one.[2]

There have been three particular shifts in the economic development debate that have gained considerable traction in recent years: the circular economy, the idea of resilience and the emerging movement campaigning for 100% renewable energy cities. The Ellen MacArthur Foundation's Circular Economy 100 business innovation programme[3] is a testament to the success of the circular economy as an idea pioneered initially by Walter Stahel & Genevieve Reday[4] and subsequently by Michael Braungart & William McDonough.[5] The '100 Resilient Cities' initiative, pioneered by the Rockefeller Foundation, has been hugely successful in encouraging cities to plan for future challenges. Cities that have committed to 100% renewable energy include Copenhagen (aiming to be carbon neutral by 2025), Frankfurt (100% carbon reduction by 2050), Malmö (100% renewable electricity by 2020), Munich (100% renewable electricity by 2015), and many others.[6] To those new to the debate, these developments have the potential to create confusion – some might well ask, 'Should we be aiming for cyclical flows, resilience or renewable energy?' The likely answer for most of the people reading this book is 'Obviously, we need all three,' but we should be aware of the potential for confusion which can obstruct progress. The case put forward in this chapter is that studying ecosystems as a model for cities and industry has the potential to unify the aims of the circular economy, urban resilience and the 100% renewable cities movement. There is potential for all to gain from a framework that integrates these aims.

The characteristics of ecosystems

At this stage it would be worth summarising some of the differences between conventional human-made systems and ecosystems:[7]

Conventional human-made systems	Biological/ecological systems
Linear flows of resources	Closed-loop flows of resources[8]
Disconnected and mono-functional	Densely interconnected and symbiotic
Resistant to change	Adapted to constant change
Wasteful	Everything is nutrient[9]
Persistent toxins frequently used	No persistent toxins[10]
Often centralised and mono-cultural	Distributed and diverse
Hierarchically controlled	Panarchically self-regulating[11]
Fossil-fuel dependent	Run on current solar income
Engineered to maximise one goal	Optimised as a whole system
Extractive	Regenerative
Use global resources	Use local resources

The right-hand list it is argued here is a comprehensive summary of the transformations we need to bring about in our industries and cities if we are to make the shift from the industrial age to the ecological age. The 'everything is nutrient' and 'no persistent toxins' characteristics of ecosystems clearly have a strong fit with the aims of a circular economy and, as Janine Benyus has observed,[12] there is much to be learned from the way that nature has evolved to make use of a limited and safe subset of the periodic table. Another leading figure in the field of biomimetics, Professor Julian Vincent, has commented that, with just proteins and polysaccharides, nature has formed compounds that have all the same properties as man-made ones stretching from polymers through to high-strength composites.[13]

A desire to run cities on 100% renewable energy is clearly consistent with the way that nearly all biological life forms have evolved[14] – most organisms 'run on current solar income'. There is also an imperative for clean energy systems to be true to the sense of that term in the way they are made and dismantled too – otherwise we will just be handing down a problematic legacy to our children. More subtly, there are distinct benefits to modelling renewable energy systems on the kind of distributed, diverse and densely interconnected characteristics of ecosystems.

Where does resilience come into the ecosystem model? Resilience is defined by Judith Rodin as 'the capacity of any entity – an individual, a community, an organisation, or a natural system – to prepare for disruptions, to recover from shocks and stresses, and to adapt and grow from a disruptive experience.'[15] The most resilient systems display three defining characteristics – they have redundancy, diversity and are self-regulating. We can see all three of these at play in biological systems. Complex and densely interconnected systems are generally more resilient than simple disconnected ones because, in the former, there is a multiplicity (and therefore a healthy degree of redundancy) of entities and flows that can continue to operate and take up the slack if one part of the system is interrupted. Similarly, self-regulating systems are more resilient than hierarchical ones and the adaptability of ecosystems means that they are much better able to respond to change than less flexible systems. Donella Meadows observed that, 'A diverse system with multiple pathways and redundancies is more stable and less vulnerable to external shock than a uniform system with little diversity.'[16]

Some of these ideas were explored by the author while working at Grimshaw on schemes such as The Eden Project and The EcoRainforest. They were taken further in writing *Biomimicry in Architecture* which concluded that, 'If waste is seen as a nutrient or an under-utilised resource then a new economic paradigm emerges and wealth can be created by consuming fewer resources.'[17] The two case studies below will show how ecosystem models can be applied to, firstly, a factory and, secondly, a project that combines agriculture and a range of technologies to produce a regenerative system.

Case study – The Sahara Forest Project
The Sahara Forest Project is a new solution to create green jobs and ecosystem vegetation through profitable production of food, water, clean electricity and biomass in desert areas. The project was jointly initiated by Exploration Architecture in 2007 and then established as a stand-alone company. It was officially launched in 2009 and the first built version was completed in Qatar in 2012.

The starting point was a belief that it would be possible to use biomimicry to develop integrated solutions to some of the major challenges facing hot arid regions. We know that many of these areas are already suffering serious water stress and nearly all the climate models predict that this will get worse with climate change. To make matters more difficult we need to plan agriculture for a global population of over 9 billion by 2050 and, in the current extractive model, we are losing substantial areas of land to desertification. Furthermore, if we are to truly address the challenge of climate change, there is an urgent need to shift from a fossil fuel economy to a solar economy. These intertwined challenges of food, water and energy security – as well as climate change and desertification – are what a number of prominent scientists have referred to as 'a perfect storm' of challenges to address in the near future.

The three core components of the Sahara Forest Project are saltwater-cooled greenhouses, solar energy systems (photovoltaics (PV) and concentrated solar power (CSP)), and technologies for desert revegetation. The synergies arising from integrating the technologies into low-waste interconnected systems improve performance and economics compared to those of the individual components.

Some of the synergies between the technologies are as follows:

• CSP needs a supply of demineralised water to keep the mirrors clean and to run the turbines.

• The greenhouses are effectively acting as cooling towers for the CSP and get rid of the excess heat.

• The CSP mirrors and PV panels make it possible for a range of plants to grow in the shade underneath and, if the mirrors/panels were placed immediately behind the greenhouse, it could extend the zone of elevated humidity behind and consequently promote more restorative growth.

• The new outdoor vegetation stabilises soil and reduces dust so that more sunlight reaches the mirrors of the CSP installation.

The saltwater-cooled greenhouses developed by the Sahara Forest Project essentially mimic and enhance the conditions in which the Namibian fog-basking beetle harvests water in a desert: evaporation of seawater is increased to create higher humidity and then a large surface area is created for condensation. Saline water is turned into fresh water just using the sun, the wind and a small amount of pumping energy.

The Sahara Forest Project Pilot Facility

© Sahara Forest Project

The first built version of the Sahara Forest Project was the Pilot Facility in Qatar which was opened during the COP18 climate change negotiations in November 2012. This was an opportunity to test the core technologies together with others that showed potential for inclusion in the system as follows:

• Halophytes (plants that can grow directly in seawater and have the potential to provide food and fodder). They also provide a way to extract nutrients from seawater and use the resulting biomass to restore the fertility of desert soils.

• Algae for biofuels and nutraceuticals.[18]

• BioRock™ (a technology that can grow elements of structure in seawater through electro-deposition of minerals onto a steel frame).

• Conventional desalination to supplement the water production in the greenhouses and thereby boost plant productivity.

• Salt processing to explore ways to extract useful elements and compounds from the brine and move towards a closed-loop operation.

Figure 1 **The technologies and resource flows of The Sahara Forest Project. In simple terms the scheme is using what we have a lot of (sunlight, seawater and carbon dioxide) to produce more of what we need**

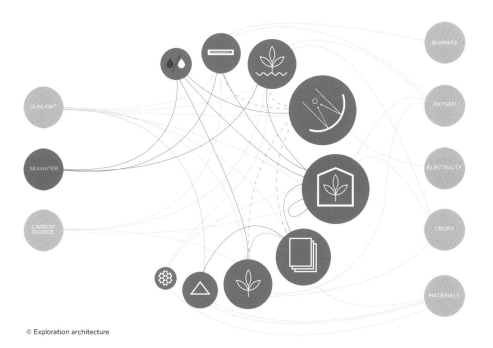

© Exploration architecture

Figure 2 **Diagram showing animal biodiversity recorded on the Sahara Forest Project Pilot Facility site, which was initially a barren area of desert. The diagram is structured according to levels of taxonomy showing class, order, family, genus and species**

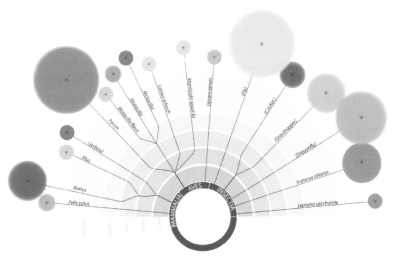

© Exploration architecture

The project succeeded in growing crops with half the amount of fresh water of conventional approaches and provided a wealth of data for the team to refine the system.[19] The next version will be on a site double the size in the Arava Valley, Jordan – a location that has ideal climatic conditions for the project. The project demonstrates the following characteristics that are typical of ecosystem models:

• It is moving towards being closed-loop although to advance this for the salt will require a larger-scale operation as many of the processes involved are only economical at large scale.

• It is densely interconnected and symbiotic (in the sense of having numerous synergies between the technologies).

• The extent to which it is adapted to constant change is debatable. In terms of its conception, the team are continuing to refine and develop the system. In terms of its operation, it has control systems that continually adapt to changes in the micro-climate.

• The axiom of 'everything is nutrient' has been followed and in most cases the outputs from one part of the system become inputs for another part. For example agricultural waste can be processed in a biochar burner to produce a soil conditioner that sequesters carbon and improves water-holding capacity of the soil. The salt processing has the potential to produce construction materials, fertilisers and other useful compounds.

• No persistent toxins have been used in the operation. The team has used biological forms of pest control in the greenhouse and will continue to develop this expertise on the Jordan project.

• The system has a degree of technological diversity and, rather than being engineered to maximise one goal, it is optimised as a whole system.

• It is run mostly on current solar income although it requires a grid connection for back-up. A larger-scale scheme, with a greater diversity of energy generation and storage, would be easier to design for full energy autonomy.

• It is regenerative in several key respects including forming a series of pathways to sequester atmospheric carbon into materials and soils. Its effect on biodiversity is described below.

• Due to the accelerated construction programme it was not possible to make extensive use of local resources but the team are working on improving this for subsequent phases.

For the first nine months of the Pilot Facility's operation the team monitored animal biodiversity[20] and Figure 2 shows what was achieved. An ecological survey carried out before construction showed that there were negligible levels of biodiversity on site apart from occasional bird sightings nearby – it was a bare patch of desert. Apart from common flies, the first animals to arrive were house sparrows which made an appearance the same day that plants were brought to the site. Soon after that we saw grasshoppers, crickets and the first butterfly. The variety of birds increased steadily through the course of the project so the next to arrive were wagtails, a rufous-tailed shrike when the halophytes were planted, then the first hoopoe (an indigenous and colourful bird not seen often in Qatar). As the desert plant species started to become more established increasing numbers of yellow wagtails, rock thrushes and a large wagtail were seen. When the algae ponds were filled, within a matter of a few days, the first dragonfly appeared. There was briefly a problematic species – rats – but this stabilised after a while with the arrival of a feral cat. Subsequently mouse tracks were found and footprints of the first truly indigenous desert mammal – a jerboa (a hopping desert rodent like a tiny kangaroo). This was the effect that was witnessed in just nine months. Over a longer time period and if the Sahara Forest Project were to be created at a larger scale the regenerative design effect would be even more pronounced.

Case study – The Zero Waste Textiles Factory

The Zero Waste Textiles Factory is a 30,000 m² facility that Exploration Architecture designed for a textile company in India. The client is a pioneer of sustainable thinking who described the brief for the project as follows:

'The idea with the new factory is to change the paradigm for factories in India. Textiles is a water- and power-intensive industry, which makes the project all the more challenging because our aim is to channel all waste from the project into closed loops, and to get as close to zero waste as possible. The structure should be designed and engineered to use the least material possible and should provide a world-class environment for the 600 people who will work at the factory.'

As with many areas of commerce, the textile industry is facing near-term increases in energy and commodities costs as well as steadily increasing levels of environmental legislation. The decision to design the factory to high standards was therefore taken in order to stay ahead of their competitors – by creating a low energy operation that approaches zero waste the company aims to meet the growing expectations from their supply chain and ensure long-term profitability.

The team used biomimicry as a design discipline to work towards the brief aims. This led to a strict north–south orientation for the building so that roof-lights with glazing facing north would provide generous amounts of natural light throughout the working environment while the sloping solid surfaces of the roof-lights are perfectly oriented for photovoltaic panels. The design team concluded that profiled aluminium was the most appropriate roofing material because of its lightweight nature (producing knock-on savings in the weight of the primary structure), full recyclability and because it maintains optimum water quality for the rainwater that is captured for use in the highly water-intensive textile processes. The design of the primary structure (steel columns and trusses) was further refined by learning from natural structures like glass sponges that show remarkable efficiency through what is known as structural hierarchy.

The client had already implemented some significant energy saving measures at their existing factory as shown in Figure 6. The new factory will take this even further with the most efficient machinery, double-sided mechanical servicing, water-cooled motors, biomimetic fans, biomass cogeneration and photovoltaics.

Figure 3 **Exterior view of the Zero Waste Textiles Factory**

Figure 4 **Truss design based on ideas of structural hierarchy found in biology**

Figure 5 **Glass sponge – a biological structure that demonstrates remarkable resource efficiency through structural hierarchy**

Figure 6 **Graph showing the energy saving measures already implemented by the client (mid-grey bars) and the new measures (light grey bars) to take the scheme through to zero carbon**

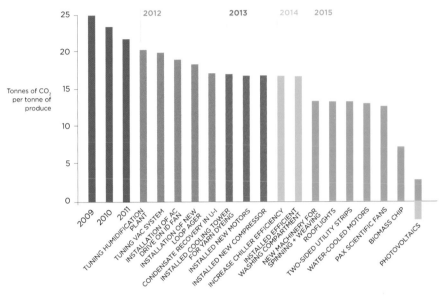

Figure 7 **Flow diagram showing a hypothetical factory without waste minimisation strategies showing a range of under-utilised resource streams (in reality, many textiles factories have transformed at least some of these into value streams)**

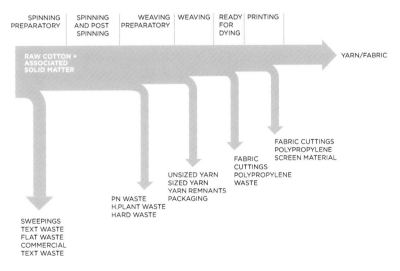

Figure 8 **Flow diagram showing how nearly all resource streams in the Zero Waste Textiles Factory are transformed into value**

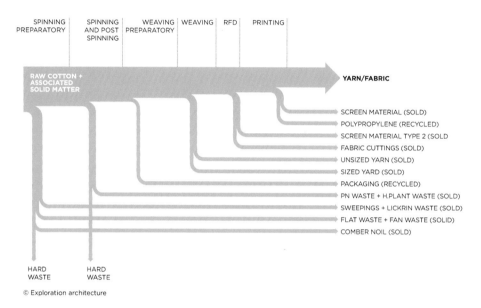

© Exploration architecture

Figure 9 **Flow diagram showing a hypothetical factory with a linear approach to water consumption**

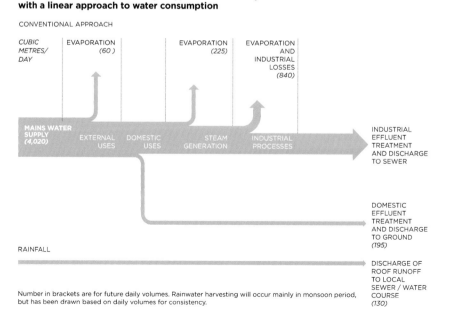

Number in brackets are for future daily volumes. Rainwater harvesting will occur mainly in monsoon period, but has been drawn based on daily volumes for consistency.

© Exploration architecture

Figure 10 **Flow diagram showing how the Zero Waste Textiles Factory can operate in a way that is close to closed-loop in terms of water use**

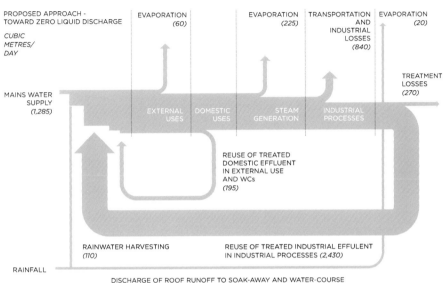

© Exploration architecture

In terms of ecosystem models, the team conceived of the factory as having three main realms: the machines and processes within the factory itself, a water strategy and an energy strategy (see Figure 10).

The machines and processes produce quite large amounts of waste fibre and nearly all of these are separated and sold for use in other applications – principally the production of lower-specification textiles. The team is working to find uses for the few remaining streams of waste fibres and is looking at the potential of making insulation and other products with commercial value. The water strategy has been designed, as far as possible, to use biological forms of water treatment – some fairly low-technology approaches such as reed-bed filtration and some high-performance biological processes. This has necessitated rethinking some of the dyeing and other treatment processes in order to eliminate, minimise or isolate problematic chemicals. The waste water treatment processes return much of the water back to the factory so that new inputs are minimised and, during the wetter times of the year, these can be substantially supplied from harvested rainwater.

The key element of the energy strategy is a shift from an existing dependence on mains electricity and process heat from a coal-fired boiler to a biomass cogeneration system (providing process heat and electricity) together with electricity from the photovoltaic panels. Anaerobic digestion is being explored

Figure 11 **Network diagram showing the main realms of the Zero Waste Textiles Factory**

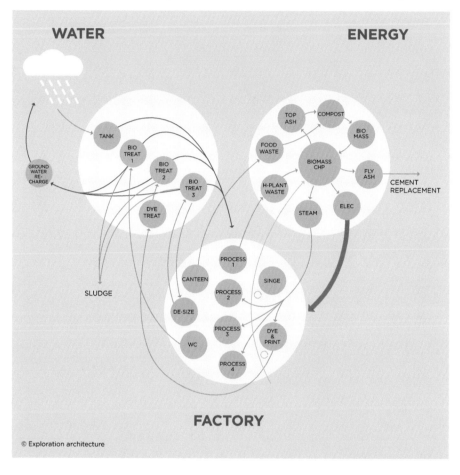

© Exploration architecture

in order to provide the small amounts of gas required for the singeing process and this would be entirely run on canteen food waste. Heat recovery from the machines allows waste heat to be fed into the cogeneration plant which increases its efficiency.

The project demonstrates the following characteristics that are typical of ecosystem models:

• It is moving towards being closed-loop in terms of water and materials.

• The elements are densely interconnected and symbiotic. There would be potential to take this even further in collaboration with the equipment manufacturers. There would also be scope to widen the system boundaries to include the production of raw cotton and end-of-life fibre/nutrient recovery from garments.

• It is adapted to constant change within the limits of what is imposed by the built infrastructure and equipment and it has control systems that continually adapt to changes in the micro-climate. Once established, major system changes are limited although there is still scope to control and improve the quality of inputs and to transform the remaining underutilised resource streams into value.

• The axiom of 'everything is nutrient' has been followed and in most cases the outputs from one part of the system become inputs for another part. There are some underutilised resources that are not currently captured such as humidity and low grade heat because they are relatively diffuse.

• The team has succeeded in designing out many of the toxins conventionally involved in textile manufacturing (mostly associated with dyeing processes) but the market was judged not to be ready for large-scale production of unbleached cotton (this is discussed further below).

• Diversity is provided at a technological level by having multiple identical machines for each stage in the process and providing compartmentalised sections to the water treatment systems. However, the factory remains fairly mono-functional compared to the complexities of real ecosystems. This could perhaps be addressed by co-locating with other industries that offer mutualistic benefits.

• It will run on current solar income once the biomass cogeneration system and photovoltaics are installed. This will be a huge improvement on the coal-fired boilers and grid electricity (also largely coal-based) that are used for the existing factory units on the site.

• It will be regenerative in terms of enhanced biodiversity on the site (partly from new planting but mainly from the plant-based water treatment systems) and life-enhancing for the people that work at the factory as it will provide light-filled workspaces with views to nature throughout.

• Local resources were explored for the structure of the building but the functioning of the factory required long-spans which can only realistically be achieved with steel. Once constructed the main resource flows, apart from energy, will be raw cotton and biomass. The team will endeavour to source these from as close to the factory as possible.

THE ECOSYSTEMS MODEL

The following is a suggested methodology for how to set about designing, or adapting, systems based on ecosystem models:

1. Visualise the key elements and flows in your system, as it is only by doing this that you are likely to really see the challenges and opportunities.

2. Convene a small group of creative polymaths to explore the opportunities presented by your system. This needs to involve at least two patterns of problem-solving – focused/deep as well as broad/creative. These sessions need to be led by an experienced workshop leader who can set and maintain the right tone as well as lead the team through 'divergent' and 'convergent' stages (the former involves opening up and exploring a wide range of possibilities; the latter involves carefully narrowing those down to the most relevant).

3. Look for synergies between technologies by assessing the inputs and outputs of each.

4. You will need to look at every challenge as an opportunity – if there is something underutilised in the system think about what you can add to transform that resource into value. Likewise, for the inputs from outside the system, think about whether you might be able to add something to your system that provides, or renders unnecessary, that input.

5. Test for resilience by seeing how you could sabotage the system – which link, if broken, would cause the system to collapse? Once you know that, you can see where you need greater diversity and multiplicity of connections to create resilience.

6. Try to be inventive with waste at every level – not just with physical resources but also financial resources and with what is arguably the most deplorable form of waste – underutilised human resources.

7. Consider opportunities to widen the system boundaries and connect with resource flows in adjoining schemes.

8. Reconsider conventional approaches to resource ownership and explore opportunities for leasing services or buying performance rather than purchasing products.

9. Use computational tools to assist with resolving complex flows and interdependencies.

10. Pursue every opportunity to reduce energy use in the system (which includes a careful consideration of layout) and then make the case for supplying all energy needs from renewables. The case should include not just financial considerations but also the less quantifiable moral ones and the benefits of demonstrating leadership.

11. It is common to run into difficulties when planning systems as complex as this and it is worth reflecting on a quotation from Ben Okri who said that '...adversity is not the end of a story but, where there is courage and vision, the beginning of a new one, a greater one than before'.

12. Look for regenerative opportunities to enhance not just the conventional focus of financial capital but also human and natural capital.

ECOSYSTEMS MODEL: A DESIGN CONCEPT

The Mobius Project

The Mobius Project by Exploration Architecture is an example of a new building type that could emerge from the transformation of cities into cyclical systems. It brings together cycles of food production, energy generation, water treatment and organic waste handling. While in the 20th century we became accustomed to separating activities into large-scale mono-functional operations, this scheme co-locates the following productive processes in a way that allows inputs and outputs to be connected up to form a closed-loop model:

• A productive greenhouse including community allotments growing a range of crops

• A restaurant serving seasonal food grown in, and locally to, the greenhouse

• A fish farm rearing a range of edible fish

• A food market

• A wormery composting system

• Mushroom cultivation using waste coffee grains

• An anaerobic digester and biomass CHP

• A 'Living Machine' water treatment system as pioneered by John Todd[21]

• Artificial limestone from waste CO_2 using accelerated carbonation technology

The innovative aspect of the Mobius Project is in the way that it co-locates and integrates these processes in synergistic cycles. The building can handle much of the biodegradable waste from a local urban area using composting and anaerobic digestion. The methane derived from this process can be used to generate electricity and heat for the greenhouse while some of the flue gases can be captured by accelerated carbonation and turned into building materials. The restaurant, apart from being supplied with fruit, vegetables and fish from the greenhouse which cuts down on food miles, can operate at close to zero waste as food left-overs can be fed to fish or composted/digested. Solids from waste water can be diverted to the anaerobic digesters while the remaining water can be treated for use as local drinking water or greywater for toilet flushing. Fertiliser from the various forms of waste handling can be used in the greenhouse and the significant surplus can help to remediate brownfield land on the outskirts of the city.

The scheme could form the centrepiece of a residential area and play an important role in generating a sense of community while addressing many of the infrastructural requirements of living in urban areas.

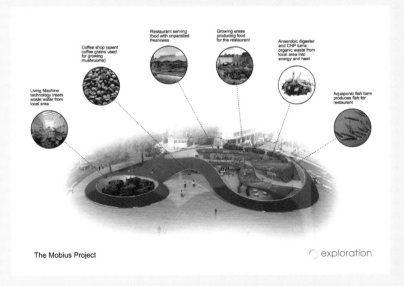

The Mobius Project

⌒ exploration

Discussion and conclusions

In the examples above it can be seen that the characteristics of ecosystems can be used as a unifying model for cities and business. It is possible to develop solutions that are cyclical, resilient, running on current solar income and, crucially, go beyond the sustainability paradigm to deliver regenerative benefits to the human and natural capital on which they depend. All of these characteristics are essential if we are to shift from the industrial to the ecological age of humankind.

There are other examples of ecosystem models such as Kalundborg in Denmark, British Sugar's plant at Wissington in the UK and George Chan's sorghum brewery in Namibia but it would be entirely reasonable to ask why there aren't more. Given the multiple advantages that ecosystem models offer, why have these ideas not been more widely adopted? Having identified the obstacles, we should also ask how we might accelerate these urgent transformations.

One reason is undoubtedly inertia. Governments have often demonstrated a lack of courage in the face of lobbying from conventional industries that resist change while the more adventurous complain that they could go much further if legislation and fiscal instruments created a level playing field. A good example, pertinent to the Sahara Forest Project, is that in several of the countries that are ideally suited to the technology the government has responded to water shortages by building energy-intensive desalination plants and making the water virtually free. A more courageous approach would be to make water more expensive with taxation and hypothecate the revenue to invest in water-saving innovation. The same approach could be applied to other resources – making them more expensive, before they become problematically scarce, would be one of the best ways to ensure that those resources are used more efficiently.[22] Clearly any such approach would need to be introduced gradually to ensure that stresses within the system can be addressed and policies adjusted accordingly. Well-designed fiscal instruments can play a part in rewarding innovation and resource efficiency; listening to laggards will achieve the opposite – perpetuating stasis and profligacy.

Another form of inertia is the substantial amounts of existing assets – buildings, equipment and infrastructure – that are often costly to adapt. If industrial processes are not co-located, then moving resources around can become self-defeating because it can use more energy than it saves. However these challenges should not be used to casually dismiss the opportunities that exist. Large-scale installations (whether a factory, an office, a water treatment facility, or even a city) have resource flows to match and, given that our conventional approaches are generally linear, there are often substantial quantities of underutilised resources that can be transformed into value.

Businesses can be nervous about transforming their processes if there is doubt about the demand or perceived value of the new product that will result. This is entirely understandable and one solution is to experiment at small scale first and go through a transition rather than rapid, radical change. An example from the Zero Waste Textiles Factory is the bleaching process. There is a limit to how much this process can be mitigated in terms of environmental impact and undoubtedly the most benign approach would be to eliminate it but currently there is almost universal demand for bleached cotton.[23] At the same time, those customers that do want unbleached cotton currently have very little to choose from. One way in which this might change would be for a textile company to launch a small-scale range of unbleached textiles alongside their existing lines (but probably under a different brand name) and market them strongly as 'value-added products'. This could be likened to the approach taken by a well-known fast food chain who presumably concluded that their brand was essentially un-transformable and they decided to buy up an emerging brand producing freshly made sandwiches in order to provide long-term security in a market that was shifting towards healthier choices.

It needs to be remembered that the system is not just the hardware but includes the people that operate it and this can be one of the weak points in terms of resilience – often new directions are championed by particular individuals and when they move on, retire or pass away, the knowledge and the energy that inspires others goes with them. Initiatives need to be backed up with deputies and apprentices to step in when necessary and the champions need to be encouraged to share their knowledge.

Complexity can be another barrier. Facilities based on ecosystem models are often more complicated to conceive and operate. When problems are encountered it can be tempting to revert to mono-functional, linear and disconnected approaches but as the Ben Okri quotation implies (See Box on pages 78-79), it is better to think about what can be added to the system to solve the problem and create more value. It is more difficult to design for complexity than simplicity, but this is the kind of complexity we need to embrace if we are really to make progress towards the ecological age.

Source: Exploration architecture

Notes

1 Quoted during course at Schumacher College 'Natural Capitalism' delivered by Janine Benyus and Amory Lovins, 23–26 September 2003.

2 Naomi Klein, *This changes everything* (London: Penguin Books, 2014).

3 www.ellenmacarthurfoundation.org/business/ce100

4 Genevieve Reday and Walter Stahel, *Jobs for Tomorrow, the Potential for Substituting Manpower for Energy*, report to the European Commission (1976).

5 M. Braungart, and W. McDonough, *Cradle to Cradle: Remaking the Way We Make Things* (New York: North Point Press, 2002).

6 Reykjavik is already supplied with 100% renewable heat and electricity due to its prodigious geothermal energy – see http://www.go100percent.org/cms/. There are also a number of countries, such as Albania, Costa Rica, Georgia, Norway, Paraguay, that are close to 100% renewable for electricity.

7 This list is based substantially on work by Janine Benyus as presented on a course at Schumacher College entitled 'Natural Capitalism' delivered by Janine Benyus and Amory Lovins 23–26 September 2003. Janine Benyus, *Biomimicry: Innovation Inspired by Nature* (New York: Harper Collins, 1998).

8 This is a summary that needs some clarification. Flows of energy are, as dictated by laws of thermodynamics, always linear. Flows of other resources such as carbon, nitrogen, water, etc. are mostly closed-loop in ecosystems although there are some limited exceptions to this. Arguably fossil fuels are an example of waste and it could be seen as ironic that we are currently getting ourselves into difficulties as a direct result of using waste from ancient ecosystems. Similarly, the carbon cycle involves some flows between atmosphere, hydrosphere and lithosphere that are linear in the short term but closed-loop over a geological timescale.

9 See note above.

10 Some biological organisms have evolved to use toxins but only for a specific purpose and all the toxins break down after use to harmless constituents.

11 Panarchy is a term used by systems theorists as an antithesis to hierarchy. The latter literally means 'sacred rules' whereas the former is used to refer to 'nature's rules' after Pan, the Greek god of nature. Panarchy (Gunderson & Holling, 2001) helps us understand interactions across scales of space and time in complex adaptive systems. The model is used to describe transitions in system behaviour and captures how the system is sustained as well as how the system evolves. The adaptive cycle is composed of four distinct phases: the r-phase (exploitation) slowly accumulates capital and connectedness to the K-phase (conservation), which eventually leads to the ff phase (creative destruction) and quickly reorganises in the Ð-phase (engine of variety). It is also possible to think of interconnected adaptive cycles across space and time (Source: Stockholm Resilience Centre, 2014). See: Lance Gunderson and C. S. Holling, *Panarchy: Understanding Transformations in Systems of Humans and Nature* (Island Press, 2001), 21.

12 Janine Benyus, 'Natural Capitalism' at Schmacher College, 23–26 September 2003.

13 J. F. V. Vincent, *Biomimetics: a review* (Proceedings of the Institute of Mechanical Engineers, Part H: Journal of Engineering in Medicine 223, November 2009), 919–939.

14 There are a few fascinating 'extremophile' organisms that eke out a living around volcanic ocean vents and, it could be argued, thrive independently of sunlight.

15 J. Rodin, *The Resilience Dividend: Managing disruption, avoiding disaster, and growing stronger in an unpredictable world* (Profile Books, ebook, 13 November 2014) Kindle Locations 125–127.

16 D. Meadows, *Thinking in Systems: A Primer* (Chelsea Green Publishing, 2008). Kindle Edition, 3–4).

17 M. Pawlyn, *Biomimicry in Architecture* (London: RIBA Publications, 2011), 63.

18 The European Nutraceutical Association defines these as 'nutritional products that provide health and medical benefits, including the prevention and treatment of disease. In contrast to pharmaceuticals however, these are not synthetic substances or chemical compounds formulated for specific indications. These are products that contain nutrients (partly in concentrated form) and mostly are assigned to the category of food.' See http://www.enaonline.org/index.php?lang=en&path=news

19 A number of reports on the Sahara Forest Project including a results report for the Pilot Facility can be found on the Sahara Forest Project website, http://saharaforestproject.com/news/downloads.html

20 It would have been even better if we had monitored floral and microbial biodiversity but our resources were limited.

21 John Todd is an internationally known eco-designer and inventor of the Living Machine waste water treatment process. See: https://www.youtube.com/watch?v=wojrOpH5O7M

22 Julian Vincent makes an observation similar to this in *Survival of the cheapest* (Materials Today, December 2002), 28–9.

23 The vast majority of printed or dyed textiles first are bleached first in order to achieve the expected quality standards.

THE CIRCULAR ECONOMY OF SOIL

L. Hunter Lovins

In a world where biodiversity seems at the service of mankind, what is our relationship to it, what role is it supposed to play? And whilst all eyes are turned towards excessive use of fossil fuels, the past 150 years of unsustainable agriculture practices have had a huge part to play not only in the current climate crisis, but also in the loss of biodiversity and ecosystem functions. In this chapter, Hunter Lovins re-establishes the fundamental roles of biodiversity and soil as natural capital, and advocates ways to reconcile farming systems with nature's cycle within a coherent 'circular economy of the soil'.

Hunter Lovins
Hunter is President of Natural Capitalism Solutions (NCS) and is co-author of *Natural Capitalism: The Next Industrial Revolution* (Earthscan, 2015).

Soil as natural capital

Humanity is fond of believing that our big brain makes success inevitable. As Jeff Wallin[1] puts it, however, we owe our existence to 15cm of soil and the fact that it rains. A handful of healthy soil has more living organisms in it than there are people on earth. A gram of fertile loam can contain up to a billion bacteria.[2] That thin skin covering the biosphere is the living heart of a circular economy upon which all life depends.

Globally, we are losing that soil and the life that is within it. Half of the topsoil on earth has been lost since the advent of 'modern'[3] agriculture. As Dr Wes Jackson of the Land Institute puts it, 'Across the farmlands of the US and the world, climate change overshadows an ecological and cultural crisis of unequaled scale: soil erosion, loss of wild biodiversity, poisoned land and water, salinisation, expanding dead zones, and the demise of rural communities. The Millennium Ecosystem Assessment (MEA) concludes that agriculture is the "largest threat to biodiversity and ecosystem function of any single human activity."[4]

Just as conventional industrial policy ignores the economic, social and business benefits of closing the loops in materials flows, conventional agricultural policy interacts with the earth as a one-way trip. Our throwaway society is impoverishing our economy. But treating soil like dirt threatens all life on the planet.

Linear use of material resources is neither economic nor sustainable. The circular economy framework that owes its emergence to the pioneering work of Walter Stahel, and was taken to scale by the Ellen MacArthur Foundation, offers an alternative to a model of growth based on depletion. It also turns out to be enormously profitable. The landmark reports, *Towards the Circular Economy,* by the Ellen MacArthur Foundation (featuring analysis by McKinsey) showed that closing the materials loops could save a trillion dollars globally each year.[5]

Michael Braungart, who defined material flows as 'technical nutrients: human artifice designed to circulate within industrial lifecycles – forever,' rightly points out that it is also important to return 'biological nutrients' to their own cycle. He describes these as, 'Raw material used by living organisms or cells to carry on life processes such as growth, cell division, synthesis of carbohydrates and other complex functions. Biological nutrients are usually carbon-based compounds.'[6]

Carbon out of place... is what is driving today?

Isn't it carbon out of place in excessive amounts as carbon dioxide in the atmosphere that is driving one of the most serious problems facing humankind today? The overwhelming consensus of the world's scientists agrees that the accumulation of carbon dioxide (CO_2) in the atmosphere is changing our climate

in ways that will become increasingly dangerous and destructive.[7] Is it possible that closing the loops in the flows of carbon – creating a circular economy of the soil – might not only forestall the predicted chaos of climate change, but also drive profitability, just as it does with the rest of the
circular economy?

This chapter advocates three ways to return farming systems to harmony with nature's cycles: regenerative agriculture, biochar and Holistic Management. Their proponents argue fiercely on behalf of their favourite approach, but practitioners of what is now called the Regenerative Economy[8] are coming to realise that they all are part of a larger system: a circular economy of the soil.

The challenge: climate destructive agriculture

Although three-quarters of the climate crisis results from burning fossil fuels, and to a lesser extent releases of various industrial gases, almost a quarter of the problem derives from agriculture. The first settlers to plough the American Great Plains unearthed three metres of dense, black soil. That black was carbon; young coal, if you will. After 20 years of conventional tillage, most agricultural soils lose 50% of their soil carbon.[9] After 150 years of unsustainable agricultural practices, that carbon-rich soil has been reduced to mere inches. The use of fossil-fuel-based fertilisers, and physical disturbances to the soil also strip it of nitrogen.[10] Both carbon and nitrogen, key building blocks of life in nature, are, when out of place, serious threats to the stability of the climate.

Soil that has been de-carbonised – where it has lost its organic matter – requires large amounts of artificial fertiliser to enable it to grow crops on an industrial scale. Producing and using all of the petrochemicals in fertiliser releases carbon and other greenhouse gases (GHGs), especially nitrous oxide, a gas 300 times more potent per tonne than CO_2 in causing global warming.[11] Ploughing and poor nutrient management releases the nitrogen from soils in quantities. Nitrous oxide (N_2O), a by-product of synthetic nitrogen fertiliser and manure from Confined Animal Feeding Operations and other industrial processes, is also a threat to the ozone layer of the atmosphere. Unlike the chlorofluorocarbons regulated by the Montreal Protocol, N_2O is not covered by any regulation, and there is no global effort to reduce its emissions.[12] In 1995 it was estimated that humans applied more than 6 million tonnes of artificial nitrogen fertiliser, resulting in human caused soil denitrification of 3–8 billion kilograms of N2O each year. By 2013, it was 100 million tons. As a result, atmospheric concentrations of N2O had risen from about 275 parts per billion (ppb) before the industrial era to about 312 ppb in 1994. Much of the increase is thought to be from human activity.[13]

A little soil and health science helps explain what is going on, literally beneath our feet. Nitrogen, necessary for life, is a key component of DNA. People and other animals cannot obtain nitrogen by breathing it in; they have to eat it. Nitrogen in molecular form (N_2) is an inert element. To be biologically available in ecosystems it must be converted to nitrate (NO_3), ammonium (NH_4), or organic nitrogen ((NH_2)2CO, otherwise known as plant protein). This biologically available nitrogen enters the soil when lightning oxidises atmospheric nitrogen and rain brings it to earth. Legumes like clover and alfalfa also 'fix' atmospheric nitrogen in the soil, using soil microbes called rhizobium to break the N_2 into forms useful to plants. Animals then get the nitrogen they need by eating plants.[14]

Figure 1 illustrates how, in healthy soil, microbes convert the nitrogen that enters the soil when living things decay back into N_2, closing the loop and completing the nitrogen cycle.[15] Artificial fertilisers used in intensive agriculture upset this balance. Excessive use of artificial nitrogen, created from natural gas, drives the cycle ever faster, as the microbes in the soil that convert organic nitrogen back into N_2 gas are fuelled by excess nitrogen and release it into the atmosphere.[16] The nitrogen in fertiliser is also lost when soil that has been ploughed up and left denuded is eroded by wind and rain. The nitrogen runoff from soil winds up in drinking water where it poisons farm animals and humans, in lakes where it promotes algal blooms[17] or in the oceans, where it is contributing to the creation of 'dead zones'.[18]

Vegetarians provocatively claim that producing red meat, dairy products, chickens, fish and eggs account for 58% of these food-related emissions. A 2006 UN report concluded that livestock were responsible for 18% of global greenhouse gases (GHGs).[19] In 2010, however, UN scientists acknowledged that claims regarding the impact of meat production were flawed. Analysts had counted emissions common to all industrial activities but neglected to do this when analysing the impact of other industry.[20] The UN has promised a revised report, but none has yet emerged.

Industrial meat production drives the emission of significant amounts of climate-destroying gases.[21] The 95 million conventionally grown cows in the US are taken off pastures where they were healthy, and 'finished' in Concentrated Animal Feeding Operations, or CAFOs. There they are fed grain and oil crops to fatten them for slaughter, food that the grazing animals were never designed to eat. As a result, meat animals now consume half of all the oil and grain crops grown in the US and the world.[22,23]

Modern agriculture worsens climate change, and, unchecked, climate change will destroy humankind's already tenuous ability to feed itself. For every 1°C rise in temperature above the norm, yields of wheat, rice, and corn drop 10%. Given that more than a billion people in the world already suffer from malnutrition, this is cause for concern.[24,25]

Figure 1 **The nitrogen cycle**

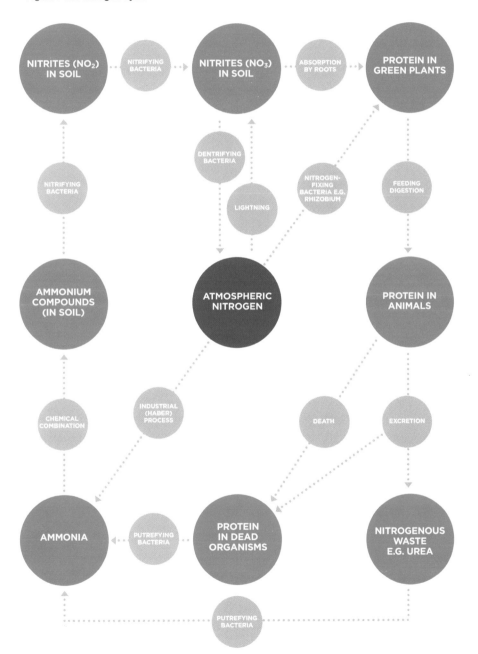

Agriculture's real impact, whether from meat production or plant crops depends on the production methods used. There are dramatically more sustainable ways of producing food. Clearly, then, one answer is to transition to agriculture that does not rely on unsustainable application of fossil-fuel-based fertiliser, and that does not decarbonise the soil.

Regenerative agriculture: there is a better way

Humanity WILL convert to sustainable agriculture; it's only a question of how hard we will make it on ourselves before we do. Agriculture as currently practiced is putting the climate at risk, and climate change left unchecked, will destroy much of industrial agriculture as it is currently practiced. Changing temperatures and precipitation levels will affect yields

Dr Stephen Chu, US Secretary of Energy, in a 2009 interview on climate risks, stated, 'You're looking at a scenario where there's no more agriculture in California. When you lose 70% of your water in the mountains, I don't see how agriculture can continue. California produces 20% of the agriculture in the United States. I don't actually see how they can keep their cities going.'[26] In June 2015 the California mountains had zero snowpack.

Critics of current agricultural practices call for a beyond-modern approach combining the best of traditional agriculture with the finest science to deliver abundant, sustainable food and high-quality ways of life to all the world's people, even in a time of climate crisis. The Rodale Institute,[27] one of the original centres of scientific research into organic agriculture, the Soil Association of the UK,[28] the Agroecology Lab at UC Davis,[29] and the Leopold Center at Iowa State University are only a few of the thousands of organisations around the world striving to build bio-diverse systems that can meet the needs of humanity while reintegrating into living systems' cycles. Such agriculture takes a longer view of production, seeking not 'to maximise yield in any optimum year, but to maximise yield over many years by decreasing the chance of crop failure in a bad year.'[30]

Studies conducted over many years by University of California, Davis, the Rodale Institute, and others have shown that such regenerative farming practices increase (not just maintain) the quantity of soil-held carbon (organic matter) through a variety of mechanisms.[31] Farming operations that use more natural agricultural practices that do not rely on chemical inputs like artificial fertilisers, pesticides, and herbicides have higher levels of beneficial soil organisms. Protozoa, bacteria by the billions, fungi, algae, and mycorrhizae, complement recognisable species from ants and earthworms, nematodes, and springtails. All of these work together in the soil to build organic (carbon) matter. Operations that do not use chemical pesticides support this soil biodiversity and more diverse farmland habitats. Farms using crop rotations

Figure 2 **Simplified soil food web**[34]

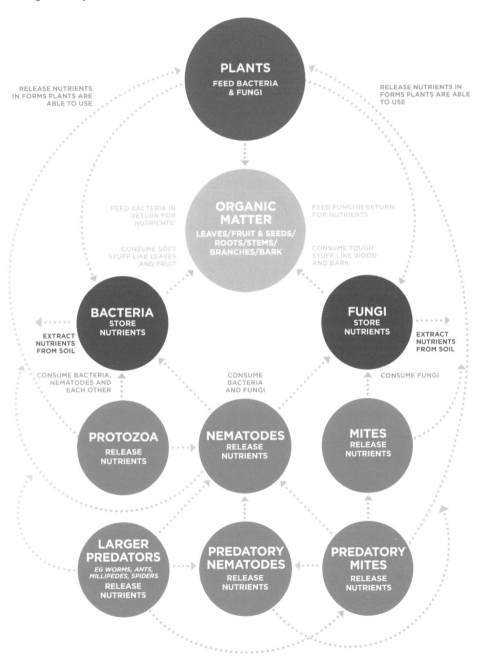

and animal manure deliver better biodiversity than fields farmed with industrial agricultural practices. Organic fields reduce nitrogen runoff and the release of nitrous oxide.[32] Systems that integrate livestock with vegetable production, use perennial pastureland, and organic production (e.g. long crop rotations, leguminous crops and cover crops, manure produced by livestock as fertiliser) deliver higher profitability while creating the circular economy of the soil, taking carbon from the air and sequestering it in the soil.[33]

Echoing a widely accepted view, Dan Charles says that, 'Without it [artificial fertiliser], human civilisation in its current form could not exist. Our planet's soil simply could not grow enough food to provide all seven billion of us our accustomed diet. In fact, almost half of the nitrogen found in our bodies' muscle and organ tissue started out in a fertiliser factory.'[35]

The United Nations would beg to disagree. Both the United Nations Conference on Trade and Development[36] and the UN Food and Agriculture Organisation recently published reports concluding that only organic, smallholder farms could feed the world. The FAO report found that protecting and empowering such 'bottom of the pyramid'[37] growers, who produce 70% of world's food, has enabled half of the world's countries to have met the Millennium Development goal of cutting malnutrition in half.[38]

Given that smallholders are the first to feel the effects of political unrest, climate-related disasters, poverty, and other issues that drive hunger, the UN's focus is a welcome antidote to the 'Green Revolution,'[39] which hit the developing world by storm in the 1960s and 1970s. In an all-out push to modernise farming throughout the world, synthetic inputs and intensive irrigation replaced traditional agriculture methods to increase yields. Many farmers took hold of these new practices, and in the short term it was a story of enormous success. Grain production doubled in less than 20 years. Previously famine-stricken regions of rural India became breadbaskets, producing enough wheat and rice to export a surplus. Farmers adopted techniques of monoculture (farmers who had previously grown as many as 30 different crops switched to growing only one cash crop, dramatically reducing biodiversity) and double-cropping (harvesting twice a year by generating a second 'rainy season' through irrigation). All of this increased yields enormously.

However, increasingly farmers found this industrialised approach did not provide a reliable, long-term foundation for agriculture. Soil fertility has declined, water pollution is rampant, workers suffer health problems including soaring cancer rates from using industrial chemicals often banned in Western countries, and fields have not sustained their peak yields. In addition, because synthetic inputs are heavily reliant on fossil fuel energy, the Green Revolution practices forced communities to become dependent on foreign inputs of oil, accompanied by significant exports of cash, to pay for these inputs. As water tables fell, farmers were forced to buy imported energy to fuel pumps, depleting the water tables ever faster. According to Daniel Zwerdling, India's once booming agriculture epicentre, Punjab, is now heading for collapse.[40] In 2011, the chairman of the Punjab State Farmers Commission stated, 'Farmers are committing ecological and economic suicide.' They are also, literally, committing suicide.[41]

This, combined with the impacts of climate change, meant that in 2009 Indian farmers came up short of food demand. Traditional water sources of local communities began failing. In Punjab, aquifers dried up, forcing farmers to dig wells deeper, driving them into a spiral of debt. Widespread applications of insecticides and pesticides are causing insects to develop immunity against the chemicals while destroying more and more crops. Farmers bought up to three times as much fertiliser as they did 30 years before to maintain yields. The Punjab State Council for Science and Technology proclaimed that the state's agriculture programme 'has become unsustainable and unprofitable.' In August 2009, India announced that it was being forced to import food, especially lentils and edible oils. 'The situation is grim, not just for crop sowing and crop health but also for sustaining animal health, providing drinking water, livelihood and food, particularly for the small and marginal farmers and landless labourers,' stated Indian farm minister Sharad Pawar. 'Food prices have risen over 10% annually.'

In contrast, shifting away from the so-called modern practices to re-focus on traditional, sustainable agricultural methods has been shown to reinvigorate communities. In 2007 the UN Food and Agriculture Organisation determined that organic agriculture would positively contribute to food security, climate mitigation, water security and quality, agrobiodiversity, nutritional adequacy, and rural development.[42]

These regenerative agriculture methods treat the farms as holistic systems, where the relationship between all inputs is considered. In best cases, farmers use only what is produced on site, e.g, manure from livestock as a fertiliser for crops in place of the synthetic fertiliser derived from natural gas. Such agricultural practices restore soil structure, build healthy topsoil, nurture soil microbes, and promote biological activity, all of which contributes to long-term productivity and nutritious crops. Water use is optimised and the best practices in irrigation are applied. Farm worker safety and investment in local dollars sustain farming communities. Additionally, this higher soil fertility also acts to sequester atmospheric carbon dioxide.

Demand for foods produced by these agriculture methods is growing throughout the world. Because more people are needed to do the work such as weeding and pest control that the chemicals were designed to do, organic farming increases employment and labour demands. The citizen-based Development Research Communication and Services Center (DRCSC) is working in West Bengal and surrounding states in northeastern India to improve the state of agriculture. Focusing on education and capacity-building as major strategies for change, the DRCSC supports organic farming as a means to ensure food and livelihood security for India's rural poor. DRCSC has built school gardens, organised workshops, created nurseries and seed centres, and even produced a documentary, each emphasising the benefits of organic farming to community stakeholders. The DRCSC's work has been so successful that some organic farmers are actually producing more than their community needs.

In the United States, an even bolder vision of regenerative agriculture is emerging at the Land Institute in Salina, Kansas.[43] Dr Wes Jackson is leading a team to shift agriculture from a single focus on monocultures of annual plants intensively managed, to polycultures of perennial plants. This is how nature grows crops.

Jackson observes that, 'Essentially all of the high-yield crops that feed humanity – including rice, wheat, corn, soybeans, and peanuts – are annuals. With cropping of annuals, alive just part of the year and weakly rooted even then, comes more loss of precious soil, nutrients, and water....' The institute is developing an agricultural system based on the ecological stability of the prairie but boasting a grain yield comparable to annual crops. Essentially all of the natural land ecosystems within the ecosphere, from alpine meadows to rainforests, are dominated by mixtures of perennial plants. By contrast, annuals are opportunists that sprout, reproduce, throw seeds, and die. Perennials stay in the soil, protecting it, better managing nutrients and retaining water. The Land Institute's long-standing mission is to use plant-breeding techniques to perennialise several major crops, such as wheat, sorghum, and sunflower, and domesticate a few wild perennial species to produce food like their annual counterparts. The institute grows them in various mixtures according to what each given landscape requires. With the pre-agricultural ecosystem as the standard, the institute is attempting to bring as many processes of the wild to the farm as possible, below as well as above the ground surface.

'Natural Systems Agriculture', should end the days in which 'agricultural scientists from industrialised societies deliver agronomic methods and technologies from their fossil-fuel-intensive infrastructures into developing countries, thereby saddling them with brittle economies.' Wes Jackson writes, 'New perennial crops, like their wild relatives, seem certain to be more resilient to climate change. Without a doubt, they will increase sequestration of carbon. They will reduce the land runoff that is creating coastal dead zones and affecting fisheries and maintain the quality of scarce surface and ground water.' In short, he hopes to rebalance living systems while producing greater economic stability all at the same time.[44]

Biochar

Carbon-based waste in the developed world tends to be thrown away, sent to landfills, where it rots, ultimately releasing methane, an even more destructive greenhouse gas than its original carbon content. In the developing world it is sometimes returned to the soil, but typically, carbon-based material piles up, especially in cities. Efforts to compost these flows so that the nutrients can be returned to the soil are beginning, but humanity needs to use the ability of plants to draw carbon from the air, finding ways to put it back into the soil on a massive scale. An important answer may be a product called biochar.

Biochar is essentially charcoal. Charcoal is an important energy source globally – nearly 3 billion people worldwide rely on burning it, along with wood (usually from local forests) for cooking.[45] Charcoal production results in deforestation, and is wasteful of the wood and the carbon. Inefficient use of charcoal also contributes to indoor air pollution and greenhouse gas emissions.

Biochar production is quite different. Created through 'pyrolysis,' the woody material is heated at low temperatures with little oxygen until it is carbonised. This produces energy (heat and power), but unlike fossil fuels it is a carbon-neutral process; it neither adds nor subtracts carbon from the atmosphere. Done intelligently, biochar production delivers usable energy in the form of charcoal, a bio-oil and syngas. The syngas can be used much like petroleum-based oil or natural gas to fuel transportation or as another substitute for charcoal.[46]

Figure 3 **The Biochar process**

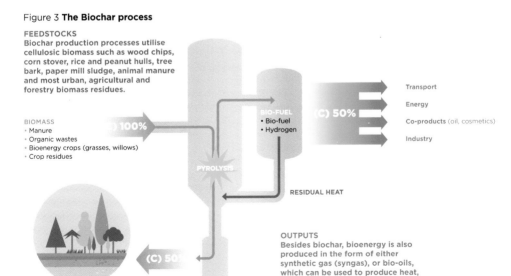

FEEDSTOCKS
Biochar production processes utilise cellulosic biomass such as wood chips, corn stover, rice and peanut hulls, tree bark, paper mill sludge, animal manure and most urban, agricultural and forestry biomass residues.

BIOMASS
- Manure
- Organic wastes
- Bioenergy crops (grasses, willows)
- Crop residues

100%

PYROLYSIS

BIO-FUEL
- Bio-fuel
- Hydrogen

(C) 50%

Transport

Energy

Co-products (oil, cosmetics)

Industry

RESIDUAL HEAT

(C) 50%

Returned to soil as **Biochar**

OUTPUTS
Besides biochar, bioenergy is also produced in the form of either synthetic gas (syngas), or bio-oils, which can be used to produce heat, power or combined heat and power.

Biochar production only turns part of the woody material into fuel. The other 50% or more of the biomass's carbon becomes the biochar, which, when placed in soil, stays there, representing a near-permanent carbon sink that has actually reduced overall atmospheric CO_2.[47]

In the soil, biochar increases water retention and crop yields, reducing fertiliser requirements. Enhancing plant growth, it thus removes even more CO_2 from the atmosphere. Because it can be made in simple, home-made devices and on a small scale, biochar production represents a start-up opportunity that can create rural jobs.[48]

Dr Tim Flannery, one of Australia's most eminent scientists and author of *The Weathermakers*, states, 'Biochar may represent the single most important initiative for humanity's environmental future. Biochar provides a uniquely powerful solution, for it allows us to address food security, the fuel crisis, and the climate problem, and all in an immensely practical manner.'[49] Flannery explains, 'Now if you used these agri-char-based technologies and you have your aggressive reafforestation projects for the world's tropics, you could conceivably be drawing down in the order of 10 to 15 gigatonnes of carbon per annum by about 2030. At that rate we could bring ourselves down below the dangerous threshold as early as the middle of this century.'[50]

'In the future, we will not be afforded the luxury of waste,' says Jeff Wallin, co-founder of the Biochar Company, the first company producing commercial biochar. 'The business case is sustainable and profitable without depending on tax subsidies or CO_2 credits, but they will help in finding interested financial partners. The environmental future is upon us and nature does not negotiate,' says Wallin.[51]

Holistic Management

Judith Schwartz's book puts the situation bluntly: *Cows Save the Planet*.[52] Her book profiles soil scientists, and the growing number of practitioners around the world who are using grazing animals to repair soil health, reverse desertification and restore the circular economy of the soil.

How much carbon dioxide from the atmosphere can be sequestered via plant photosynthesis in properly managed grasslands and how fast? The grasslands of the world are the second largest store of naturally sequestered carbon after the oceans. Grasslands co-evolved with pre-industrial grazing practices: sufficient herds of native graziers, dense packed because they are pursued by healthy populations of predators. The three-metre-thick black soil of the historic grasslands of the Great Plains of the US represented massive carbon reserves. Most of that carbon reserve is gone, but it can be regenerated.

Adam Sacks, writing for *Climate: Code Red*, cites studies showing that capturing one ton of carbon per acre per year on average is reasonable on well-cared-for grasslands.[53] 'We are only beginning,' he observes, 'to understand the potential of intensive planned grazing with animals that break capped soil surfaces with their hooves, fertilise, moisturise and aerate the ground, and make earth hospitable to thousands of vital soil organisms.'

'There is no climate-saving strategy that has anywhere near the potential of soils,' Sacks argues. 'There are roughly 12 billion acres of grassland worldwide, mostly ruined by human misuse, which we can restore. At a modest one ton per acre we can pull twelve billion tons of carbon out of the atmosphere every year. That's 6 parts per million (ppm) – and even if we foolishly continue to add 2 ppm annually, it's still less than a 30-year trip back to a stable pre-industrial 280 ppm, down from today's perilous 393.'[54] Since Sacks wrote this, the concentration of carbon dioxide in the atmosphere has risen to 403ppm.

The approach Sacks is advocating was developed by Allan Savory. The Savory Institute[55] restores the vast grasslands of the world through the teaching and practice of 'Holistic Management' and 'Holistic Decision Making'. The institute enables livestock farmers to turn deserts into thriving grasslands, restore biodiversity, bring streams, rivers and water sources back to life, combat poverty and hunger, all while putting an end to global climate change.[56] Holistically managed grazing animals are, it turns out, one of the best ways to reclaim depleted land. It is also one of the more important ways to create healthy communities of soil microorganisms. This, in turn recarbonises the soil, and restores natural nitrogen cycles. It is one of the fastest ways to profitably create the circular economy of the soil.

Figure 4 **Regenerative grazing system**

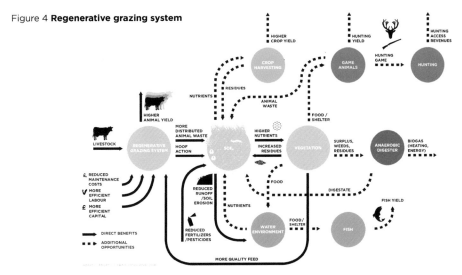

The conventional wisdom is that reduced grazing is better – it sounds right. More herbivores, such as elephants or cattle, means more stress on the vegetation leading to less output and falling soil quality. But this is a partial understanding. Allan Savory came to realise that, in evolutionary terms, the grasslands developed in the presence of very large herds of herbivores and that this characteristic – of a large herd grazing everything, churning up the soil with their hooves and depositing faeces and urine and slobber before moving on, had a particular relevance to how the grassland worked as a system.

Taking it to the other extreme, Savory found evidence that leaving a semi-arid grassland without cattle or other herbivores means it doesn't thrive, it becomes 'stagnant' – sub-optimal but reasonably stable. Nutrients are not returning to the soil as they are locked up in the dead stalks and stems of the earlier years, since rainfall is low and bacteria and fungi cannot get to work as they would prefer. Moreover, sunbaked, bare earth develops a crust so that rain runs off more easily, land erodes and water which runs off is not available for plants – and brings flooding downstream. Some woody perennial plants begin to dominate and species diversity in the system declines.

In savanna that is intensely grazed by herds which then move on, the situation is very different. The stomachs of the cattle act as bioreactors, the water needed by bacteria and the bacteria themselves are active and the resulting manures and urine are rich in minerals and usable and accessible, the hooves break up the soil surface and the non-discriminatory grazing leaves spaces for plants which would lose out in the ungrazed regime – particularly annual grasses. It is the way the grasses react which is most interesting. Once heavily grazed, the grasses adapt their root structure to the needs of regrowth, effectively 'dropping' some roots since the structure above ground is much reduced – as the plant grows again the roots will regrow. This process 'pulses' carbon into the soils, but the key is that the new plant growth isn't immediately or too soon grazed again. That herd needs to be long gone and for quite a while. In conventional cattle grazing the interval is too short and the pressure on the habitat too limited to get the broad spectrum regrowth – the animals are choosy eaters if they can be and the energy of the grasses is never fully rebuilt. In the holistic management system at Savory Institute cattle grazing is established to mimic the grazing patterns of herbivores in natural savanna ecosystems – this ensures more effective nutrient cycling and build-up of soil organic matter resulting in enhanced vegetation growth and cattle grazing land.[57]

Holistic management

© Faunggs-CC Flickr

The Lovins ranch

© H. Lovins

Savory points out that even achieving zero emissions from fossil fuels would not avert major catastrophe from climate change. Grassland and savanna burning would continue and desertification would accelerate as soils become increasingly unable to store carbon or water.[58] Averting disaster, Savory argues, will require a global strategy to cut carbon emissions, substitute benign energy sources for fossil fuels, and implement effective livestock management practices to put the carbon already in the atmosphere back into the soils.[59]

Profitable Holistic Management is a key way to reduce biodiversity loss and biomass burning and reverse the desertification that is not caused by atmospheric carbon build-up. (Not all loss of soil is caused by global warming. Bad agricultural practices can desertify ground, cause erosion, chaining, etc.) Awarded the 2010 Buckminster Fuller Challenge for their decades of work, Savory's Africa Centre for Holistic Management in Zimbabwe and the Savory Institute are transforming degraded Zimbabwe grasslands and savannas into lush pastures with ponds and flowing streams, and demonstrating how this approach to climate protection also enhances African agricultural livelihoods. The Award celebrates initiatives that take a 'comprehensive, anticipatory, design approach to radically advance human well being and the health of our planet's ecosystems'. The Fuller award recognised that Savory's work accelerates the development and deployment of whole-systems solutions to climate change, and sustainable development.

What's holding it up? This approach to land management contradicts accepted practice and theories of removing land from animal grazing. The vitriol leveled against Allan Savory is daunting. Despite this, Holistic Management is now successfully practised on more than 40 million acres around the world. Re-establishing the symbiotic balance between plant growth and herd animals is helping land managers bio-remediate barren land back to thriving grasslands, and increasing crop yields and ensuring food security for millions of people.[60]

Savory's approach works. In the 1990s this author undertook to rehabilitate almost 1,000 acres of degraded western rangeland. Taken out of cattle production for 20 years, the land had suffered erosion and been overrun by noxious weeds. Its prior owners believed the conventional wisdom that removing grazing animals from land would increase its health. This may be true of intact wilderness, where intact predators still drive native grazing herds to pack up and move across the land. But most of the planet's agricultural land is rapidly releasing stored carbon, nitrogen and other greenhouse gases, so the approach that nature is somehow spiritual and will heal itself is clearly wrong. Working with Allan Savory, we restored cattle to the ground, and managed the land based on the principles of Holistic Management. Within two years the water table rose, and wetland plants returned (the seeds had always been there, just waiting for the right conditions). Endangered species not seen in two decades flourished. Even sceptical government officials acknowledged this evidence of an ecosystem returning to health. The value of the property also rose. Many others are enjoying the success of Holistic Management as well.

In the Australian desert, the company Sustainable Land Management has shown that it can double the carrying capacity of cattle on what had historically been desertified Australian range, achieve superior weight gain while buying no feed, double plant diversity, and restore the grasslands even in the face of a drought. The company is attracting foreign investment to a region of Australia typically struggling to achieve economic development, and rehabilitating the local economy. Patagonia, the clothing company partnered with Ovis XXI and the Nature Conservancy to use Holistic Management to regenerate the grasslands of Patagonia while increasing economic viability.[61]

From Montana to Hawaii, Grasslands Llc is using Allan Savory's approach to heal grazing land and rural communities.[62] It is enabling conservation buyers to afford to save historic ranches like the charismatic Hana Ranch on Maui from becoming luxury housing.[63]

In 1961 Joel Salatin began farming what he describes as the Shenandoah Valley's most worn-out, eroded, abused property. He describes how Savory's approach of Holistic Management turned a destitute farm into a prosperous operation supporting 35 farm-based ventures.[64] Joel speaks often about his success using Savory's approach, moving cows daily using portable electric fencing to mimic how predators naturally control overgrazing on grasslands.[65] Selling high-end vegetables, meat, eggs and forest products within a 100-mile radius, Polyface Farm is a profitable enterprise that validates the Salatin family's mission to develop emotionally, economically, and environmentally balanced agricultural practices that fit within living systems' cycles.

Dan Daggett[66] has profiled a dozen small grazing operations that are reclaiming land by managing cattle in harmony with the ecology that is there, not against it. Daggett shows that while humans have come in recent years to behave as an alien species rapaciously taking from the land what they desire, for most of our history we lived on land as natives, working with place and the natural cycles in ways that enhanced our homes, and us. Daggett argues that we all need to become native to the places that support us.

Conclusion

The economics of the circular economy are compelling to companies. The elegant engineering of biological and technical nutrient material flows inspires environmentalists as well. The latest Club of Rome report shows that implementing a circular economy in Sweden could cut carbon emissions by 70%, while saving money and adding 100,000 jobs to the Swedish economy.[67] It is time now to apply these concepts at scale to our relationship with the living systems that sustain us. Adam Sacks quotes Allan Savory: 'Global climate change and land degradation have to be put on a war footing internationally – meaning that all nations need to pull together and treat this threat as we would a war ... Only through uniting and diverting all the resources required to deal with climate change and land degradation can we avert unimaginable tragedy. We have all the money we need. All we cannot buy is time.'

Global restoration of grasslands can re-establish soil integrity and biodiversity as it sequesters massive amounts of carbon from the atmosphere. Regenerative agriculture can stabilise local and, eventually, global weather patterns, restore a balanced hydrological cycle, create meaningful jobs, particularly in third-world countries; produce high-quality animal protein without synthetic fertilisers and destructive factory farming; and support local communities worldwide in sustainable living.

This is the circular economy of the soil.

©José Pedro Cosat- Flickr CC

Notes

1 Founder of The Biochar Company, https://www.soilreef.com/company/soilreef-company.php

2 http://www.soils4teachers.org/biology-life-soil

3 'Modern' in the sense of humans cultivating the soil.

4 Dr Wes Jackson, *The 50-Year Farm Bill* (The Solutions Journal, 1/ 3, 7 July 2010).

5 http://www.ellenmacarthurfoundation.org/publications

6 http://www.braungart.com/en/content/terminologie

7 http://www.ipcc.ch/pdf/assessment-report/ar5/syr/AR5SYRFINALSPM.pdf

8 www.capitalinstitute.org

9 Pacific Northwest Direct Seed Association, http://www.directseed.org

10 J. T. Houghton et al. (eds.), *Climate Change 1995: The Science of Climate Change*, published for the Intergovernmental Panel on Climate Change (New York: Cambridge University Press, 1996).

11 Baggott et al., *Greenhouse Gas Inventories for England, Scotland, Wales and Northern Ireland*, Division Research Programme of the Department for Environment, Food and Rural Affairs. November 2006, www.airquality. co.uk/.../0509211321Reghgreport2003MainText Issue1.doc

12 A. R. Ravishankara et al., *Nitrous Oxide (N2O): The Dominant Ozone-Depleting Substance Emitted in the 21st Century* (Science 326/5949, October 2009).

13 In 1995 it was estimated that humans applied more than 6 million tonnes of artificial nitrogen fertiliser, resulting in human caused soil denitrification of 3–8 billion kilograms of N_2O each year. By 2013, it was 100 million tons. As a result, atmospheric concentrations of N_2O had risen from about 275 parts per billion (ppb) before the industrial era to about 312 ppb in 1994. Much of the increase is thought to be from human activity. See J. T. Houghton et al., *Climate Change 1995: The Science of Climate Change* (New York: Cambridge University Press, 1996).

14 The Nitrogen Cycle, http://users.rcn.com/jkimball.ma.ultranet/BiologyPages/N/NitrogenCycle.html

15 Dr John A. Harrison, *The Nitrogen Cycle: Of Microbes and Men* (Vision Learning, Vol. EAS-2/4, 2003; http://www.visionlearning.com/library/moduleviewer.php?mid=98).

16 J. T. Houghton et al., *Climate Change 1995: The Science of Climate Change* (New York: Cambridge University Press, 1996).

17 United States Environmental Protection Agency, *Harmful Algal Blooms* (http://www2.epa.gov/nutrientpollution/harmful-algal-blooms).

18 David Biello, *Oceanic Dead Zones Continue to Spread* (Scientific American, 15 August 2008; https://www.scientificamerican.com/article/oceanic-dead-zones-spread/).

19 FAO Newsroom, *Livestock a major threat to environment* (FAO News, 29 November 2006).

20 Richard Black, *UN body to look at meat and climate link* (BBC News, 24 March 2010; http://news.bbc.co.uk/2/hi/science/nature/8583308.stm).

21 Methane, a particularly potent greenhouse gas, is produced by enteric formation (burping and flatulence) from cattle (1,792 million tonnes CO_2-equivalent each year.) Jessica Bellarby et al. *Cool Farming: Climate Impacts of Agriculture and Mitigation Potential* (Greenpeace International report, January 2008). This argument forgets that cows aren't really adding more methane to the planet so much as cycling compounds already in circulation. Methane emissions from enteric fermentation represent the transformation of carbon already in circulation between the earth and the atmosphere, and the number of cows roaming the planet today is not significantly larger than the herds of prehistoric bison and other ungulates. For more on this argument see: Suzanne Nelson, *Beef and Dairy Can Be Good For the Planet* (Indy week, 5 March 2008; http://www.indyweek.com/gyrobase/Content?oid=oid%3A194735).

22 US Department of Agriculture, Economic Research Service, *Feed Grains Database: Yearbook Tables* and *Oil Crops Yearbook* http://www.ers.usda.gov/data-products/feed-grains-database/feed-grains-yearbook-tables.aspx; http://www.ers.usda.gov/data-products/oil-crops-yearbook.aspx

23 In 2008, 70–80% of grains grown and acreage farmed was used to produce America's 11 billion meat, milk, and egg-laying animals, 95% of which were raised in confinement. This includes nearly 69 million pigs, and 300 million commercial laying hens in battery cages, ten billion meat chickens, and half a billion turkeys that live in abusively close quarters. In addition, about 33 million beef cows and 9.7 million dairy cows are confined in crowded feedlots or dairy barns, that foster diseases.

24 Lester R. Brown, *Plan B 4.0: Mobilizing to Save Civilization* (Earth Policy Institute/W. W. Norton, 2009; www.earthpolicy.org/index.php?/books/pb4/pb4presentation).

25 In 2010, then the hottest year ever (2014 now holds that record and 2015 is on track to beat it) unprecedented floods on three continents and heat and drought in Russia contributed to soaring wheat prices, and as food riots ensued across North Africa, the Arab Spring. Lester Brown, *Rising Temperatures Raise Food Prices: Heat, Drought and a Failed Harvest in Russia* (Earth Policy Institute, 10 August 2010; www.earth-policy.org/plan_b_updates/2010/update89).

26 Jim Tankersley, *California farms, vineyards in peril from warming, U.S. energy secretary warns* (Los Angeles Times, 4 February 2009; http://www.latimes.com/news/local/la-me-warming4-2009feb04,0,7454963.story).

27 Rodale Institute website, *Our Work: FST Fast Facts* (http://rodaleinstitute.org/our-work/farming-systems-trial/farming-systems-trial-fst-fast-facts/).

28 Soil Association website, http://www.soilassociation.org/

29 http://www.plantsciences.ucdavis.edu/plantsciences/

30 Janet Cotter and Reyes Tirado, *Food Security and Climate Change: The answer is biodiversity* (Greenpeace International, June 2008).

31 L. Drinkwater, et al., *Legume-based cropping systems have reduced carbon and nitrogen losses* (Nature 396, 1998), 262–5; D. Pimentel et al., *Environmental, Energetic, and Economic Comparisons of Organic and Conventional Farming Systems* (BioScience 55, 2005), 573–82; E. E. Marriott and M. M. Wander, *Total and labile soil organic matter in organic and conventional farming systems* (Soil Science Society of America Journal 70, 2006), 950–9.

32 D. Gabriel et al., *Beta diversity at different special scales: Plant communities in organic and conventional agriculture* (Ecological Applications 16, 2006), 2011–21, cited in: http://www3.interscience.wiley.com/journal/123417154/abstract?CRETRY=1&SRETRY=0

33 Union of Concerned Scientists, *Agricultural Practices and Carbon Sequestration* (1 October 2009; http://www.ucsusa.org/sites/default/files/legacy/assets/documents/food_and_agriculture/ag-carbon-sequest-fact-sheet.pdf)

34 http://happyfood-funnyfarm.blogspot.com/20090201archive.html

35 Dan Charles, *Fertilized World* (National Geographic, May 2013; http://ngm.nationalgeographic.com/2013/05/fertilized-world/charles-text?source=podrelated).

36 United Nations Conference on Trade and Development, *Trade and Environment Review 2013: Wake Up Before It's Too Late* (September 2013; http://unctad.org/en/pages/PublicationWebflyer.aspx?publicationid=666).

37 The 80 people at the apex of the global development pyramid have as much wealth as the bottom 3.5 billion poorest. See: https://www.oxfam.org/sites/www.oxfam.org/files/fileattachments/ib-wealth-having-all-wanting-more-190115-en.pdf

38 Food and Agriculture Organization of the United Nations, *The State of Food Insecurity in the World* (2015; http://www.fao.org/3/a4ef2d16-70a7-460a-a9ac-2a65a533269a/i4646e.pdf).

39 Unlike the term 'green' used today to indicate sustainability and living in harmony with nature, the term 'green' was used to indicate a resistance to communism, mirroring images of 'red'. The name was given by the US State Department, William Guad, in 1968. He explained that if people were well fed by the high-yielding crops of the new modernised agriculture system, they would be less motivated to become communist.

40 Daniel Zwerdling, *India's Farming 'Revolution' Heading for Collapse* (National Public Radio, 13 April 2009; http://www.npr.org/templates/story/story.php?storyId=102893816).

41 Somini Sengupta, *On India's Farms, a Plague of Suicide* (New York Times, 19 September 2006; http://www.nytimes.com/2006/09/19/world/asia/19india.html?r=3). For more recent information see: Dr Vandana Shiva, *Save our annadatas* (20 May 2015; http://www.navdanya.org/blog/?p=2136).

42 *Report on the International Conference on Organic Agriculture and Food Security* (Nay 2007).

43 The Land Institute website, http://www.landinstitute.org/

44 Ibid.

45 Lawrence Berkeley National Laboratories, *Cookstove Projects* (http://cookstoves.lbl.gov/).

46 International Biochar Initiative, *Biochar Technology* (http://www.biochar-international.org/technology).

47 International Biochar Initiative website, http://www.biochar-international.org/.

48 International Biochar Initiative, *Farming* (http://biocharfarms.org/farming/).

49 Tim Flannery, *An open letter on Biochar* (http://www.biochar-international.org/timflannery).

50 Scott Bilby, *Flannery talks biochar and why we need to move into the renewable age, Beyond Zero Emissions* (Beyond Zero Emissions, 11 January 2008; http://beyondzeroemissions.org/media/radio/tim-flannery-talks-bio-char-and-why-we-need-move-renewable-age-080111).

51 Jeff Wallin at the 2012 US Biochar Conference (http://2012.biochar.us.com/profile/165/jeff-wallin).

52 Judith Schwartz, *Cows Save the Planet* (Chelsea Green Publishing, 2003); See also Allan Savory, *Cows Can Save the World* (Range magazine, summer 2015; http://www.rangemagazine.com/features/summer-15/range-su15-sr-cows_save_world.pdf).

53 Central Minnesota Sustainable Development Partnership, *A Landowner's Guide to Carbon Sequestration Credits* (http://www.cinram.umn.edu/publications/landownersguide1.5-1.pdf), 8.

54 Adam Sacks, *Putting Carbon Back in the Ground – The Way Nature Does It* (Climate Code Red, 7 March 2013; http://www.climatecodered.org/2013/03/putting-carbon-back-into-ground-way.html)

55 Savory website, http://savory.global/

56 *Introduction to Savory Hubs*, video (https://www.youtube.com/watch?v=SKWeqkq6tP4).

57 *Circular Economy: Innovation and Enterprise MBA Handbook 2014* (University of Bradford, 2014)

58 Allan Savory, *A Global Strategy for Addressing Global Climate Change* (2008; http://savory.global/assets/docs/evidence-papers/climate-change.pdf).

59 Ibid.

60 K. T. Weber and S. Horst, *Desertification and livestock grazing: The roles of sedentarization, mobility and rest* (Pastoralism: Research, Policy and Practice, 2011, 1/19, October 2011; http://www.pastoralismjournal.com/content/1/1/19).

61 https://www.youtube.com/watch?v=Jt3O4v-v3tU

62 Grasslands, LCC website, http://www.grasslands-llc.com/

63 Grasslands, LCC, *Hana Ranch, Maui, Hawaii* (http://www.grasslands-llc.com/#!hana/ckwm).

64 Salatin's land supports a number of ventures – he calls it 'enterprise stacking' – including pigs, poultry, eggs, turkeys, beef, rabbits, plus forestry and market gardening; they also offer farm tours, run an on-line store, and produce educational videos. See www.polyfacefarms.com/

65 Joel Salatin, Polyface Farms (Meet the Farmer.TV; https://www.youtube.com/watch?v=FrxmgR-vYms)

66 Dan Daggett, *Gardeners of Eden, Rediscovering our Importance to Nature* (Thatcher Charitable Trust/EcoResults, Santa Barbara, 2005).

67 Anders Wijkman, *Circular economy could bring 70 percent cut in carbon emissions by 2030* (The Guardian, 15 April 2015; http://www.theguardian.com/sustainable-business/2015/apr/15/circular-economy-jobs-climate-carbon-emissions-eu-taxation).

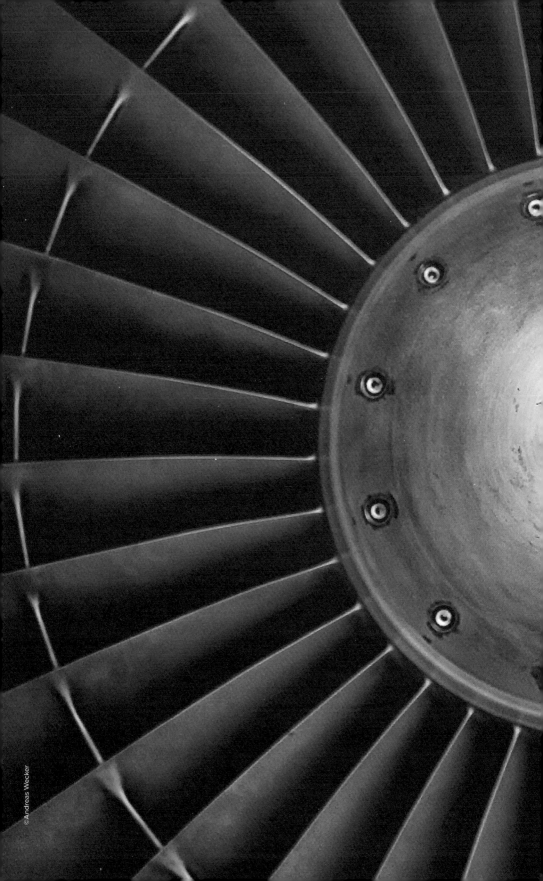

REMANUFACTURING AND THE CIRCULAR ECONOMY

Nabil Nasr

This chapter critically considers a range of remanufacturing definitions and descriptors. It briefly examines the history and profile of the current global remanufacturing industry. As 'servitisation' leads companies to focus on selling product functions or service rather than products, the chapter examines how it has the potential to facilitate product remanufacturing in a circular economy. The chapter considers the importance of incorporating the principles of 'design for remanufacture' to optimise the utility of products and maximise the contribution of remanufacturing in a circular economy.

Nabil Nasr
Nabil is Associate Provost for Academic Affairs and Director of the Golisano Institute for Sustainability at Rochester Institute of Technology. He is founder of the Center for Remanufacturing and Resource Recovery – a leading source of applied research and solutions in remanufacturing technologies.

Introduction to remanufacturing

Remanufacturing is a proven industrial process by which discarded, retired or non-functional products or modules are processed and returned to 'like new' condition. Lund[1] offers a widely accepted definition:

(Remanufacturing is), ... an industrial process in which worn-out products are restored to like-new condition. Through a series of industrial processes in a factory environment, a discarded product is completely disassembled. Usable parts are cleaned, refurbished, and put into inventory. Then the product is reassembled from the old parts (and where necessary, new parts) to produce a unit fully equivalent and sometimes superior in performance and expected lifetime to the original new product.'

A number of other industrial processes are used to repurpose products for second use, and such products may be promoted as 'remanufactured' although they do not meet the definition. This creates confusion in the market and can impact the perception of true remanufactured products. Terms used to describe 'repurposed products' include:

- Refurbished
- Refinished
- Overhauled
- Reset
- Refined (oil)
- Recycled
- Rebuilt
- Restored
- Recharged (batteries)
- Repaired

These descriptors do not reflect remanufacturing's business model or the scope of industrial operations that make remanufacturing a unique area of today's global economy.

Remanufacturing (often shortened to 'reman') is a closed-loop industrial process that intentionally recaptures the value-added component of a product so that it may lead additional useful lives rather than being landfilled or recycled. The cornerstone of reman is full restoration – a high-quality process through which products are systematically disassembled, cleaned, and inspected for wear and/or degradation. Any substandard or degraded components are replaced, feature upgrades can be incorporated, and the product is reassembled. Quality testing is typically performed to ensure performance meets original specifications. At the end of the process, the remanufactured item emerges functionally equivalent to new production, and often it is supported post-sale with the same kind and length of warranty coverage as a newly manufactured product.

Remanufacturing is often compared with recycling even though the two processes differ significantly. Recycling reduces products into raw material, which can then be used again. In contrast, remanufacturing retains the geometrical shape of the product, and is therefore able to capture both the materials and the value added (the labour, energy, and manufacturing processes) which were embodied in the original product during initial manufacturing. In many cases, the ratio of total energy required for new production compared to that required for remanufacturing is approximately 6:1.[2] Research by Adler[3] found that a typical reman operation (diesel engine cylinder head remanufacturing), required less energy and produced fewer greenhouse gas emissions than new production of the same component. Recapturing (and retaining) the value-added component of a product is both environmentally and economically beneficial. Remanufacturing is often referred to as the 'ultimate form of recycling' because it preserves the embodied energy contained in a product. By implementing a remanufacturing strategy, disposal costs (both financial and environmental) can be avoided, the value embodied in the product can be recouped, and resources can be used more efficiently, thus helping advance the circular economy model.

History of remanufacturing
Automotive industries were early practitioners of remanufacturing. By 1910, automobile tyre remanufacturing (usually termed 'retreading' in this industry sector) was an established business. In the early 1930s Ford Motor Company began to apply remanufacturing principles and practices to the rebuilding of automobile engines. After World War II, Caterpillar, Xerox, and other multinationals, as well as many smaller independent companies, adopted the remanufacturing concept.

Remanufacturing entered a new era with the environmental movement of the early 1970s, driven by awareness of the environmental consequences resulting from the world's industrial appetite for resources, including consumption of fossil fuels, a finite resource that contributes to climate change. Remanufacturing gained recognition as a preventive step towards a more sustainable, non-linear and low-waste economy.

Recognising the need to curb resource depletion and waste generation, the US President's Council on Sustainable Development in 1998 recommended remanufacturing as a potential means to 'close the loops of material and energy flows,' citing reman's cost and energy efficiency for products at the end of their initial life cycles. There was also growing appreciation of remanufacturing's inherent benefits over recycling.

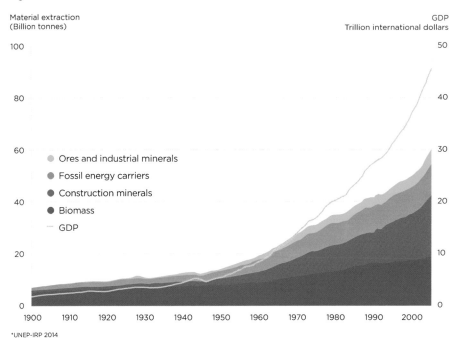

Figure 1 **Global material extraction & GDP***

Material extraction
(Billion tonnes)

GDP
Trillion international dollars

- Ores and industrial minerals
- Fossil energy carriers
- Construction minerals
- Biomass
- GDP

*UNEP-IRP 2014

United States remanufacturing segments and sectors

Remanufacturing activities in the United States are broadly divided into two primary industry segments: military and civilian (i.e. non-military).

Military (vehicle, aircraft, and equipment): The US Department of Defense is the largest remanufacturer in the world. Military remanufacturing includes ground vehicles, aircraft, weapon systems, ships, and stationary equipment. Activities in this area include refurbishment, upgrade, conversion, and complete remanufacturing. It is often referred to as 'turning the odometer back to zero' when remanufacturing is completed.

Non-military: According to USITC:[4] 'The remanufacturing-intensive sectors that account for the majority of remanufacturing activity in the United States include aerospace, consumer products, electrical apparatus, heavy-duty and off-road equipment, information technology products, locomotives, machinery, medical devices, motor vehicle parts, office furniture, restaurant equipment, and retreaded tyres.'

Reman industry profile

The global commercial remanufacturing industry is characterised by predominant emphasis on the automotive sector. However, global

Figure 2 **Remanufacturing in the US[4]**

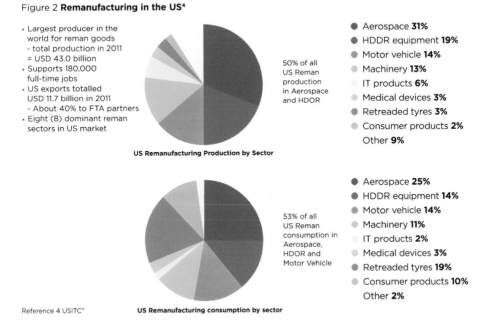

- Largest producer in the world for reman goods
  - total production in 2011 = USD 43.0 billion
- Supports 180,000 full-time jobs
- US exports totalled USD 11.7 billion in 2011
  - About 40% to FTA partners
- Eight (8) dominant reman sectors in US market

50% of all US Reman production in Aerospace and HDOR

US Remanufacturing Production by Sector

- Aerospace **31%**
- HDDR equipment **19%**
- Motor vehicle **14%**
- Machinery **13%**
- IT products **6%**
- Medical devices **3%**
- Retreaded tyres **3%**
- Consumer products **2%**
- Other **9%**

53% of all US Reman consumption in Aerospace, HDOR and Motor Vehicle

US Remanufacturing consumption by sector

- Aerospace **25%**
- HDDR equipment **14%**
- Motor vehicle **14%**
- Machinery **11%**
- IT products **2%**
- Medical devices **3%**
- Retreaded tyres **19%**
- Consumer products **10%**
- Other **2%**

Reference 4 USITC"

remanufacturing activities also encompass aerospace industry; toner cartridges; office furniture and equipment; transportation, construction and electrical equipment; medical devices; machine tools, compressors, heavy machinery, and others.

Although it is an enterprise of worldwide scope and significance, remanufacturing is possibly the industry most neglected by researchers. Until recently only two major surveys of US remanufacturing have been conducted;[5] and both assessed a limited number of broad indicators including number of firms, total annual sales, total direct employment, and number of product areas served.

In 2011, the US International Trade Commission performed a new survey of the industry. Its report, *Remanufactured Goods: An Overview of the U.S. and Global Industries, Markets,* and Trade stated that: 'U.S. production of remanufactured goods totaled at least USD 43.0 billion in 2011. U.S. production of remanufactured goods grew from USD 37.3 billion in 2009 to USD 43.0 billion in 2011. Remanufactured goods are estimated to have accounted for about 2% of total sales of all products (new and remanufactured) in the industry sectors noted above during the 2009–11 period. U.S. production of remanufactured aerospace products, heavy duty off-road (HDOR) equipment, and motor vehicle parts together accounted for 63% of total U.S. production of remanufactured goods. Small and medium-sized enterprises (SMEs) comprise an important share of remanufacturing production and trade. For instance, SMEs are estimated to have accounted for 25% (USD 11.1 billion) of U.S. production of remanufactured goods, and 17% (USD 1.8 billion) of U.S. exports in 2011.'

Products from Remanufacturing: Remanufactured products include CAT scanners, printing presses, marine engines, tyres, fuel pumps, fitness equipment, postage meters, and toner cartridges. Today, remanufacturing is expanding into areas formerly dominated by new production, e.g. medical devices. According to MDDI,[6] 'The remanufacturing of medical devices is a growing phenomenon within the health-care industry. The types of devices that are currently [remanufactured] range from machines such as neonatal monitors and anesthesia vaporizers to devices used in surgery, such as forceps, endoscopes, and cytoscopes.'

Geographic survey of reman industries

USA: Contemporary US remanufacturing is a major business, with approximately 73,000 remanufacturing firms generating nearly USD 43 billion in annual sales. The automotive parts segment alone accounts for annual sales of close to USD 6.2 billion.[7]

Europe: Nations of the European Union have active remanufacturing efforts, often driven by EU legislation. The Waste Electrical and Electronic Equipment Directive (WEEE), passed by the European Parliament in 2002, sets collection, recycling and recovery targets for all types of electrical goods by manufacturers for electrical and electronic equipment in the 28 European Union member states and affects anyone who does business with European countries. The directive has stimulated interest in practices that improve recovery and recycling rates.

Worldwide: India, China, Japan, Australia and other Asian nations have less developed remanufacturing activities. Major corporations such as Caterpillar have invested in dedicated, state-of-the-art remanufacturing facilities in Singapore and China. Asia is also host to numerous smaller operations, notably toner cartridge remanufacturer/suppliers.

Economics of remanufacturing: The effects of remanufacturing extend far beyond the actual remanufacturing process. According to Lund,[8] 'Remanufacturing industry sales are greater than the value of shipments of the entire consumer durables industry (appliances, furniture, audio & video, farm & garden equipment).' The following are two major reman industry segments:

• *Aftermarket automotive parts:* One of the largest and most prosperous remanufacturing segments. According to the Production Engine Remanufacturers Association (2013):[9] 'There are nearly 6,000 companies in North America remanufacturing engines in one form or another. At USD 2.5 billion dollars, the engine remanufacturing industry remanufactures approximately 2.2 million engines annually in North America.'

• *Tyre retreading:* Within this remanufacturing sector, 'Retreaded tyres hold an 80% share of the replacement market for aircraft landing gears, since nearly all air carriers procure retreads when available. Off-road machines, such as earth excavators, are other big users of retreads.'[10]

Reman and the circular economy

Mass production, and high levels of consumption and disposal are forcing society to face constraints on the availability of resources. Closing the loop with regard to the material flows associated with the product life cycle or service delivery to consumers would be an important step toward establishing a circular economy. Product remanufacturing is a key element of an overall product life-cycle strategy that can help achieve this goal (refer to Figure 3).

Figure 3 **Remanufacturing in the product life cycle**

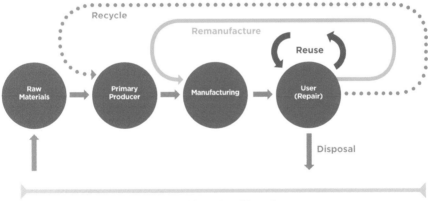

In order to realise all the advantages that remanufacturing can offer to the circular economy, several conditions must be met. Chief among them is the design of the collection system – the supply chain that sources and delivers discarded/worn product 'cores' suitable for remanufacturing to the company performing this work. Organising and maintaining such a collection system is often expensive for the remanufacturer. For example, vehicle engine remanufacturers may need to provide secure shipping containers so that engine cores can be transported to their facility without incurring damage en route. Consequently it is in the interest of the remanufacturer – once its collection system is established – to create an incentive for end-users to turn in their discarded/worn-out goods rather than disposing of them in landfills.

Appeals to recycle generally lack the economic incentive to affect some consumer behaviour, and as shown above, remanufacturing contributes considerably higher value to the circular economy than recycling. However, once a collection system for remanufacturable cores is set up and functioning, the remanufacturer then may select the optimal cores to remanufacture, with the remainder of the received product being recycled, refurbished, refinished, etc., at the same location (refer to the 'repurposed product' terms in Section 1). The exception is *repair*, which is generally handled at dedicated service shops specialising in this activity, e.g. vehicle engine and transmission repair shops. Thus reman can not only provide economic value and incentive, it can help facilitate other processes that help divert materials from ultimate disposal, and thus promote the circular economy model (refer to Figure 4).

Product service and reman
Many manufacturing companies are currently making efforts to servitise their businesses. Servitisation is the phenomenon of manufacturing companies adding services to their total offerings.[11] Manufacturing companies, especially those based in developed countries, contend with market saturation and commoditisation in many product areas; in response, they servitise their businesses to increase profits. This movement toward servitisation provides opportunities to increase economic profits and develop closed-loop industrial systems including the adoption/incorporation of remanufacturing. As servitisation leads companies to focus on selling product functions or service rather than products, companies are motivated to take responsibility for the entire life cycle of products and thus to reduce the costs associated with product life cycles by developing closed loops of material flows that, in turn, help enable the circular economy.

This movement to servitisation provides companies with opportunities to increase profits and facilitate product remanufacturing. These potentials have been discussed in terms of their relevance for a functional economy,[12] for product service systems,[13] and for industrial product service systems.[14]

Figure 4 **The role of remanufacturing in the circular economy model**

PRINCIPLES

1

Preserve and enhance natural capital by controlling finite stocks and balancing renewable resource flows – for example, replacing fossil fuels with renewable energy or using the maximum sustainable yield method to preserve fish stocks.

2

Optimise resource yields by circulating products, components and materials at the highest utility at all times in both technical and biological cycles – for example, sharing or looping products and extending product use cycles.

3

Foster system effectiveness by revealing and designing out negative externalities, such as water, air, soil, and noise pollution; climate change; toxins; congestion; and negative health effects related to resource use.

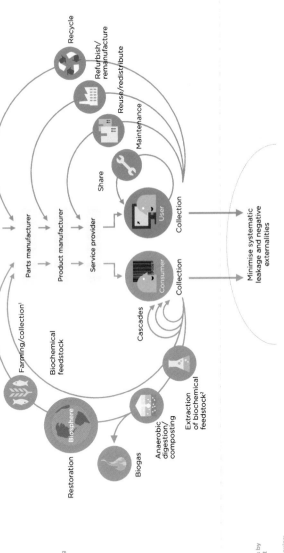

Renewables   Finite materials

Renewables flow management

Regenerate   Substitute materials   Virtualise   Restore   Stock management

Farming/collection[1]   Parts manufacturer   Recycle

Biochemical feedstock   Product manufacturer   Refurbish/remanufacture

Biosphere   Service provider   Reuse/redistribute

Restoration   Share   Maintenance

Biogas   Consumer   User

Anaerobic digestion/composting   Collection   Collection

Extraction of biochemical feedstock[2]   Cascades

Minimise systematic leakage and negative externalities

1 Hunting and fishing
2 Can take both post-harvest and post-consumer waste as an input.
Source: Ellen MacArthur Foundation circular economy team. Adapted from the Cradle to Cradle Design Protocol by Braungart & McDonough

Servitisation facilitates remanufacturing in the following seven ways:

1. When customers focus on the functions provided by products rather than the product, they become less sensitive to the appeal of new products; thus, they are more likely to accept remanufactured products.

2. In terms of selling products, the price of remanufactured products is usually much lower than that of new products. For example, remanufactured auto parts may cost 20-50% less than equivalent new production. This cost differential may become narrower in the cases of customers who are covered by servitisation contracts; they may not be as concerned about the price difference between new and remanufactured products since product performance is guaranteed.

3. Original Equipment Manufacturers (OEMs) often fear cannibalisation of new products by remanufactured products – especially when competitors, e.g. independent remanufacturers, supply remanufactured products. In the case of servitisation, because it is more difficult for competitors to imitate the business,[15] competitors are less likely to capture the business' revenue.

4. Servitisation enables OEMs to take responsibility for the full product life cycle rather than merely the phases leading up to product sales.[16] This becomes even more significant when OEMs retain ownership of the products as in use-oriented or result-oriented services. With servitisation, OEMs are motivated to further reduce the total costs of ownership (TCO), and remanufacturing provides a means to reduce these costs.

5. If OEMs are motivated to remanufacture their products, they generally become motivated to implement Design for Remanufacturing practices, which can substantially reduce remanufacturing costs and thus enhance their bottom-line profits from reman activities.

6. With servitisation, returning used products becomes easier. This is the case especially when OEMs retain ownership of products. Even if other companies (e.g. leasing companies) own the products, it is usually more efficient to accept bulk returns of used products from large-scale product owners than to receive one-by-one returns from large numbers of individual end users.

7. Servitisation enables OEMs to easily monitor the usage of products. When products are directly sold, customers may refuse this monitoring. If OEMs retain the ownership of products, monitoring is simplified. Even when customers own the products, they are more likely to accept usage monitoring if it is linked to valuable services such as preventive maintenance. If the conditions of usage and products are known, this tends

to facilitate remanufacturing, which can reduce the costs associated with the remanufacturing process.

On the other hand, servitisation does not automatically lead to remanufacturing. For example, servitisation can lead to less responsible user behaviour[17] and hence to decreased product life and reduced ability to remanufacture products. However, servitisation has the potential to facilitate product remanufacturing and thus the circular economy; realising this potential is a significant challenge for industry.

Anatomy of remanufacturing

Remanufacturing is distinguished from other industrial activities by four key factors which will be briefly reviewed in this section.

Collection

Because remanufacturing does not begin with processing raw materials, it depends on a steady supply of customer returns and/or worn and end-of-life products which are suitable for remanufacturing; these are called 'cores.' Cores can range from discarded cellphones to complete worn-out marine diesel engine assemblies. For many firms, ensuring a steady supply of cores to remanufacture is a concern and business challenge.

Processes

For a product to be classified as remanufactured, it must go through several production steps. Remanufacturing begins with complete disassembly of the product followed by thorough cleaning and inspection of reusable parts. Parts that pass inspection according to their design specifications or are restorable through a series of processes are processed and inventoried. These parts are then fed to an assembly process (which could be identical to or different from the original product assembly method) and are mixed with new replacement parts for worn and non-restorable parts to make up a remanufactured product. The percentage of new parts in a remanufactured product varies considerably based on product type, condition, and cost. Remanufacturing also enables certain older products (e.g. copiers, vehicle electronics) to be upgraded with advanced technology that was unavailable during initial production, thus increasing the products' utility and perceived value.

Marketing

Marketing remanufactured products can be distinctly unlike new product marketing in some areas. For example, finished remanufactured products are marketed and sold at a discount from new production. Also such products must carry labelling that indicates they are remanufactured (i.e. not new). Reman marketing must also strive to overcome any lingering negative perceptions by consumers that the remanufactured products are 'used' or otherwise inferior to new. In response, reman products often carry a warranty comparable to new products, reflecting the remanufacturer's commitment to assuring that their production is functionally equivalent to newly manufactured goods. Such guarantees help overcome consumer uncertainties concerning product quality and performance.

Logistics/policy

Unlike most new manufactured products, remanufactured goods can be significantly more difficult to export and sell worldwide. Even with the reman industry's worldwide scope and the economic, social and environmental advantages that come from its products, the benefits of remanufacturing are not widely understood by governments or consumers.

A major challenge is that many countries that bar or restrict the importation of remanufactured goods represent key markets. A 2012 US International Trade Commission report[18] about the importation of pre-owned ('used and refurbished') capital medical equipment in countries around the world hints at the magnitude of the problem for US remanufacturers looking to gain access to key markets. The report's review of import regulations from 106 countries found that although only 21 of the countries are known to bar or restrict the importation of pre-owned medical devices, the combined population of these countries (about 3.4 billion people) represents 58.6% of the total population of potential U.S. export markets (i.e. world population minus US population). The report also points out that the population in many of these countries is largely at the low or middle-income level where buyers might be attracted to the lower cost of remanufactured products.

Market access information for other remanufacturing sectors such as the automotive parts industry is limited. A report issued by the US Trade Representative in 2010[19] acknowledged that many countries limit trade of remanufactured automotive parts, and noted that these barriers exist because countries associate remanufactured goods with used goods and waste. The report also said the barriers can be an excuse to protect domestic firms.

Design for remanufacturing

Another major challenge for the reman industry is that many potentially profitable products were never designed to be remanufactured. Most products are designed for a single life cycle and then are discarded; however, the discarded product still has significant residual value, and if recovered, could save money and natural resources. The recovered value and environmental benefits can be increased by incorporating the principles of Design for Remanufacturing (DfReman). DfReman can be a viable opportunity to maximise the utility of products and value to businesses and consumers while also maximising the amount of waste that can be diverted from landfills.

Figure 5 **How remanufacturing is implemented in various stages of a typical product delivery process**

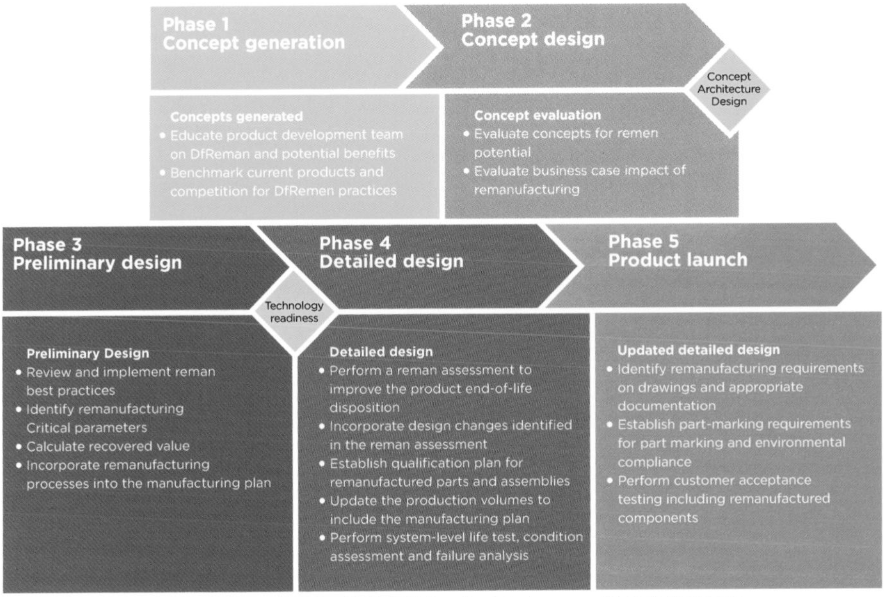

Phase 1 Concept generation		**Phase 2** Concept design	
			Concept Architecture Design
Concepts generated • Educate product development team on DfReman and potential benefits • Benchmark current products and competition for DfReman practices		**Concept evaluation** • Evaluate concepts for remen potential • Evaluate business case impact of remanufacturing	

Phase 3 Preliminary design	**Phase 4** Detailed design	**Phase 5** Product launch
Technology readiness		
Preliminary Design • Review and implement reman best practices • Identify remanufacturing Critical parameters • Calculate recovered value • Incorporate remanufacturing processes into the manufacturing plan	**Detailed design** • Perform a reman assessment to improve the product end-of-life disposition • Incorporate design changes identified in the reman assessment • Establish qualification plan for remanufactured parts and assemblies • Update the production volumes to include the manufacturing plan • Perform system-level life test, condition assessment and failure analysis	**Updated detailed design** • Identify remanufacturing requirements on drawings and appropriate documentation • Establish part-marking requirements for part marking and environmental compliance • Perform customer acceptance testing including remanufactured components

© N. Nasr and B. Hilton, Design for Remanufacturing, 2008 CIRP International Conference on Life Cycle Engineering

Products that incorporate DfReman principles from their conception can display greater economic, environmental and social benefits to manufacturers and society than products that incorporate remanufacturing strategies as an afterthought to product design.

Rationale and objectives

There are economic and environmental benefits to purposely designing products to take advantage of remanufacturing. It has been suggested that decisions made during the product design phase influence more than 75% of the economic cost connected with a product as well as 75% of its environmental and social impacts.

DfReman tools implemented at the start of the design cycle can maximise the full potential of reman. Designers must consider beyond the product's initial useful life and take into account its end-of-life options, including reuse, remanufacturing and recycling.

Design engineers may need to change current practices to make best use of DfReman assets and resources. Examples include changing from a commonly used material to a more robust material to enable a part to withstand additional life cycles, or making an assembly more modular to enable quick disassembly/reassembly or replacement. Some of these new design decisions may increase the product's initial cost, but the long-term economic and ecological benefits could be substantial.

Methodology

A product design team is required to balance many 'top priorities' within the constraints of the product launch such as cost, form, fit, function, quality, and delivery. Typically, however, environmentally preferable end-of-life strategies are considered only after a product has been manufactured and released to the market. Maximising the economic and ecological benefits of remanufacturing can be achieved only if the end-of-life strategy becomes a top priority and is integrated throughout the product delivery process, from concept generation through product launch. Figure 3 shows an example of the ways that remanufacturing can be typically implemented during the various stages of a typical product delivery process.

The design team needs to be equipped with tools specifically designed to facilitate reman. These tools provide guidance for selecting the proper design attributes to maximise remanufacturing. DfReman may be new to the team and can directly conflict with previous training. For example, a product designed for remanufacturing is easy to disassemble, thus enabling the recovery of high-value components. Designing a product for disassembly might conflict with designing a product for quick and economical assembly; for example, products designed for assembly may include snap-joints for rapid assembly, but these joints can be difficult to disassemble without damaging the components.

Best practices are normally used to guide the design team in making decisions that will optimise reman. DfReman best practices result in simpler reman processes including disassembly, cleaning, inspection, renewal, and reassembly processes. Remanufacturing best practices recognise that all components eventually lose their value, and so designing for eventual recycling is also important.

Checklists are used to educate the engineering team on targets or deliverables through the various product delivery process stages. Because, with some products, it can take a year or more to design and develop a new product, checklists can remind a veteran engineering team or educate new team members of what requirements must be met at the current programme stage.

Other tools such as decision trees can help guide engineers through key choices, such as the recovery of each component or assembly. Finally, assessment tools are used to evaluate and compare concepts. According to Nasr and Thurston[20] the evaluation process includes:

• Value and cost of component(s).

• Technical feasibility of remanufacturing (i.e. Can the condition be assessed for reuse? Can the component be extracted without damage? Is there a known process for restoration to like-new condition?).

• Economic feasibility of remanufacturing. This includes recovered value at end-of-life (i.e. the cost to extract from product, and the cost to convert to like-new condition).

• Disposal options and environmental impact or legislation.
Metrics such as the recovered value and ecological impact are used to compare various designs; this maximises the recovery of the final product and helps promote the circular economy.

Case studies
This section examines servitisation and remanufacturing in two representative product areas using case studies from the automotive and heavy duty industry sectors.

Automotive: CARDONE Industries
The auto parts remanufacturing industry is among the world's largest remanufacturing sectors, accounting for an estimated two-thirds of global remanufacturing activities.[21] Engines, transmissions, starter motors, alternators, steering racks, and clutches are the principal remanufactured auto parts. Such parts usually cost 20–50% less than new parts.[22] Auto parts remanufacturing saves both material and energy; e.g. the material used for remanufacturing alternators is about one-fifth of that used in manufacturing a new product, and the energy consumed is about one-seventh.[23]

CARDONE Industries is the largest family-owned remanufacturer of automotive parts in the world. It employs 6,000 people and has several divisions with facilities in the United States, Canada, and Mexico. CARDONE currently services 40,000 parts numbers, contributing significantly to the industry's sophisticated and efficient supply chain or loop. CARDONE and the remanufacturing service part sector at large sells millions of remanufactured parts through companies such as NAPA, AutoZone, CARQUEST, Goodyear, Advance, and through car dealerships. Historically, the automotive remanufacturing sector grew alongside the independent aftermarket. During World War II, the company founder helped remanufacturing become a primary source for civilian and commercial fleet parts replacements as resources were directed to national defence.

Remanufacturing and recycling – CARDONE Industries

Corporate goal: Zero discharge for environmental waste

• Largest family-owned automotive remanufacturer in the world

• Employs 5,550 people worldwide

• Remanufactures over 65 different product lines

2014 accomplishments:
The remanufacturing of used parts is not the only area in which CARDONE is demonstrating leadership. In addition to the 73,000 tonnes of discarded or non-usable auto parts that CARDONE remanufactured, the company also recycled the waste and by-products generated during the remanufacturing process.

17,504 tonnes of scrap metal was recycled.

7,127 tonnes of cardboard (product packaging returned with the core) were recycled into new paper products.

915 tonnes of municipal trash were recycled into electrical energy, the equivalent of approximately 503,250 Kwh.

207,000 litres of waste oil recovered from cores and cleaning processes were recycled into fuel.

712 tonnes of wood skids were sent to a recycler and reused.

40,000 litres of alkaline washer bath were recovered for reuse.

41 tonnes of electronic boards, PC monitors and telecommunications equipment were recycled.

Source: CARDONE Industries, Inc. 2015

The ability of remanufacturing to supply service parts for all makes and models and years of vehicles for the motoring public at lower prices is the key to growth and development of the sector, according to CARDONE. The number of part numbers the company services is growing at the rate of 3,000 to 5,000 annually. As the volumes in those parts increases, the company sees both an opportunity and challenge. The increasing amount of technology being used in vehicles is another opportunity. An energetic remanufacturing industry makes it easier to sustain the technologies. Today's automotive sector is made up of about 3,800 automotive remanufacturing companies ranging in size from 10-20 people to 5,000–6,000 people. The companies represent USD 1 billion in sales and employ more than 350,000 people in the United States.

At CARDONE, commitment to quality helped it achieve ISO 9001, QS-9000 and ISO 14001 standards. In 2003, CARDONE became the first national remanufacturer to achieve TS16949, an internationally accepted standard to ensure parts meet the quality requirements established by automotive societies in the United States, the United Kingdom, Italy, France and Germany. With their manufacturing facility located in Belgium, CARDONE has become a supplier of remanufactured brake calipers and steering products to the European market.

Long before 'green' was fashionable, CARDONE's focus on remanufacturing parts such as power steering pumps, wiper motors, rack and pinions and brake master cylinders and calipers reduced energy consumption, waste and pollution. The company estimates that its reman efforts consume only 15% of the energy required to produce new parts.

According to CARDONE, today's economic indicators point to a growing remanufacturing industry that will continue to create jobs and benefit the environment. As the company moves forward the family's third generation is already in place to carry on the company's successful business.

Heavy duty: Caterpillar, Inc.
Components of construction machines and mining machines are another representative area for remanufacturing. 'Heavy duty' refers to equipment such as on-highway trucks, mining, heavy construction, marine, electrical power generation and rail. Today's heavy duty sector is made up of fewer than 20 Original Equipment Manufacturers (OEMs) like Caterpillar as well as dozens of smaller companies that focus on specific components, products, markets or technologies. Caterpillar is the largest OEM of construction and mining machines.

Since 1973, Caterpillar has remanufactured diesel engines and components for its own machines and power systems. In 2004, the company created Cat Reman, a global remanufacturing organisation focused on the heavy duty market.

Currently Caterpillar remanufactures more than 700 products, including hydraulics, drivetrain and fuel systems. Its operations include 3,000 employees and 18 facilities worldwide. Caterpillar is applying remanufacturing to an increasing number of products, and the USD 1 billion Remanufacturing & Components business is one of the company's fastest-growing divisions.

According to Caterpillar, salvage technology and quality processes are continuing to evolve, and advances in these areas will be critical for the industry. At Caterpillar, considerable effort is centred on cleaning and metal deposition, a process used to put metal back on and restoring material to its like-new state. Reversing the effects of fatigue is another area of interest.

One of the greatest challenges for Caterpillar and for the sector as a whole is creating a common understanding among governments and regulatory bodies about what remanufacturing is and how it contributes to the environment and the economy, according to a Caterpillar Remanufacturing & Components spokesperson. 'Remanufacturers in general want open trade and stable regulations and want to be able to sell our products anywhere in the world,' he said. 'There is so much confusion and misunderstanding of the remanufacturing practice.'

In 2011, Cat Reman opened a new facility in Singapore to serve as the regional source for remanufactured major components, including mining truck engines, transmissions, final drives and torque converters. It also opened a facility in Shanghai, China, and is the first foreign company licensed to assist the Chinese government in the development of a reman industry.

Discussion and conclusion

Remanufacturing is a key enabler to circular economy by giving products multiple life cycles and incorporating incremental upgrades. However, global remanufacturing intensity is still very low due to market challenges and also industrial challenges. Those are also referred to as external and internal challenges. Chief among those challenges are market restrictions for trading reman products as well as lack of market awareness of the value of reman products. In addition, at the firm level, there is lack of investment in reman technologies, infrastructure, and supply chain development which limit the potential growth of this industry. Progress in addressing those factors is needed to realize the great promise for contributing to the growth of the circular economy model.

Alone of the product-recovery manufacturing processes, remanufacturing retains the geometrical shape of the product, it preserves the materials and the added value embedded in the original product. These features indicate that, generally, remanufacturing is more advantageous to other end-of-life processes in terms of energy and material savings and economic benefits. For these important reasons, remanufacturing holds great promise for contributing to the global adoption of the circular economy model.

Notes

1 R. T. Lund, *Remanufacturing* (Technology Review, 87(2), 1984), 19–23, 28–29.

2 N. Nasr, *Reman for success* (Industrial Engineer, 42(6), 2010), 26.

3 D. P. Adler, *Comparing energy and other measures of environmental performance in the manufacturing and remanufacturing of engine components* (M.S. Michigan Technological University, 2004).

4 US International Trade Commission (USITC), *Remanufactured Goods: An Overview of the U.S. and Global Industries, Markets, and Trade* (Investigation No. 332-525; USITC Publication 4356. Washington: US International Trade Commission, 2012).

5 R. T. Lund, *The Remanufacturing Industry: Hidden Giant* (Boston: Boston University, 1996); R. T. Lund and W. M. Hauser, *Remanufacturing – An American Perspective* (Annals of 5th international Conference on Responsive Manufacturing & Green Manufacturing, Ningbo: China, 11–13 January 2010).

6 Medical Device and Diagnostic Industry, *Remanufactured Devices: Ensuring Their Safety and Effectiveness* (1 January 1997; http://www.mddionline.com/article/remanufactured-devices-ensuring-their-safety-and-effectiveness).

7 USITC, *Remanufactured Goods*.

8 Lund, *The Remanufacturing Industry*.

9 Production Engine Remanufacturers Association, *How large is the total remanufacturing industry?* (http://www.pera.org/faq).

10 G. Ferrer, *The Economics of Tire Remanufacturing* (INSEAD Centre for the Management of Environmental Resources, France: Fontainebleau, 1996).

11 S. Vandermerwe and J. Rada, *Servitization of business: adding value by adding services* (European Management Journal, 6(4), 1988), 314–24.

12 O. Giarini and W. R. Stahel, *The Limits to Certainty – Facing Risks in the New Service Economy* (Boston: Kluwer Academic Publishers 1989/1993).

13 M. Goedkoop, C. van Halen, H. te Riele, and P. Rommens, *Product Service Systems, Ecological and Economic Basics* (Amersfoort: Pre consultants, 1999); A. Tukker, *Eight types of product-service systems: Eight ways to sustainability? Experiences from SusProNet* (Business Strategy and the Environment, 13(4), 2004), 246–60; E. Sundin and B. Bras, *Making functional sales environmentally and economically beneficial through product remanufacturing* (Journal of Cleaner Production, 13(9), 2004), 913–25.

14 H. Meier, R. Roy and G. Seliger, *Industrial product-service systems – IPS2* (The International Academy for Production Engineering, CIRP Annals – Manufacturing Technology, 59(2), 2010), 607–27.

15 Ellen MacArthur Foundation; McKinsey Center for Business and Environment; SUN; Drawing from Braungart & McDonough, Cradle to Cradle (C2C).

16 E. Sundin and M. Lindahl, *Rethinking Product Design for Remanufacturing to Facilitate Integrated Product Service Offerings*, IEEE, 2008 IEEE International Symposium on Electronics and the Environment, San Francisco, USA, 19–22 May 2008.

17 Tukker, *Eight types of product-service systems*.

18 USITC, *Remanufactured Goods*.

19 US Trade Representative, *National Trade Estimate Report on Foreign Trade Barriers* (Washington: Executive Office of the President, 2010).

20 N. Nasr and M. Thurston, *Remanufacturing: A key enabler to sustainable product systems* (The International Academy for Production Engineering, Proceedings of 13th CIRP International Conference on Life-Cycle Engineering, Leuven, Belgium, 31 May–2 June, 2006).

21 USITC, *Remanufactured Goods*.

22 Ibid.

23 H. Y. Kim, V. Raichur, and S. J. Skerlos, *Economic and environmental assessment of automotive remanufacturing: alternator case study* (American Society of Mechanical Engineers, Proceedings of the 2008 International Manufacturing Science and Engineering Conference (MSEC 2008), Evanston, IL: USA, 7–10 October 2008).

24 Adler, *Comparing energy and other measures of environmental performance in the manufacturing and remanufacturing of engine components*.

See also:

International Trade Administration, *Global Import Regulations for Pre-Owned (Used and Refurbished) Medical Devices* (Washington: US Department of Commerce, 2008)

Lundmark, P., Sundin, E., and Bjorkman, M., *Industrial challenges within the remanufacturing system* (Proceedings of Swedish Production Symposium, Stockholm: Sweden, 2–3 December 2009)

Maurer, C., *The US President's Council on Sustainable Development: A Case Study* (Washington: The U.S. President's Council on Sustainable Development. 1998/1999)

Matsumoto, M., and Nasr, N., *Remanufacturing as an enabler for service models* (Rochester: Rochester Institute of Technology, 2015)

Annex 1 **System factors affecting reman intensity**

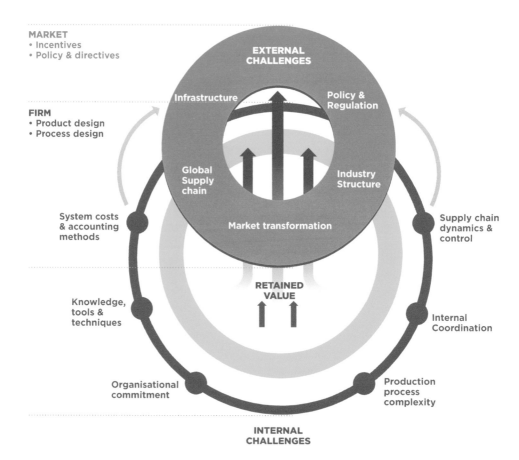

Annex 2 **Levers for increasing reman intensity** *Mechanisms for closing 'gaps'*

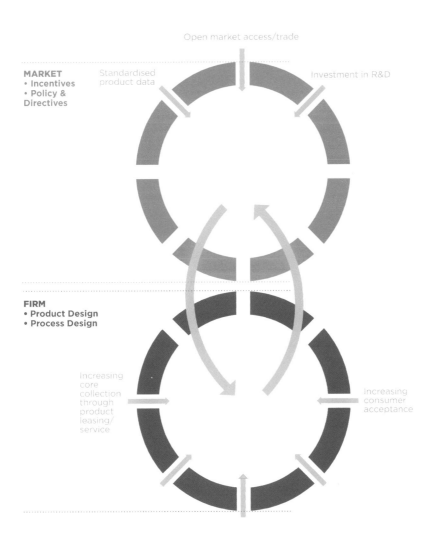

*Circular Economy and Remanufacturing, 2015 Nasr et al., CIRP Winter Meeting.

Source: Circular Economy and Remanufacturing, CIRP Winter Meeting, 2015, N. Nasr, C. Kreiss, and J. Russell.

SELLING ACCESS OVER OWNERSHIP, CUI BONO?

Ken Webster

7

In developed nations, there is evidence of a shift towards embracing a new way of accessing goods and services. With the emergence of new technologies, apps and websites, a whole generation has wider access to informal goods; but this chapter argues that as they rent, borrow, lend, swap and share products more and more, they will own virtually nothing. The rise of the 'internet of things', the demographic and economic trends, and the quest for efficiency from unused assets, can only accelerate such a trend. But is favouring use over ownership a choice, an opportunity or a necessity, asks the author?

Ken Webster
Ken is Head of Innovation at the Ellen MacArthur Foundation. His background is in economics education, teaching, teacher training and curriculum development. He writes extensively on the circular economy and its connections with systems thinking. He has been working at the Foundation since the end of 2009 and was part of its establishment in 2010.

The circular economy presents a number of business and economic advantages, particularly in producing net material cost savings, in the potential of more intense use of assets ranging from buildings to heating systems, in selling products as services in suitable markets, and in creating new flows (as 'waste becomes food' and natural capital is restored or regenerated). There are other advantages, as highlighted by reports produced by the Ellen MacArthur Foundation (*Towards the Circular Economy* Volumes 1–3 and *Growth Within*).[1] The circular economy is also a response to a number of drivers including the 3 billion new consumers anticipated by 2030, energy and materials costs increases (and volatility) and the impact of information and communications technologies. The last apply to the tracking and tracing of systems which are increasingly supplying feedback around technological performance, products, components and materials status (location, quality, and history). It includes the emergence of entirely new industries around, say, digital manufacturing and financial innovation.

This paper looks at the proposal that in developed nations fundamental changes in the economy writ large, many of which are revealing the possibilities of a circular economy (as noted above), will continue to shift the advantage towards the owners of assets and providers of rental/performance models especially in terms of the ability of firms to earn income in the long term.

The growing productivity and efficiency of production, the supply side, is but half of the circular flow of income. The demand side may be underconsidered. Changes here include the evidence that, broadly, wages are stagnant or falling as a share of GDP, and long-term economic growth is on a downward trend in the developed world (see Figure 1). The overhang of private debt and its servicing is a constraint on spending for groups in debt and, on the other side, the creditors do not spend all that they receive. Unemployment is high for younger generations especially and this group is increasingly working on a freelance or contract basis in an increasingly casualised market. As a result they are not as able easily to aspire to the sorts of purchases upon which earlier generations based their lifestyles: houses, holiday homes, cars, fitted kitchens, bathrooms, and large durables – heating systems, washing machines, furniture, and so on.

Within the existing demographic there is a tendency for older people – the over-55s, who comprise an increasing proportion of the population – to save more and spend less, and such spending on durables or housing that there is focuses on replacement rather than on additional items. Following the financial crash of 2007/8 a significant drag on consumption is the application of public spending cuts under the heading of 'austerity'.

The picture on the demand side is nuanced by those workers who are entering the rump of the linear economy as full-time employees or who have access,

Figure 1 **GDP growth rate for 13 OECD countries (average)**

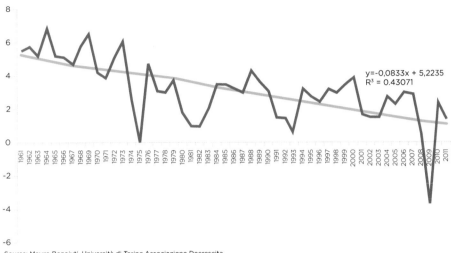

$y=-0,0833x + 5,2235$
$R^3 = 0.43071$

Source: Mauro Bonaiuti, Università di Torino,Associazione Decrescita

perhaps through family, to assets themselves. However, the 'disadvantaged' will be an increasing proportion of the demographic over the next decade.[2] Housing price inflation for those on the outside of this market further depresses spending on consumer items through rising rents (and mortgages for new buyers), and a significant debt overhang from the years leading up to the financial crash and its aftermath has dampened prospects for growth in private and public sectors. It hardly need be said that a rise in interest rates[3] marking the end of an unprecedented period of near-zero costs for new money will impact consumer spending and increase the tendency to save or pay down debt rather than spend.

In these circumstances consumers will increasingly become users, only partly from choice, or through expert marketing and adroit business models making a convincing proposition. There is evidence of some shift towards embracing access over ownership, or a long-term ownership ethos – but primarily because it is the available and affordable alternative. The concentration of assets as evidenced in the housing market also presents business opportunities, as rentiers are less interested, say, in the ownership of household durables and more interested in asset performance, how tenants use them and ease of maintenance. The much-anticipated 'internet of things' can only accelerate such a trend. The existence of these trends – the demographic shifts, income-strapped users, the asset owner seeking efficiencies, the internet of things and the manufacturer looking for additional income – is clearly synergistic, will be increasingly attractive, and could be energetically exploited.

Development of current trends

It was the mark of the modern industrial society in a post-war phase to see a continuation of rising incomes decade upon decade and for consumer *expectations* to rise in parallel. This began to unwind at the end of the 1970s. The exploration of the multiple social, economic and political factors at play at that time cannot be readily undertaken in a short chapter but a useful tour *d'horizon* came from Adam Curtis the BBC film-maker in his three-part series *Century of the Self.*[4]

The graphic below illustrates just one point at which disconnection occurred. There was, and in the popular imagination *still* is, a sense of entitlement around earnings, home ownership, pensions and wealth accumulation. Things could only get more and they could only get better. If a modern industrialised system depends on cheap energy, cheap and available materials and access to credit, it also depends upon confidence and expectation when it comes to employment and income in order that, for example, debt might be repaid, cars parked or garaged and stuff moved and used.

APPEAL OF A
SHARING ECONOMY
(BY)**DEMOGRAPHIC:**

GEN X
MILLENNIAL
BOOMER

31%

24%

15%

SOURCE: CAMPBELL MITHUN, CARVONVIEW; BASE: 383 RESPONDENTS   CampbellMithun

This is changing. In developed nations, looking at the tail-end of Generation X and the so-called Millennials,[5] there are clear trends towards a very different expectation, and it is the possibility of downward mobility. This is leavened by the existence of a sizeable rump of full-time workers in salaried employment, some of whom are very well remunerated indeed, and an earlier generation willing to spend on their children from the wealth accumulated in better times. It is also leavened, it should be emphasised, by a remarkable fall in the marginal cost of everything digital and beyond (music, film, publishing, 3D printing, iFixit repair, and make-your-own-crafts-and-sell-them-on-etsy).

The result is that networking and access, in particular to informational goods such as music, film, transit, carshare/rental, social interaction, and collaboration, has become easy. This masks the fundamental shifts in the economy by *making living 'light' and rewarding flexibility.* It can be exciting, and fashionable brands have been quick to exploit this digitally connected bohemian, someone OK to spend £3 on a latte, and more on eating out, if the funds are there, but who is disdainful of everything mundane, who would rarely be seen in any of the large stores offering washing machines, heating systems, large kitchen appliances or conservatories, but might be attracted to repair/fixit culture or a sweatshirt which can last 30 years (see box) or Fairphone 2 (see box), a subscription to Car2Go and their Oyster card. It is remixing necessity as opportunity.

In an extended essay in Washington Monthly entitled *The Post Ownership Society: How the 'sharing economy' allows Millennials to cope with downward mobility, and also makes them poorer*[6] Monica Potts writes of her own experience and of those around her:

'The car service smartphone apps Uber and Lyft have finally allowed me to get a ride from my house and friends' houses in neighbourhoods like Columbia Heights or Petworth – they're sometimes cheaper than traditional cabs, and they're always more reliable. Using Capital Bikeshare means we didn't even have to own our own bikes.

Other products and services have made my life easier still. At a slight premium, I can have food delivered straight to my door rather than worrying about cab trips back and forth from the supermarket. Amazon Prime's free two-day delivery obviates long trips to Target or spending a fortune at a hardware store for household goods. If we have to pick up extra hours of work to cover the cost of rent or lattes and drinks, we can have our washing done by the online service Washio, or send someone else to the grocery store for us with Instacart. These companies mostly make money by charging fees per transaction or fixed membership fees. Saving time is important, too – there is always more work to do.

These are the benefits of the sharing economy. They help us manage, and sometimes afford, our lives. We can live in relatively cheaper neighbourhoods, far from the city centre and reliable public transportation, because we can always pull up an app. Everyone uses Uber and Lyft and Zipcar: the waitress at the brick-oven pizza place that opened in Bloomingdale four years ago, especially when she needs to get home after a late shift; the kid who quit his job at the coffee shop to be a theater set designer; the vintage-clothing store owner who also makes money as a freelance journalist. Facets of the sharing economy provide opportunities for coping with downward mobility, even if some older folks may not understand how using a $600 smartphone to summon a college-educated Uber chauffeur amounts to thrift...

But before we get too excited about all the low-cost goods and services our generation can summon with an app, we need to understand that even these features of the 'sharing economy' are making some people above us very rich while we become a generation that owns virtually nothing.'

The future is very uncertain; and, as one 29-year-old Millennial interviewed said,

'I never know whether to save for a house deposit or start a pension fund. Ha! Me and my friends (most of whom are either self employed or minimum wage/basic salary and all have student debt) are very worried about our futures. But, at the same time we don't want to 'conform' or bow down to 'the man'. We're certainly not settling down anytime soon! When we all hit 60, who knows what state the government will be in...'

Phone hacking at FairPhone

© Fairphone

Business opportunities aimed at a generation owning very little: built to last...

1 A 30-year sweatshirt?

The 30-year sweatshirt from designer Thomas Cridland 'will retail for £55 each. Far more than the average Primark men's sweatshirt – most are under £10 – but if you work on the cost-per-wear principle, seven wears of a Primark (the average before the garment is discarded or put away) will cost you £1.43 a time.

Worn once a week, for just one year, a ... 30-Year Sweatshirt will cost you £1.06 a go. Throw it on every Sunday for the full guaranteed term and it will come down to 0.04p a wear.

And if, on one of those outings – Cridland will keep a record of the date of sale – you rip or tear it, or if it should come apart anywhere, send it back and it will be repaired, return postage paid.'

2 Built to upgrade and repair and with good conscience

Fairphone 2: Its advantages displayed: -

'...the phone is designed to be modular, it will be quite simple for users to replace internal components. ... Need a better camera/more RAM/a faster processor? Replace the old one! In all fairness, most users will probably have a tough time doing this by themselves, as replacing the camera is not as easy as removing a LEGO bloc – like on the Project Ara prototype. Take the handset to a smartphone repair shop, however, and the trained professionals there should not encounter any major setbacks.'

'Like its predecessor, the Fairphone 2 will use conflict-free tin and tantalum from the Democratic Republic of Congo. The company is also working to get fairly-traded gold and tungsten into the second generation device, a move that's been made possible thanks to having greater control over its own supply chain.'[8]

As Monica Potts makes clear, life and work still come with aspiration, for in a fluid networked economy there is the possibility that entrepreneurial start-ups can become the next Airbnb or Lyft; or simply, in collaborating or circulating around, say, the FabLabs or urban food scene, will secure a better and perhaps more satisfying quality of life for those who cherish autonomy.

Self-awareness is high; this generation is both better educated and better connected and has a strong sense of personal entitlement but often clear preferences, encapsulated between the adverts 'Because you're worth it' (L'Oréal) and Patagonia's 'Don't Buy this Jacket'.

But there is a darker side:

'The oldest of us are now reaching our mid-thirties. A couple of years ago, it seemed as if I woke up one day and suddenly felt like an adult. Nothing had changed materially about my life, but my experiences and responsibilities totalled up in a way that equalled grownup. And yet, I still lived in a tiny apartment with an Ikea dining table, a bookshelf I scored from my kerb, and a couch I carted home when it was discarded from my office. I never expected to be rich, but I did expect to someday have real furniture and maybe even a house. Achieving those things was always in the future, at some relatively well-moneyed point that I was expecting would roll around – until I realised the future had dawned and the financial stability hadn't appeared.'

What current trends certainly do not do is promise the stability and job security which favours the retailer of household durables, automobiles or the stuff which requires U-Haul to move and many rooms to store it, or wall space to hang it. If so, where can manufacturers and retailers find a market? Perhaps it is with the owners of assets used by the target group rather than the erstwhile customers themselves. Follow the money.

The Millennials along with other members of what is termed the middle classes are increasingly spending the money they have in a non-discretionary manner. Economist Michael Hudson discusses the residual in the USA:[9]

'How can American industry compete when some 40% of the salaries it pays its employees must be paid for housing, 10% more for credit-card and other bank debt, 15% for FICA wage withholding for Social Security and Medicare, and 15% more for income tax withholding and for sales taxes? Before employees can start buying the goods and services they produce, they must spend about three-quarters of their income on the Finance, Insurance and Real Estate (FIRE) sector and taxes that have been shifted onto their shoulders.'

The rapidly growing realisation that finding a way into the fully employed job category – or trying to – requires extended and often specialist education has both increased the competition for entry into university but increased the cost and the duration, as more and more employers demand Masters or Doctorate level or supplementary courses. This additional cost has increased quite significantly ahead of household income, adding another factor which constrains expenditure on consumer goods and services.[10]

A business too soon?

Straightforward rents for housing are rising faster than incomes in major cities like London, Copenhagen and Seattle, while the welfare net frays in a post-crash austerity atmosphere and because the tax base is already shrinking – there are fewer people of working age and they earn less while the number of older people increases rapidly. Minimum wages are also stagnating in real terms. Figure 2 maps the USA minimum wage in inflation-adjusted dollars (top line).

Figure 2 **Minimum wage 1938–2012 (USD/hour)**

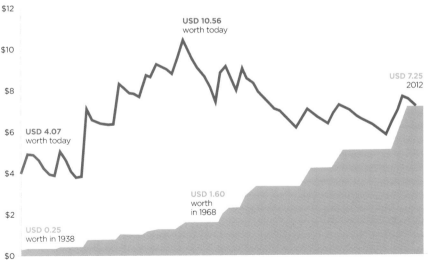

Source: Bureau of Labor Statistics

● Inflation adjusted

● Minimum wage

The opportunity is there to provide low-cost access to products sold as services to sophisticated users, but are consumers really ready for products as services?

An app-based collaborative consumption model seems well advanced in the anecdotes above but recent academic studies of product service systems[11] have cast doubt on whether the customer is ready for these models. Or indeed whether these models are sufficiently well developed as yet. In an interview for *The Independent* Tom Bawden writes:

'The internet has led to the emergence of numerous sites that allow people to rent, borrow, lend, swap and share products rather than buying new ones.

However, such schemes will never replace purchase capitalism because people are culturally programmed to amass as many possessions as possible.

"The sharing economy is a credible way to help tackle today's consumer society," said Laura Piscicelli, a researcher at Nottingham Trent university. "What we've identified in this study, though, is that people's individual values may prevent 'collaborative consumption' from becoming mainstream."[12]

The study appeared in an issue of the *Journal of Cleaner Production* (June 2015) dedicated to product service systems and the editors of the journal state quite clearly their view on the slow take-up of such systems: it lies not only with customers.

'The basic reason is that sustainable product service systems (PSS) are usually considered to be *'radical innovations,'* because they challenge existing customer/user habits, company organisational structures and regulatory frameworks. In other words, their introduction and *'scaling-up'* require fundamental changes in behaviour and practice that are implemented by individuals, groups, business communities, policy actors and society-at-large. Consequently, the introduction and scaling-up of PSS innovations is not under the control of a single actor (or a small network of actors). In fact any changes in the factors that form the boundary conditions (i.e. existing institutions, dominant practices, rules and interests) are resisted at multiple levels, and strategies for changes must be addressed holistically if they are to be brought about.'

In contrast, this paper argues that 'purchase capitalism' in the future might be increasingly constrained to a shrinking customer base – at least in the developed world – around those living amongst their own (property-based) assets and/or in full-time employment. As time goes on the new normal of an increasingly polarised economy will disrupt purchase capitalism because the emerging system conditions are very unfavourable towards it. Throughput is challenged by resource and energy constraints, whilst spending is constrained by debt, by the uncertainty of casualised labour markets, technologically instigated structural unemployment and falling real wages. Overproduction is endemic and asset price inflation benefits economic rent-seeking activities, which further crimps the possibilities of 'purchase capitalism'. It may not be a case of choice of one mode or another, in the future, so much as necessity for significant consumer segments to accept product service systems.

Changes wrought by the burgeoning information technology revolution have favoured productivity and have lowered costs of production or the cost of providing services, and often make good sense in terms of resource use, especially if taken to include a circular economy context around materials flows and energy use. If these cost reductions are significant, and rebound effects do not overwhelm the resource impacts then there is a case for saying that the purchasing power released can generate economic growth from 'within' the system. This is basically the argument of the Ellen MacArthur Foundation/SUN/McKinsey report *Growth Within*[13]. In the context of this chapter of *A New Dynamic* the question might be how the welcome additional monetary flows are circulated. How much becomes compensation for falling real wages; how much is captured by increasing charges and economic rent in housing, education, health and taxation; and how much is spent on goods and services. There is potential for all three and this must be seen as a worthwhile direction of travel.

However, looking again at the business opportunity for asset owners then choosing to operate a service or performance contract commercially the development of *Growth Within* strategies could add impetus to both revenues and efficiencies. Manufacturers working with now smaller economies of scale (due to stagnant demand) coupled with changed business models could exploit new B2B opportunities alongside traditional B2C customer arrangements.

Although this business opportunity 'bundle' can be seen as an outcome of a number of very large trends in process now in the developed world, it is bound to be criticised at a deeper level, beyond business and economics. In some real sense ownership implies rights to determine what a person's relationship is with products and property, to have the right to use, abuse, abandon or dispose, and for much of human history this ownership was reserved to a small group. Democracy and property-owning are deeply entwined as any historian of democracy and the extension of the voting franchise can demonstrate. For successful product service systems in an extension of a revival of a rentier-dominated system a user might wish to know how they are to be protected from excessive rent-seeking, from disconnection or exclusion or unfair contracts, no matter how cheap or effective the general user experience might appear. To take an extreme example, could a dispute with a particular taxi driver lead to exclusion from the whole platform? As always the resources question is connected to the question of social justice and what is often termed 'inclusion'.

Conclusion

The argument in this paper is that although selling products as services is difficult and at an early stage the barriers to change are being weakened through four main trends.

Firstly there is the information technology revolution which is enabling the products providing the service or the performance to be closely and cheaply monitored, to be easily accessible by users, to be a bundled package perhaps (washing powder, water and electricity to run the motor in the case of a washing machine?) and intercepted in a timely manner for the purposes of maintenance and repair or, importantly from a cost basis, for the assessment and evaluation of user behaviour.

The second trend is the narrowing of the ownership base of assets like housing and office space and aircraft etc. which gives rentiers opportunities to extract more revenue and perhaps, like the government of the USA, rely on, or even *mandate suppliers* to supply services or performance not products. This may be the B2B dynamic which manufacturers seek, rather than relying on finding individual customers for sales, individuals who may have a greater attachment to ownership as the research for the *Journal of Cleaner Production* suggests.

The third trend is that as wages stagnate[14] or fall this leaves customers less able to afford big-ticket items associated with, in particular, housing and transport. The availability of credit is reduced and lower incomes undermine the potential for expanded product sales in a significant and growing segment of the demographic, which is itself ageing overall.

The fourth trend is the shift from product to service to platform or network which not only often increases the degree of casualisation of the workforce and the number of self-employed or contract operators involved but provides new business opportunities for successful platforms that can offer low user cost.

The impact on physical resource use in all four contexts is likely to facilitate a reduction in both materials and energy terms while potentially securing a greater proportion of a customer's non-discretionary spending – by capturing it as part of a rental or leasing bundle perhaps – if wages continue to fall and growth falters according to prediction. The rebound effect, the tendency for additional resources to be dragged into use will therefore be progressively more muted.

Notes

1 Ellen MacArthur Foundation, *Towards the Circular Economy 1* (2102), *2* (2013), and *3* (2014); Ellen MacArthur Foundation, SUN, McKinsey Center for Business and Environment, *Growth Within: A Circular Economy Vision for a Competitive Europe* (2015); all available at http://www.ellenmacarthurfoundation.org/publications

2 For jobless growth see: World Economic Focum, *Top 10 trends of 2015: Persistent jobless growth* (http://reports. weforum.org/outlook-global-agenda-2015/top-10-trends-of-2015/2-persistent-jobless-growth/).

3 For interest rates see: Andrew Oxlade, *Interest rate predictions on the move: 'First rise in December 2016'* (The Telegraph, 5 November 2015; http://www.telegraph.co.uk/finance/personalfinance/interest-rates/11032396/ Interest-rates-predictions-When-will-the-Bank-Rate-rise.html).

4 Adam Curtis, *The Century of the Self* (2005; available at thoughtmaybe.com/the-century-of-the-self/).

5 https://en.wikipedia.org/wiki/Millennials

6 www.washingtonmonthly.com/magazine/junejulyaugust2015/features/thepostownershipsociety055896. php?page=all

7 Mihai A., *The Fairphone 2 is a modular smartphone that doesn't compete against Project Ara* (PhoneArena, 16 June 2015; http://www.phonearena.com/news/The-Fairphone-2-is-a-modular-smartphone-that-doesnt-compete-against-Project-Ara_id70519).

8 Jo Best, *Fairphone 2: The ethical Android handset is back with a smart modular construction* (ZDnet,16 June 2015; http://www.zdnet.com/article/fairphone-2-the-ethical-android-handset-is-back-with-a-smart-modular-construction/).

9 Michael Hudson, *Obama's Master Class in Economy Demagogy 101* (Counterpunch, 25 July 2013; www. counterpunch.org/2013/07/25/obamas-master-class-in-economic-demagogy-101/).

10 For rising education costs see: *Growing numbers of students priced out of going to university as college costs jump a staggering 250PERCENT in the past 30 years while median income has stagnated* (Mail Online, 15 June 2013; http://www.dailymail.co.uk/news/article-2342279/Growing-numbers-students-priced-going-university-college-costs-jump-staggering-250PERCENT-past-30-years-median-income-stagnated.html).

11 Carlo Vezzoli, Fabrizio Ceschin, Jan Carel Diehl and Cindy Kohtala (eds.), *Special Volume: Why have 'Sustainable Product-Service Systems' not been widely implemented?* (Journal of Cleaner Production 97, 15 June 2015; http:// www.sciencedirect.com/science/journal/09596526/97), 1–136.

12 Tom Bawden, *'Sharing Economy' won't become widespread because people crave their own material goods, says study* (The Independent, 12 June 2015; www.independent.co.uk/news/science/sharing-economy-wont-become-widespread-because-people-crave-their-own-material-goods-says-study-10317074.html).

13 http://www.ellenmacarthurfoundation.org/books-and-reports

14 In a situation where private debt cannot be expanded further to maintain or extend inequality the emphasis would shift to depressing wages to extend the gap between labour and capital's share of GDP according to Ari Andricopoulos, *Why was r greater than g? Will it continue? And how to reverse it* (Notes on the Next Bust, 16 June 2015; http://www.notesonthenextbust.com/2015/06/why-was-r-greater-than-g-will-it.html) and Steve Keen.

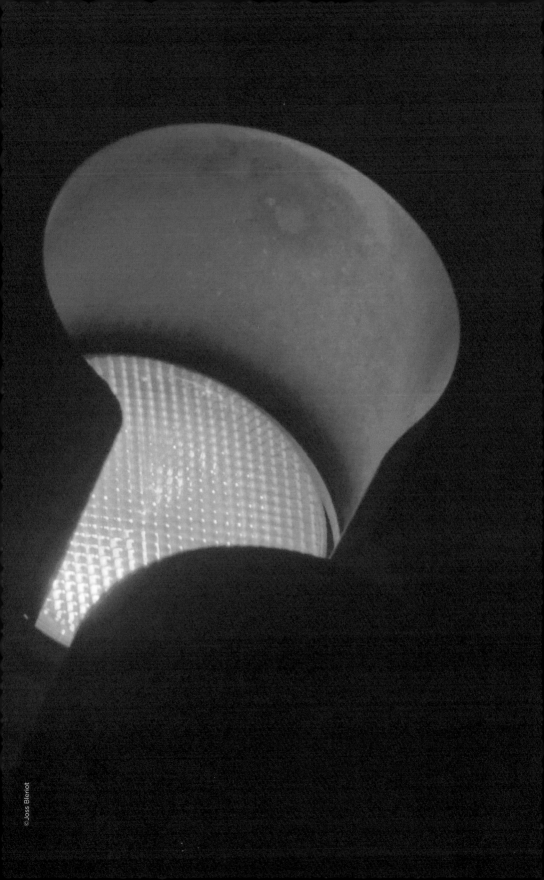

BROADER LESSONS FROM SELF-ORGANISING TRAFFIC LIGHTS IN CITY TRANSPORT SYSTEMS

Dirk Helbing and Stefan Lämmer

The focus in this chapter is the problem of coordinating incompatible traffic flows at road intersections to examine effects of decision-making in complex dynamic systems. The example of traffic lights developed here has resource consumption implications but the key point demonstrated by this urban transport case study is that understanding systems with feedback presents a more accurate way of modelling systemic activity, and it potentially overthrows the largely one-dimensional decision-making still dominating discourse in economics. This work suggests that a devolved decentralised but feedback-rich ('circular') economy may offer distinct advantages to business and to the economy as a whole.

Dirk Helbing
Dirk is Professor of Computational Social Science at the Department of Humanities, Social and Political Sciences at ETH Zurich. He is internationally known for his work on pedestrian crowds, vehicle traffic, and agent-based models of social systems.

Stefan Lämmer
Stefan is chair of Transport and modelling at the Technical University of Dresden.

A central proposal in a circular economy is that it is feedback-rich and that insights from modelling complex adaptive systems can bring benefits through system optimisation. In addition, complexity and computational social science question the common notion that economies are more efficient if agents act selfishly or a centralised regulatory top-down control is exerted. The reality illustrated here is that a feedback-rich environment where suitable 'rules of the game' are established allow the system to self-organise towards greater effectiveness overall than if operating in a top-down or selfish actor mode. The example of traffic lights has resource consumption implications but this is perhaps not the main point; the point is that understanding systems with feedbacks presents a more accurate way of modelling systemic activity, and it potentially overthrows the largely one-dimensional decision-making still dominating discourse in economics.

This suggests that a devolved decentralised but feedback-rich ('circular') economy may offer distinct advantages to business and to the economy as a whole.

This chapter uses the problem of coordinating incompatible traffic flows at road intersections – based on simulations of traffic flows in urban networks – to examine effects of decision-making in complex dynamical systems. Inspired by the observation of self-organised oscillations of pedestrian flows at bottlenecks, a self-organisation approach to traffic light control is presented. The problem can be treated as a 'multi-agent' problem with interactions between vehicles and traffic lights. Specifically, this self-organisation approach assumes a priority-based control of traffic lights by the vehicle flows themselves, taking into account a short-term anticipation of vehicle flows and 'platoons'. The considered local interaction approach leads to emergent vehicle coordination patterns known as 'green waves' and achieves an efficient, decentralised traffic light control. This 'green wave' (the click, click, click of a sequence of green traffic lights that allows platoons of vehicles to move smoothly through intersection after intersection) is an ultimate goal in traffic regulation. When this happens, no drivers have to wait very long and road sections don't become so filled up with cars that there's no room for entering vehicles when the light turns green.

The need to rethink city traffic congestion

Imagine cars control traffic lights rather than the other way round. This revolutionary new concept can dramatically reduce travel times and vehicle emissions in urban areas. While it sounds like fantasy, such a 'user-oriented control strategy' is cheap to implement and will soon be reality in cities all over the world. Coping with variability by designing in more flexibility, this novel complexity management approach for transport systems has a wider applicability and will be a central success principle of smart cities and business supply chains in the future.

Traffic jams and road congestion do a lot more than annoying millions of people every day. In the United States, delays by backed-up traffic cost nearly USD 100 billion each year, and waste more than 10 billion litres of fuel, not to mention countless human hours of waiting time. The UK government estimates that reducing traffic congestion by 10–30% would potentially save GBP 800 million to GBP 2.4 billion each year. Across Europe every day, traffic jams block some 7,500 kilometres of European highways. And then there is all the extra CO_2 and other pollutants spewed into the atmosphere. In coming decades, as developing nations become more industrialised, these problems will only grow worse. Is there any solution? The best current methods for managing traffic aim at reducing congestion by road pricing and by better coordinating cyclic on-off operations of traffic lights with actual vehicle flows. For example, a control centre switches between several control strategies over the day: traffic lights offer longer green times during peak hours, and there are special programmes for Friday afternoons, for soccer games, or rock concerts. However, the traffic conditions for which the signal schemes were optimised never occur exactly. Indeed, real traffic flows naturally exhibit large fluctuations in the number of vehicles arriving at an intersection during any one cycle. These fluctuations cause trouble for current 'top-down' traffic management, as do other variations associated with road accidents or weather conditions, which cause further departures from the average norm. What can we do? We can build more roads, of course, and try to reduce traffic loads by encouraging people to ride bikes or share their cars with others. But there is another way – by getting traffic lights to organise their own operations, and dropping the arbitrary constraint that lights should always operate in a pre-determined regular fashion.

The idea to investigate self-organising traffic lights was born when the authors noted that, when crowds of people are trying to move through a bottleneck, such as through a door connecting two hallways, there is a natural oscillation – a mass of people from one side will move through the door while the other people wait, then suddenly the flow switches direction.[1] This looks as if there was a traffic light managing movement of people, but there is not. It's actually the build-up of pressure on the side where people have to wait, which eventually lets the flow direction turn, and this observation has stimulated investigations whether the same principle could be applied to road intersections. Several studies show that in such a setting, traffic flows control the traffic lights rather than the other way around.[2]

Self-organisation as a concept of the future

Most current thinking about traffic management is focused on the idea that traffic lights should cycle on and off in a regular and predictable way in order to facilitate their synchronisation. The idea appears so logical and obvious that it has been the dominating 'top-down' control paradigm since the invention of coordinated traffic light control. It turns out, however, that it is unnecessarily restrictive, and less orderly patterns can be far more efficient, reducing travel times for all, and making traffic jams far less frequent.

The key innovation to avoid traffic jams is to give each set of traffic lights some simple operating rules and let them organise their own on-off schedules in response to changing traffic conditions. This can already be realised if lights share information with neighbouring lights and follow a simple strategy. First, each light senses the local traffic conditions and calculates how long it should stay green to clear its incoming roads. Second, lights communicate with one another to inform each other of arriving vehicle platoons. In many cases, this allows nearby lights to dissolve vehicle queues just before the platoon arrives. Moreover, spill-over effects that could obstruct adjacent intersections are avoided. As demonstrated in computer simulations,[3] and real-life implementations,[4] lights operating this way can reduce average delay times by up to 40%.

Surprisingly, this improvement comes with the lights going on and off in a seemingly chaotic way, not following a regular pattern as one might expect. Self-controlled traffic lights do not follow a fixed schedule. Instead they flexibly respond to the actual traffic situation. If the actual situation changes due to unexpected arrival or turning flows, or due to an accident or building site, the green and red times will adjust accordingly: the lights compensate for fluctuations and perturbations. This new kind of control does not try to impose a certain flow rhythm as classical control approaches do. Rather, the principle is to create small platoons of vehicles and use gaps opening up in crossing traffic flows to clear the way for them. In this way, the system uses the variability of traffic as an opportunity to serve other flows. Rather than fighting fluctuations, the solution is a flexible response!

The whole point is to avoid stopping an incoming platoon, as much as this can be done. The new paradigm works extremely well: gaps between platoons are used as opportunities to serve flows in other directions, and this local coordination naturally spreads throughout the system.

Surprisingly, short delays can improve the system performance altogether. This paradoxical 'slower-is-faster effect' is known to occur in many complex systems.[5] Therefore, you can increase the throughput – speed up the entire system – if you delay single processes within the system at the right time, for the right amount of time.

Remarkably, lights working in this self-organising way reduce travel times, even though the lights are no longer periodic and their behaviour is actually quite unpredictable. The scheme also eliminates other irritating problems, such as

©Stephen Chipp - CC Flickr

©Dickson Phua- CC Flickr

drivers having to wait a long time at empty intersections because the lights' schedules are determined by the traffic flow at busier times, or lights cycling even in the middle of the night when there is almost no traffic at all. Rather, self-organising traffic lights simply switch to green if there is a need for it. In case of no arriving vehicles, all traffic lights are red in order to be ready to switch to green as soon as a car or a pedestrian arrives.

Some details of self-organising traffic lights

In more detail, the self-organisation approach works as follows: based on measurements of the inflows into the road sections, the system at each intersection anticipates the vehicle flows that will arrive at the traffic lights a short time later. These anticipated flows can be used to determine the expected delays to all traffic streams, imposed by the respective traffic lights. Then, 'traffic pressures' are calculated based on the temporal increase of the stream-specific cumulative delays, and at each intersection a green light is given to the traffic stream exerting the highest traffic pressure. According to this principle, traffic streams control the traffic lights rather than the other way round. To avoid instabilities, large queues are cleared, whenever needed. The resulting control principle is self-organised and decentralised. It reacts flexibly to the actual local situation rather than an average, 'typical' situation, and the short-term anticipation of vehicle flows reaches a coordination of neighbouring traffic lights and vehicle streams. In fact, self-control does not fight fluctuations in the flow by imposing a certain flow rhythm. It uses randomly appearing gaps in the flow to serve other traffic streams. The order in which roads are being served changes steadily over time and, therefore, the self-control principle can exploit advantages of non-periodic solutions. This principle does not only reduce average delays, it also increases the predictability of travel times.

Strikingly, the superior performance of this decentralised self-control concept results from the combination of two strategies that are inferior in separation – one for stabilisation and another one for optimisation. Together this allows for a sequence of traffic phases that flexibly adjusts to the actual flow conditions and avoids spill-over effects, which would cause a rapid spreading of congestion. See Figure 1 opposite.

Instead of searching out a monstrous solution space for the optimal solution and evaluating a myriad of switching sequences, the novel prioritisation approach just tries to keep vehicle platoons going. The formula, according to which the priority of each flow is calculated, considers the queue lengths as well as the arrival times of vehicles. Meanwhile, a stabilisation of queues and red-time durations results from the decentralised supervision of instabilities, which the local travel time minimisation may cause. The proposed supervisory concept also makes sure that all network flows get a green light regularly and

Figure 1 **Traffic intersection with an inflow sensor to anticipate the arrival flow and an outflow sensor to determine the time when queues have resolved (top). A real-time control-loop is continuously regulating the green lights according to the current traffic state (bottom). The self-control is based on three principles: anticipation, optimisation, and stabilisation**

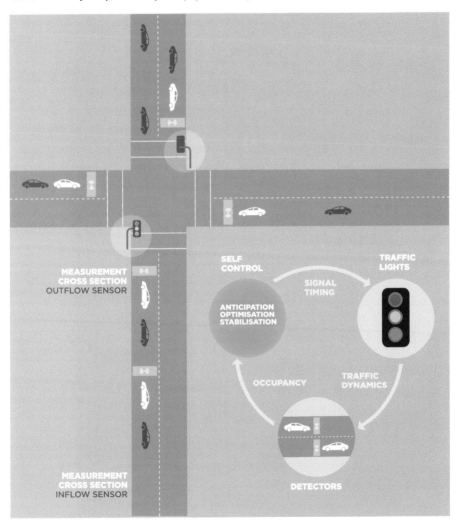

for long enough. In addition, it enables flexible responses to local fluctuations in the demand, and it favours a self-organised coordination of traffic flows. The superior performance of this adaptive self-organising control scheme has been demonstrated in a detailed pilot study of a road network consisting of 13 traffic-light-controlled intersections located in the city centre of Dresden, Germany. The city was using an adaptive state-of-the-art control supporting green waves, but it could not prioritise public transport without causing large-scale congestion. Dresden Mitte train station lies between two main parallel roads. No less than seven bus and tram lines cross the network every 10 minutes in opposite directions, and 68 pedestrian crossings lie within that area. Due to the irregularity of the network topology, and the relatively high traffic load, local traffic authorities agree that this part of Dresden is the most challenging to control.

Figure 2 **Road network in the city centre of Dresden, Germany**

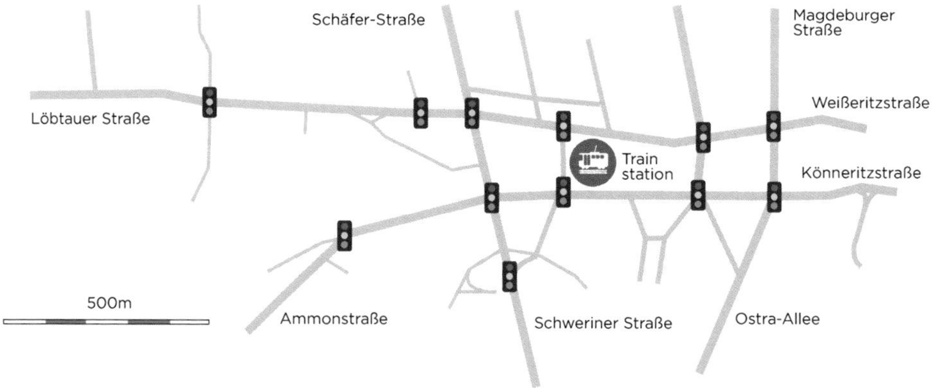

Simulations for measured traffic conditions in Dresden show that the self-organising traffic light control can reduce delays of trams and buses by more than 50% in comparison with the current top-down traffic management system. Cars and trucks travel faster through the network as well, while pedestrians wait 36% less time for the next green light. These significant reductions in waiting times for all modes of transport were found for a wide variety of different traffic demands. See Figure 3 and 4.

Figure 3 **Dresden pilot study. Comparison with a state-of-the-art 'top-down' control, the flexible self-control approach reduces the average delay for all modes of transport**

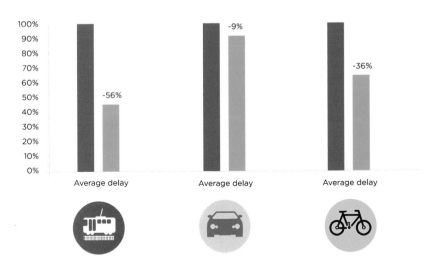

State-of-the-art 'top-down' control
Flexible self-control approach

Figure 4 **Dresden pilot study. Resulting reduction of the total delay as a function of the traffic volume for trams and buses, and for other vehicles**[6,7]

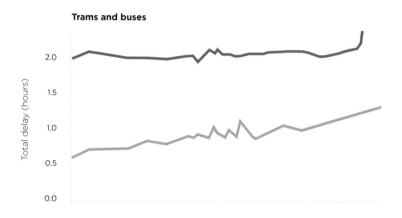

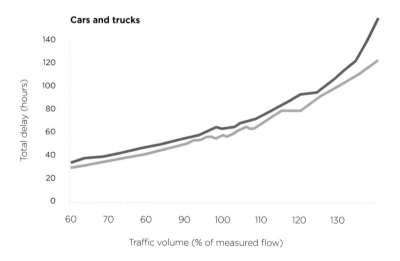

● State-of-the-art 'top-down' control
● Flexible self-control approach

Innovative enhancements of the self-organising approach

This technique of self-organising traffic management differs from previous top-down signal control approaches in the following points:

1. It reaches a superior performance by a non-periodic service and is much more flexible. Nevertheless, a periodic traffic light behaviour may emerge if the street network has a grid-like geometry and if the incoming flows and turning fractions (or the boundary conditions) are periodic.

2. The variation of waiting times is surprisingly small, i.e. the average waiting times are largely predictable, even though the sequence and duration of green times are hardly predictable.

3. Simulations indicate that a substantial reduction of the average travel times, and therefore also of the fuel consumption and CO_2 emission, can be achieved.

4. The greatest gain in performance compared to previous traffic control approaches is expected (i) for strongly varying inflows, (ii) irregular road networks, (iii) large variations of the flows in different directions and among neighbouring traffic lights, or (iv) at night, where single vehicles should be served upon their arrival at the traffic light.

Several traffic authorities in Europe and elsewhere are now considering self-organising lights as a practical solution of problems caused by looming traffic congestion.

Since the new technique optimises traffic for the actual conditions, rather than some calculated average conditions, it is based on the operation of two traffic detectors or sensors per lane for each traffic light. However, the technique avoids the need for excessive road constructions, the use of expensive wires, or a central supercomputer. The decentralised approach instead uses conventional microcomputer and detection technology on a local level, which makes the system much cheaper to install and maintain, more robust in the face of sudden changes in traffic conditions and less vulnerable to hardware failures. Moreover, newly controlled traffic lights can be integrated into an already existing network (and even fit into a network of classically controlled traffic lights). There is no need of an excessive reprogramming.

Conclusion

It is clear that, as systems get more and more complex, top-down regulation can no longer achieve efficient and satisfactory solutions. Instead, we can build on self-regulation, such as found in ecological, social and immune systems. Ants, for example, work in an entirely self-organised and largely decentralised way without a hierarchical system of command. The same applies to social animals like termites, flocks of birds, or schools of fish. The ecological and immune systems also function in a decentralised and highly efficient way, due to the evolutionary principles of mutation and selection. The advantage of this self-regulation approach has been illustrated here by the example of urban traffic light control.

In summary the self-regulation approach coordinates traffic lights and traffic flows based on local interactions. While the self-regulation is based on a decentralised bottom-up approach rather than a centralised top-down approach, it surprisingly reaches a superior performance.[8] Studies comparing self-regulated traffic lights with state-of-the-art top-down traffic control approaches show that shorter waiting times can be simultaneously reached for individual traffic, public transport, pedestrians, and bikes.[9] Self-controlled traffic also reduces environmental pollution without having to impose travel restrictions, and it makes travel times more predictable. From the above example, we can draw a number of important conclusions:

1. In complex systems with strongly variable and largely unpredictable dynamics, bottom-up self-regulation can outperform top-down optimisation by a central regulator (an urban traffic control centre).

2. When taking into account the situation of interaction partners ('neighbours'), a high system performance can be reached even for strong interaction effects because of coordination between neighbours.

3. A top-down central traffic regulator fails to be efficient due to the complexity of the optimisation problem, which cannot be solved in real-time even with a supercomputer. In contrast, the self-organisation approach can overcome the problem by flexible local adaptation. Such self-organisation is based on suitable local interaction rules and can produce resource-efficient solutions delivering high system performance. The recent trend towards replacing many signalised intersections by roundabouts and changing urban spaces regulated by many traffic signs in favour of designs supporting a considerate interaction and self-organisation of different traffic participants suggests an ongoing paradigm shift from regulation to self-regulation (Hamilton-Baillie, 2008[10]). These solutions also tend to be resilient to perturbations (such as accidents, road works, etc.).

Finally it should be noted that the above conclusions are also relevant to other complex dynamical systems. It has been demonstrated that a similar approach can be applied to logistic problems and supply chain management as well as to administrative systems and procedures.[11] The method was recently patented in USA, Japan, China, and a number of EU countries, including Germany.[12]

Acknowledgment
Our thanks to Craig Johnson and Ken Webster for their support in producing this chapter.

Notes

1 D. Helbing and P. Molnár, *Social force model for pedestrian dynamics* (Physical Review E 51, 1995), 4282–6.

2 D. Helbing, S. Lämmer, and J.-P. Lebacque, *Self-organized control of irregular or perturbed network traffic* in: C. Deissenberg and R. F. Hartl (eds.) Optimal Control and Dynamic Games (Springer, Dordrecht, 2005), 239–274. D. Helbing and S. Lämmer, *Method for coordination of concurrent processes for control of the transport of mobile units within a network* (WO/2006/122528, 2006). S. Lämmer *Reglerentwurf zur dezentralen Online-Steuerung von Lichtsignalanlagen in Straßennetzwerken* (Dissertation, TU Dresden, 2007, http://www.qucosa.de/fileadmin/data/qucosa/documents/736/1194272623825-4259.pdf). S. Lämmer and D. Helbing, *Self-control of traffic lights and vehicle flows in urban road networks*. JSTAT P04019 (2008).

3 S. Lämmer and D. Helbing, *Self-control of traffic lights and vehicle flows in urban road networks*. JSTAT P04019 (2008). S. Lämmer and D. Helbing, *Self-stabilizing decentralized signal control of realistic, saturated network traffic* (2010, see http://www.santafe.edu/media/workingpapers/10-09-019.pdf). S. Lämmer, *Simulationsstudie Bahnhof Dresden Mitte. Praxistauglichkeit und Einsatzmöglichkeiten einer neuartigen voll-verkehrsabhängigen Lichtsignalsteuerung* (internal report, 2009, available on request). S. Lämmer, J. Krimmling, A. Hoppe, *Selbst-Steuerung von Lichtsignalanlagen – Regelungstechnischer Ansatz und Simulation* (Straßenverkehrstechnik 11, 2009; http://stefanlaemmer.de/Publikationen/Laemmer2009.pdf), 714–21.

4 S. Lämmer, *Die Selbst-Steuerung im Praxistest* (Submitted to Straßenverkehrstechnik, 2915, see http://stefanlaemmer.de/Publikationen/Laemmer2015.pdf).

5 D. Helbing, T. Seidel, S. Lämmer and K. Peters, *Self-organization principles in supply networks and production systems* in: B. K. Chakrabarti, A. Chakraborti, and A. Chatterjee (eds.), Econophysics and Sociophysics – Trends and Perspectives (Wiley, Weinheim, 2006), 535–58. C. Gershenson and D. Helbing, *When slower is faster* (2015, in preparation; look for preprint at www.arXiv.org).

6 S. Lämmer, *Simulationsstudie Bahnhof Dresden Mitte. Praxistauglichkeit und Einsatzmöglichkeiten einer neuartigen voll-verkehrsabhängigen Lichtsignalsteuerung* (internal report, 2009). S. Lämmer and D. Helbing, *Self-stabilizing decentralized signal control of realistic, saturated network traffic* (2010).

7 Ibid.

8 S. Lämmer and D. Helbing, *Self-stabilizing decentralized signal control of realistic, saturated network traffic* (2010). D. Helbing, *Economics 2.0: The natural step towards a self-regulating, participatory market society* (Evolutionary and Institutional Economics Review 10, 2013), 3–41.

9 S. Lämmer and D. Helbing, *Self-stabilizing decentralized signal control of realistic, saturated network traffic* (2010).

10 .Hamilton-Baillie, B (2008) 'Shared space:reconciling people, places and traffic' Built Environment vol 34 number 2
https://www2.bristol.gov.uk/committee/2008/sc/sc026/1217_15.pdf

11 D. Helbing and S. Lämmer, *Supply and production networks: From the bullwhip effect to business cycles* in: D. Armbruster, A. S. Mikhailov, and K. Kaneko (eds.), Networks of Interacting Machines: Production Organization in Complex Industrial Systems and Biological Cells (World Scientific, Singapore, 2005), 33–66. D. Helbing and S. Lämmer, *Method for coordination of concurrent processes for control of the transport of mobile units within a network* (WO/2006/122528, 2006). D. Helbing, T. Seidel, S. Lämmer and K. Peters, *Self-organization principles in supply networks and production systems* in: B. K. Chakrabarti, A. Chakraborti, and A. Chatterjee (eds.), Econophysics and Sociophysics – Trends and Perspectives (Wiley, Weinheim, 2006), 535–58.

12 D. Helbing and S. Lämmer, *Method for coordination of concurrent processes for control of the transport of mobile units within a network* (WO/2006/122528, 2006).

See also:

Helbing, D., Siegmeier, J,. and Lämmer, S., *Self-organized network flows* (Networks and Heterogeneous Media 2(2), 2007), 193–210

Kesting, A., Schönhof, M,. Lämmer, S., Treiber, M,. and Helbing, D., *Decentralized approaches to adaptive traffic control* in D. Helbing (ed.), Managing Complexity: Insights, Concepts, Applications (Springer, Berlin, 2008), 179–200

Lämmer, S., Donner, R., and Helbing, D., *Anticipative control of switched queueing systems* (European Physical Journal B 63(3), 2008), 341–8

Seidel, T., Hartwig, J., Sanders, R. L., and Helbing, D., *An agent-based approach to self-organized production* in C. Blum and D. Merkle (eds.) Swarm Intelligence Introduction and Applications (Springer, Berlin, 2008), 219–52

CHALLENGES AND CAPABILITIES FOR SCALING UP CIRCULAR ECONOMY BUSINESS MODELS – A CHANGE MANAGEMENT PERSPECTIVE

*Markus Zils, Phil Hawkins and
Peter Hopkinson*

Considering the increasing number of successful circular economy business models, the question is no longer whether the economic opportunities are there, but rather how to manage the transition from a linear to a circular model. Having described Ricoh's circular economy business model in the first volume of *A New Dynamic*, the authors here focus their attention on how it has grown and developed over the years, exploring the scaling-up of remanufacturing and reuse activities. Drawing some wider lessons from this business case, this chapter discuss the challenges and key options facing businesses that are building circular business models.

Peter Hopkinson
Peter is Professor of Innovation and Environmental Strategy at the University of Bradford's School of Management. Peter is director of the academic collaboration with the Ellen MacArthur Foundation and leads the new online MBA in Innovation, Enterprise and Circular Economy, as well as the executive education course for the Global CE100.

Markus Zils
Markus is Managing Director of Returnity Partners, Formerly Principal, McKinsey Company Inc, he contributed to the report *Towards The Circular Economy: Economic and business rationale* for an accelerated transition (Ellen MacArthur Foundation with analytics by McKinsey, 2012 and 2013).

Phil Hawkins
Phil is General Manager, Business Development Office at Ricoh UK Products Ltd and Ricoh Industrie France SAS.

The circular economy aims to provide alternatives for conducting business in such a way that a linear 'take, make, dispose' economy can be upgraded to an economy that is restorative by design. One of the aims for such an economy is to deliver superior utility on the back of substantially improved resource, component and product productivity. The great appeal to businesses is that this transition could be self-reinforcing by being profitable rather than solely requiring costly regulation. At the core of this drive lies the innovation of business models which allow us to generate, capture and distribute the benefits of offering more circular products, services and solutions. So far so good: few people would argue against such an ambition. As shown in this book, there are now many good examples of circular economy business models, for example, Nabil Nasr's remanufacturing case studies point to the opportunity and potential success of circular business models. For those on the outside of such cases, the scale of these business models is impressive and might seem an obvious future strategy for any business making and selling technical products with high material values. For those businesses seeking to shift from a linear to a circular model the process of how to manage the transition is a key question. The change management involved inevitably presents numerous challenges and requires specific capabilities which are less well understood or explained than the clear material and economic benefits of a successful transition.

In this chapter therefore we present an insider perspective from Ricoh's circular economy business model that has grown steadily over a number of years and is now at a point of significant scale. The early stages of this story feature in the three EMF/McKinsey reports *Towards a Circular Economy 1, 2, and 3* as well as the first volume of *A New Dynamic*.[1] Here we update the story and shift our attention to what happens when the company begins to scale up remanufacturing and reuse activities, and in particular seeks to bring more of its own product back than has hitherto been possible. The chapter discusses challenges and capabilities that are relevant and important to any business seeking to set up, implement and scale up an asset recovery and reuse programme whilst at the same time running a business manufacturing and selling new products.

In the first part of this chapter we discuss briefly what we mean by the term 'business model' and some of the key options and issues facing businesses that are transitioning from linear to circular or building a circular business model within a traditional successful linear business organisation. In the second part we present the asset reuse and remanufacturing programme in Ricoh Global. Finally we draw some conclusions and wider lessons from this business case for wider discussion and debate.

What is a business model?

Business models are stated as being a key building block for the circular economy, along with design, reverse logistics and system conditions. In this respect, it is useful to ask ourselves exactly what is meant by this term.

In fact the term 'business model' is very difficult to define with any consistency and many definitions exist. For example Baden-Fuller and Mangematin[2] define a business model in terms of:

'A model that links the workings inside the firm to outside elements, including the customer side, explaining how value is created and how that value is captured or monetised'

Amitt and Zott[3] reviewed over 1,000 papers with the term 'business model' in the title and found widely different uses of the term but also some common elements and presented the following definition:

'...[business model is a]...system of interconnected and interdependent activities that determines the way the company does business with its customers, partners and vendors – a bundle of activities (an activity system), conducted to satisfy the needs of the market along with the specification of which parties conduct which activities and how these are linked to each other'

Whilst these are both interesting definitions, 'How do you plan to make money or a profit?' seems a good place to start with any business model and actually helps cut through a lot of the confusion. Ultimately, profit is what is left over from revenues after subtracting the cost. To understand how to maximise profits we need to ask three simple questions.

- **How do you create value?**
- **How do you capture value?**
- **How do you share value along your value chain?**

How you expect to make money is one part of your business model, but when you expect the money is another important factor. Some companies run up costs and spend cash months (even years) before a revenue stream begins to flow.

In the circular economy various models have been proposed that will shift payments from one lump sum (make-sell model) to spreading the purchase price over monthly instalments (often at greater overall cost to the consumer). In some business models, customers also have the choice to pay as they go or to prepay for unlimited use of a product or service (e.g. mobile phone services). A rental or hire model offers customers the option to buy or rent/

hire, alongside schemes to finance their purchases. A performance-based business model involves an agreed contract with payment for guaranteed use and outcome. Each option has different financial consequences for the business and revenue and balance sheet. Even at this basic level we can begin to see how internal discussions in a company about a shift from linear to circular, or scaling up a circular offer, might begin to create some challenges and anxieties within a business setting. To develop this further we need to remind ourselves how a linear business model works and why it is successful. To explore this a little further we describe below some of the key features of a generic manufacturing company operating largely in the technical cycle.

The success of the linear business model

The basic model at the heart of most manufacturing and sales-based business models that forms our traditional understanding of linear value creation is a one way 'take, make, sell' transaction relationship. Some of the key features of the success of this model involve :

• **Become leaner, meaner and more efficient** – Toyota's inspired lean manufacturing principle is taught to engineers and business administrators alike.
• **Gain scale** to drive down unit costs on operating expenses and capital employed.
• **Increase scope of activities** to be able to reduce margins, if under pressure, without needing to finance too many intermediaries.
• **Offer most competitive prices** on the back of low unit costs (if operating in a competitive environment) or maximise returns on investment by increasing margin (if operating in a less competitive environment).

While the above description is very simplistic it leads to two important consequences, which create linear 'lock-in' into the 'take, make, dispose' economy: a low cost, point of sales, transaction focus (and not quality); and no systematic end-of-use revalorisation (recovery of value).

In many cases, one outcome of this approach is that less effort is put into designing products that last or are repairable. As a result, material productivity is reduced. As companies can also boost revenues by increasing the number of sales to customers, there is even a natural incentive to reduce durability on purpose so as to stimulate replacement sales (also known as planned obsolescence). This creates a high correlation between low cost and reduced quality in terms of durability and usage extension. As there is no value seen or recognised after this usage cycle, it can lead to materials being (temporarily) lost to landfill or (for good) to incineration.

The emerging circular business models

In order to beat the linear model, innovation in circular business models is required to deliver superior business and financial performance. This circular business model innovation will need to address the three 'value' questions identified above. These questions are central to any business intending to develop circular economy business models or to scale them up. In the case of businesses already operating a successful linear model the questions become more complex as not only is there a need to develop and scale up the circular model, but also to assess how any such models at scale will impact on the existing linear model. While the list of levers and case examples on how to create value from circularity is long and well defined,[4] the challenge frequently revolves around the question of how to *capture* the value, i.e. make it worthwhile for the companies or consortium of players to reap back the additional costs or investments for closing the loop on products, components or materials. There are many options for capturing value but the most common in a circular economy business model are resale, performance-based delivery, and internalisation (see box on next page). Another key challenge relates to how to share the value along the value chain. To achieve this may require innovative collaboration between players upstream and downstream of a company's core value chain, and new collaborations.

Having defined the term 'business model', and reminded ourselves about some of the key features of the linear business model and what is needed to compete with this model, we now turn attention in the second half of the chapter to explore further how this works in practice, with the benefit of insights and lessons learnt from Phil Hawkins, the Project Manager for Ricoh's 3R programme. The case demonstrates how one circular economy business model answers the three key questions addressed above:

• **How to create value?**
• **How to capture value?**
• **How to share value?**

Challenges and opportunities at Ricoh

Ricoh is a global Japanese print and document management business. Ricoh's business fundamentals display all three of the value capture opportunities described previously. A cornerstone of Ricoh's business model is leasing print machines on a print-per-page basis – effectively a performance-based model. Many of its assets remain the title of Ricoh in a service contract and are therefore returned at the cessation of the contract for potential reuse. Toner and cartridges are refreshed in the field as required. Cartridges are returned for refill and resale.

The company has a long-established asset reuse and remanufacturing business model so has a clear desire to continually seek ways to improve design,

CIRCULAR VALUE CAPTURE OPPORTUNITIES

Resale of circular goods and services

In many situations, reusable materials, components or products can be offered to the marketplace in the same way as new products. In many cases an option is for the original equipment manufacturer (OEM) or an intermediary to buy the product back, refurbish it and then sell it as 'good as new' or 'near new'. However sales force and market development professionals frequently want to make sure that selling of reused materials, components or products does not cannibalise the existing top line of the linear business. Another key concern is rooted in the belief that reintroduced products do not deliver the same utility, quality or performance of new products. To counter these worries some companies have offered their own labels for refurbished products to differentiate from new products, or given out the same warranties as for new products in order to build consumer confidence in the refurbished products (e.g. John Deere).

Performance-based delivery

In performance-based or utility delivery models, the core idea is to find a form of pay-per-use remuneration for the provider (e.g. power by the hour, rate per mileage). The benefits for the user are the reduced upfront expense, the reduced risk of (premature) failure, reduced maintenance costs and the ability to control expenses by adjusting usage behaviour. The benefits for the provider of the performance-based delivery model are the ability to translate any improvements in durability and reduced operating costs (e.g. for maintenance), into an increase in sales margins, improved long-term customer relationship and an ability to maintain control over the product, components and materials during the usage cycle (which in turn improves collection and revalorisation rates at end of use). The drawback is the increased risk profile and financing of working capital.

As the performance-based delivery model creates a continuous incentive for the user and provider, Walter Stahel[5] has rightfully identified the move from sales to performance-based models as one of the greatest thrusts in the circular economy.

Internalisation

In many cases, companies can deploy circular practices in their upstream operations to improve their cost competitiveness and to improve resilience against commodity price fluctuations. There are many ways this can be achieved, from material input sourcing to shared services. In these instances the (new) product is delivered to customers, without declaring the circular elements of this offering.[6]

Figure 1 **The Ricoh Comet Circle**[7]

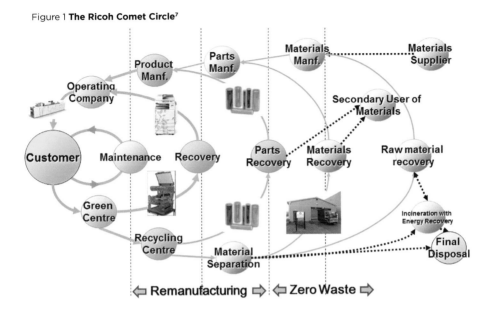

manufacturing efficiencies and internalise cost savings. As a consequence no Ricoh materials in the remanufacturing sphere are sent to landfill, as all products, components and materials are reused apart from a residual amount for energy recovery.

The Ricoh Comet Circle (see Figure 1) was a pioneering product and materials recovery and recirculation framework that recognised the material and business benefits of equipment maintenance services, product and parts recovery and recycling. It has served the company well in spotting materials leakage and opportunities for value creation.

Since 2004 Ricoh has slowly grown a remanufacturing and asset reuse strategy including installation of a separately branded 'GreenLine' product line. The GreenLine brand historically operated across many different models and machine configurations, with little or no standardisation across countries or operating companies. However, by 2013, GreenLine had grown to a substantial operation with sales of around 10,000 machines per annum, raising one of the key questions for Ricoh – how to feed and grow this thriving business.

As these initial capabilities around GreenLine and parts and supplies (P and S) have matured, Ricoh has found itself in a position to 'industrialise' this approach and prepare to scale up operations. Ricoh's business model rationale for scaling up extensive remanufacture and reuse of assets is compelling. Reusing assets allows the company to service the print offer at a lower cost than through virgin assets.

Figure 2 **Ricoh's asset cascade**

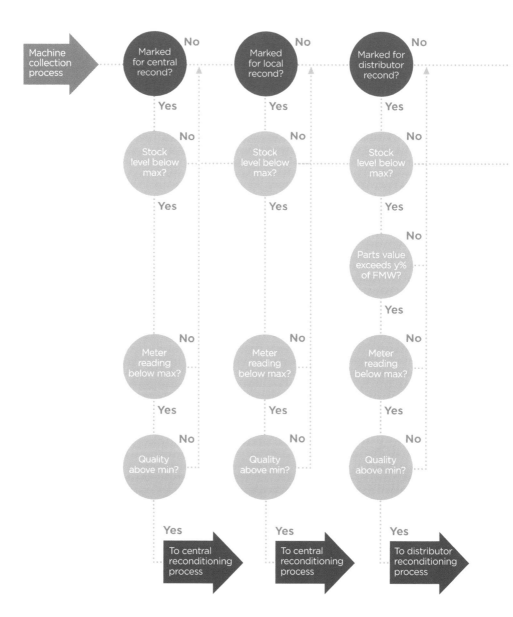

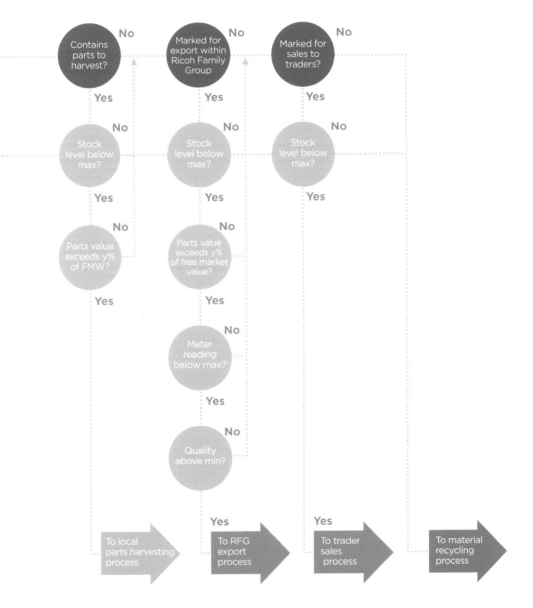

Through the utilisation of remanufacturing technologies within its own EU-based remanufacturing plants, the company is able to offer as-new part and product performance to the customer whilst internally reducing the cost to supply and service (internalisation).

The scale-up programme is known as '3R' (recover, reuse, recycle) and covers machines, parts and supplies and traders. Ricoh's 3R business model is based upon a value realisation cascade (Figure 2), a decision tree which defines the optimum value that the company can realise from returning assets: both hardware (machines), as well as consumables and spare parts. This cascade involves optimising the opportunities for value creation, capture and distribution across the full remanufacture and reuse value chain.

The value realisation cascade is aligned to the Ricoh Comet Circle by the creation of maximum value through product reuse in the market (the inner loops of the circle) and as a source of competitive advantage. The Ricoh GreenLine brand was established to overcome market perceptions about remanufactured machines being viewed as 'second-hand products' and is a key element of defining product quality and standards that are sold within these inner loops.

The opportunity to scale up leads to new requirements for the company, notably an ability to track and monitor assets and their condition, and unearths new challenges. In the next part of this chapter we focus on the following:

• **Value creation – identifying and avoiding loss of assets:** how does Ricoh track, identify and value lost assets?
• **Value capture – the feedstock management and recovery challenge:** how does Ricoh recover assets and ensure sufficient feedstock for refurbishment and remanufacturing operations? In relation to the maximisation of network profits, how does Ricoh identify and enable the maximum profit opportunity for the company including what product to place where (market, segment)?
• **Value sharing – the incentive alignment challenge:** how does Ricoh align global manufacturing and sales targets across business units and geographies?

Value creation – identifying and avoiding loss of assets
A perspective that Ricoh is currently grappling with is that of assets sold outside of a Ricoh service contract. Despite the Comet Circle being long established and very successful, the company typically faces leakage of approximately 40% of all assets in use. These assets are not dumped but instead many end up being sold through dealer and distribution channels. At end of usage or contract the asset title belongs either to the dealer or possibly to the actual end user. In this case recovery of the asset is no longer within Ricoh's direct control.

Figure 3 **Asset reuse and value in the market for different models of Ricoh print machines**

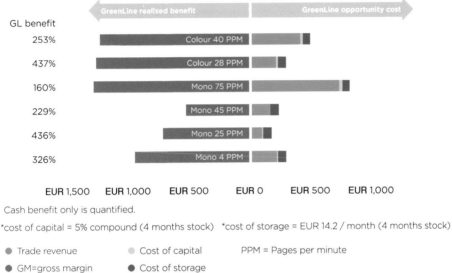

Cash benefit only is quantified.

*cost of capital = 5% compound (4 months stock) *cost of storage = EUR 14.2 / month (4 months stock)

● Trade revenue   ○ Cost of capital   PPM = Pages per minute
● GM=gross margin   ● Cost of storage

Avoiding such losses (via the secondary market) is a profitable exercise as machines with little repair/refurbishment needs can be brought back into the market and for each machine saved a customer is recovered for Ricoh's service business.

From a circular economy perspective this recovery linked with remanufacture and reuse extends product life, enables repeat circulation of technical materials at high quality and significantly increases the utility and performance per kilo of material deployed compared to the single usage or sub-optimal resale outside of Ricoh's strict quality control processes.

As an illustration of the value creation potential for Ricoh, Figure 3 shows the asset reuse value in the market to Ricoh compared to resellers. 'GreenLine opportunity cost' in this graph shows the value of GreenLine to resellers.

Recognising that Ricoh has defined three levels of reused hardware offered to the market, the company has defined a model by which it decides which machine types and configurations it will place into the GreenLine remanufacturing process. This enables products to be made available either to new channels and segments or towards the 'balanced deployment concept' (where a customer takes a mix of new and remanufactured GreenLine products). Phil Hawkins describes five criteria by which the company evaluates the GreenLine offer to the market:

1. Market pricing – the competitive price that the market will support for a GreenLine product.

2. Market quality – the level of quality that the market will expect from the product in use.

3. Software compatibility – in balanced deployment contracts software compatibility becomes important. As an example, machines of different age of manufacture/remanufacture may use different software (e.g. Windows 8 vs. Windows 7) hence an end user might not be able to deploy a single operating system with its entire fleet.

4. Flexibility of configurations – if Ricoh is targeting a segment or channel that requires flexibility of the offer, there is an obvious cost implication for the company, which may determine the ability to meet the market price. Consequently this would affect where and how Ricoh would produce such an offer.

5. Availability of asset over time – Ricoh recognises the need to manage asset usage cycles. If a particular model is likely to be unavailable or in poor condition at the end of its first usage, then the launch of a GreenLine product is precluded.

Figures 4 and 5 present two examples for two different machines of the model Ricoh use to assess potential target interventions.

In the case illustrated in Figure 4, the company evaluated the launch of a 20 pages per minute (ppm) mono remanufactured machine to the market. The last date of original manufacture was 2008 and it was sold in high volumes meaning feedstock potential was high. An apparently obvious candidate for GreenLine remanufacture, it was, however, ruled out on the basis of software compatibility with the new equivalent model in the market and the highly competitive pricing in the market for this segment of product (20ppm mono) at the time. The company was unable to realise value from its plentiful feedstock and chose instead to either recover and reuse components (parts) from the returning assets or simply dispose of them on the spot market for trade machines.

In the case illustrated in Figure 5, the company evaluated the launch of a 40ppm colour machine to the market. The last date of original manufacture was 2009 and again it was sold in high volumes meaning feedstock potential was high. In this case, however, Ricoh was able to proceed to launch a GreenLine offer. The positioning and pricing took some time for the company to clarify, but once this was agreed the cost-effective provision of the offer to the market was relatively straightforward for the company.

Figure 4 **GreenLine remanufacture (20 ppm mono machine)**

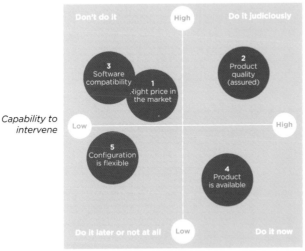

*Resource implications
(cost/time) of intervention*

Figure 5 **GreenLine remanufacture (40 ppm colour machine)**

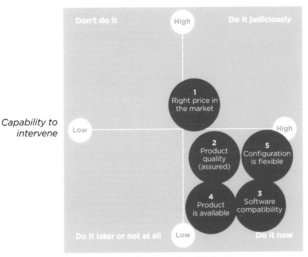

*Resource implications
(cost/time) of intervention*

Value capture – the feedstock management and recovery challenge
To scale up both GreenLine and other asset reuse initiatives requires an ability to recover and deploy sufficient feedstock for refurbishment and remanufacturing operations. Ricoh targets the capture of these used assets via a number of differing routes. Consumables, being user replaceable, are obtained through Ricoh's online collection system (www.ricoh-return.com). Empty toner cartridges are returned directly to Ricoh's market place remanufacturing facilities, with toner cartridges being repatriated via the company's European supply chain into markets across the EU. Approximately 60% of Ricoh's machines in field (MIF) are leased directly by the company, and maintained through its own field service engineers (FSE). Consequently the company has developed a sophisticated return, remanufacture and reuse process for all parts replaced by FSE in the course of a machine contract. Parts are returned directly to EU remanufacturing plants, from where they are again repatriated via the Ricoh EU supply chain into the FSE network across the EU.

The key feedstock challenge for Ricoh is the coordination and capture of these used assets. Feedstock volatility is a major issue for two key reasons: sporadic flows create variable and unpredictable utilisation of remanufacturing and reuse capacity which in turn reduces the fixed cost recovery or creates additional costs; and limited visibility of supply or ability to forecast supply accurately makes it difficult to set production and sales targets, balance out trade-offs between second life and new assets and add risks and costs in terms of needing to hold excess inventory or potentially running out of stock.

The potential mismatch of supply and demand requires a shift in approach from individual products to a network profit approach (see below). Asset tracking and more specifically the matching of feedstock to demand is a challenge that Ricoh is now currently seeking to address. As the GreenLine offer gains traction in the market, the dispersion of potential feedstock and its allocation to meet demand is a balance that the company strives to achieve. Particularly in terms of its hardware reuse offering, the company is developing three differentiated concepts for the market. Figure 6 demonstrates each of these concepts and highlights the need for rapid decision-making, balancing the level of intervention required, time to market, demand and ultimately value recovery and capture.

The ability to match feedstock with the sources of demand has required the company to undertake the construction of a complex system to visualise the end-to-end supply and demand landscape within Europe at a virtual level – this enables the physical execution of supply chains on demand to facilitate lowest cost as demonstrated in Figure 7.

To operate a virtual network of end-of-usage asset management in a dispersed supply chain requires the organisation to both track assets in usage and to

Figure 6 **Refurbished and remanufactured Ricoh machines**

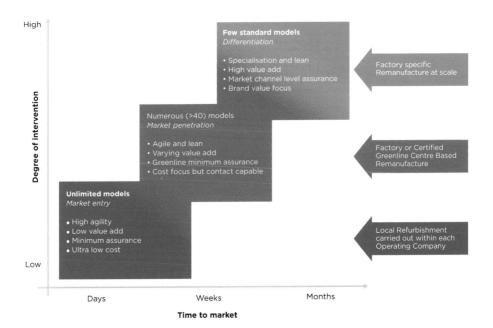

determine how and where end-of-usage asset treatment should take place. Any Ricoh assets that do not fall into one of the three reuse options (Figure 6) need to be treated at the lowest possible cost in situ, or traded at the maximum commodity price on the spot markets.

Phil Hawkins describes this trading process as being 'Ricoh's last resort: our aim is to reuse assets wherever possible, and to do this we not only need to understand where they are, but also when they will become available (end of contract) and their likely condition at end of contract (to facilitate the decision of which level of reuse they will be subjected). To enable the company to manage these intelligent asset tracking systems we trace an asset through its first usage based on its serial number.' Using serialisation as the key technique to identify assets allows Ricoh to understand where assets are, how they have performed (service history) in their first usage, when they are due for contract termination, and the level of profitability of each asset. This last facet is particularly important, as Hawkins notes, because 'it allows us to chase assets. If we need an asset for remanufacture and none is available we may incentivise our sales teams to chase assets for us. Both the company and the customer win in this relationship; the customer will receive a new machine at an attractive price, whilst the company recovers high potential assets in terms of condition to feed the remanufacturing offers within Europe.'

Figure 7 **Virtual and physical network for Ricoh machine reuse**

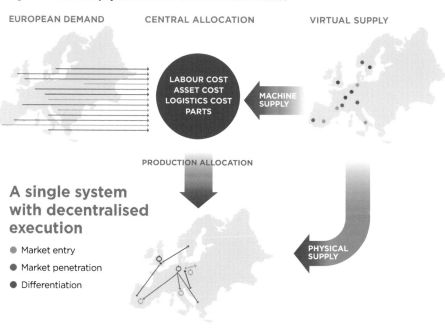

The maximisation of network profits

As Ricoh's 3R grows the need to be able to predict future demand and optimise the maximum profit opportunity across the network becomes critical to the success of the programme.

The graph in Figure 8 illustrates the maximisation of network profits issue more specifically. Up to 2013, Ricoh managed country-specific asset reuse across its 21 operating divisions. It was apparent when the 3R programme began to be rolled out that there were significant differences in performance across geographic regions, which made it difficult to scale up and optimise a reuse strategy across such a large scale. Figure 8 demonstrates that, by product category (supply vs. spare part) and by country, the company has mixed success.

The company is now focused upon the rectification of potentially sub-optimal behaviours across its European operating companies. An asset return in country x may have little value other than to be traded, at the same time however country y may be able to resell that same asset within the GreenLine programme. The issue for Ricoh is how to manage the opportunity loss (short-term cash inflow from a traded asset) in country x, to allow country y to realise the great long-term gain.

Figure 8 **Reusable Ricoh parts and supplies return ratio per operating country in 2013**

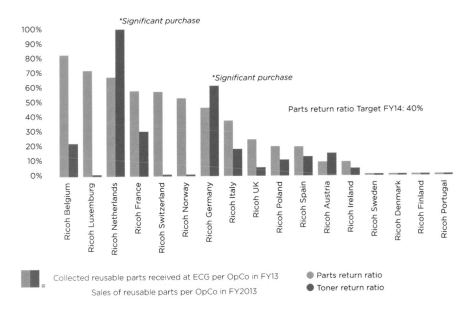

Value sharing – the incentive alignment challenge

A business such as Ricoh, despite having many impressive circularity characteristics, is also a business where much of its turnover and profits come from sale of new equipment. Huge amounts of capital, fixed assets, collateral and human resources are committed to this goal. Hence sales and marketing teams, financial targets, performance bonuses and overall strategy will potentially be affected by the scale-up of 3R. Growing a 3R business may be perceived as a threat to new machine sales with the potential to cannibalise new sales and hence impact on manufacturing output and a raft of performance metrics.

The 3R programme is responding to these challenges in these ways:

Alignment of sales targets across business units and geographies

Ricoh recognises the need both to feed a fixed infrastructure for the production of new machines and to balance this with an ambition to grow the reuse business; the alignment of sales targets across geographic and commercial boundaries is a constant iteration of price and margin alignment for the company. Naturally sales teams will strive to achieve their personal commission targets. Within a major corporate such as Ricoh it is feasible to steer a sales team to sell new or remanufactured products by simply adjusting their incentives.

Alignment of global manufacturing targets (especially as the need for new machines might ultimately be reduced in saturated markets) and the ability to optimise the fixed costs of the manufacturing operations globally
Ricoh's heritage is as a manufacturing company. The implications of this in terms of fixed infrastructure and organisational agility (or lack thereof) is compounded by the sale of remanufactured assets within mature markets. From a fixed asset perspective the company is asset-heavy; factories cannot be taken on and off stream in an instant. Yet from an efficiency perspective in dynamic and volatile markets, the company needs to be asset-light, unless it is able to protect its sales channels such that fixed assets are pushed towards their productivity frontier.

The effect of cannibalisation will be to increase the marginal costs of Ricoh's fixed infrastructure (in this instance the level of production output for new machines might drop, reducing economies of scale and increasing the cost of production per machine). An asset reuse strategy also requires the company to focus its marketing and sales strategy for remanufactured machines towards growing new businesses such as SMEs and non-traditional customers incrementally – possibly increasing costs. To cultivate this approach the company has established a dual sales approach to the market. Either remanufactured machines are sold into discrete channels, segments or markets within which the company has little or no presence with new machines, or via a so called 'balanced deployment' approach, whereby contracts are won on the basis of a mixed fleet of new and remanufactured devices.

Conclusions and wider lessons

The case study presented in this chapter is specific to one company in one sector. In the language of circular economy it operates primarily in the technical material cycle. The case explores a business programme – 3R – to illustrate a business model including the selling of performance (via a leasing model), resale and internalisation that enables the company to create and capture value from the reuse and remanufacture of physical assets.

The 3R programme represents a transformational circular business model involving a shift from a single remanufactured product line (GreenLine) split into geographic market responsibilities to a potential network/matrix type of business managing product loops and cascaded service offerings across national markets and product segments. At this point the company needs actively to engage with its dealer and distributor network to incentivise and facilitate returns to feed the cascade.

A scaled-up 3R business model presents challenges and profitable opportunities to Ricoh. It also requires specific managerial skills that form part of the new 'circular economy' business professional role. Indeed, this shift in model also requires a paradigm shift in management thinking and capabilities. Going forward, Phil Hawkins picks out three key challenges that relate to the value creation, capture and sharing questions identified earlier in this chapter:

Need for end-to-end visibility

Without end-to-end visibility Phil Hawkins states, "we will only ever be sub-optimal, continue to leak assets and lose opportunities". This is fundamental to the value creation stage of scaling up. Ricoh is just beginning to grasp the need for this capability and is actively exploring how this might be delivered as 3R progresses.

The shift from single products to matrix/cascades

Ricoh has been evolving its thought processes over time by reflections of learning through practice. Before the global economic downturn Ricoh's often fragmented 3R offerings were positioned largely from a corporate social responsibility perspective and marketed accordingly. In the years since the downturn, market pressure has become so intense, and points of differentiation so limited, that the company has had to focus much more on its capabilities and the development of these in a much more dynamic matrix of offers and product reuse cascades. Hawkins comments that 'the development of the asset cascade concept and the technologies, systems and process that underpin this has taken the organisation on a journey where if we get it right then we can create greater value without burdening ourselves with even more infrastructure and capital costs'. In essence, Ricoh is looking at the flow of products and materials that they have manufactured that disappear into the outer loops of the Comet Circle and work with clusters or networks of partners who have specialisation to support the shift towards the inner loops of Comet Circle.

Management capabilities and skill set requirements

The lessons Ricoh has taken from the last few years suggests that it has had to develop resilience in its managerial team in terms of expectations. Hawkins comments: 'I often use the term amongst my team and peers that working within 3R is analogous to looking for diamonds amongst a field of wet mud. We think there are diamonds in there, and fortunately most of our peers lack the vision to look for them. But it is hard heavy work and we fail more often than we succeed. Hence we need to adopt a mentality of 'fail quick, fail cheap, learn and move on' '. It is clear that the management skills sets need to be well aligned to the core new business model at Ricoh.

Notes

1 Ellen MacArthur Foundation, *A New Dynamic Volume* 1 (2013); *Towards the Circular Economy 1* (2102), *2* (2013), and *3* (2014)

2 Amitt, R. and Zott, C. (2012). Creating value through business model innovation, *MIT Sloan Management Review,* Spring, vol. 53, no. 3, pp.31–49.

3 Baden-Fuller, C. and Mangematin, V. (2013). Business models: A challenging agenda, *Strategic Organization,* November.

4 See for example Ellen MacArthur Foundation, *Towards the Circular Economy 1–3.*

5 W. Stahel, *The Performance Economy* (London: Palgrave-MacMillan, 2010).

6 A good example of this trend is the increasing drive of corporations to procure services instead of products or capital items. For example, cloud-based software-as-a-service solutions turn investments into previously fixed IT infrastructure from a fixed capital to an operational expense. This has immediate (likely positive) implications on financial performance for the company. In this instance the service providers benefit by driving up computer productivity as they are able to achieve better utilisation of higher-performing, larger computer systems, which in turn drives resource productivity and makes it more cost competitive.

7 For Ricoh's Comet Circle concept (1994) see: *A New Dynamic Volume 1,* 163.

CITIES AS FLOWS IN A CIRCULAR ECONOMY

Michael Batty

This chapter explores the nature of flows in cities which drive the circular economy. Flows and interactions between economic activities can be measured with respect to information, materials, people movements, and social linkages. It examines the nature of locating activities in cities and argues that it is the interactions between activities that give the city its form and structure. This chapter considers how cities currently function but then suggests that if we regenerate activities by internalising energy and material flows, then we would have much greater control over the shape and size, avoiding some of the excesses of the modern city such as urban sprawl, segregated communities, and urban blight.

Michael Batty
Michael is Bartlett Professor of Planning at University College London where he is Chair of the Centre for Advanced Spatial Analysis (CASA). He has worked on computer models of cities and their visualisation since the 1970s and has published several books, such as *Cities and Complexity* (MIT Press, 2005), and most recently *The New Science of Cities* (MIT Press, 2013).

The context: flow, not form; process, not product

The great challenge in understanding cities and their growth is in getting to grips with the way they process materials and information to provide the kind of environments that enable them to work efficiently and equitably in the forms and functions that are currently portrayed in most of our cities on the planet. Cities are places where people come together to pool ideas, to engage in social interactions, but, most of all, to generate greater prosperity for themselves in organising their labour in such a way as to raise their productivity over and above any other form of spatial organisation such as that associated with agrarian society. This does not mean that cities are in any sense ideal, far from it. The spatial forms that we have invented often contain as many diseconomies as economies, and they are not necessarily superior to other forms of spatial organisation with respect to their sustainability. But there is little doubt that cities by their very nature provide much greater opportunities for their populations to develop and indulge their social and economic interests and skills. The simple fact is that putting people in close contact with one another generates interactions that lead to a more fulfilling life. In one sense, this is a truism but it is an essential construct in thinking about how cities might evolve in the future and, particularly, how they might evolve into a form that is consistent with a circular economy where materials and information are balanced in a more sustainable fashion than currently characterise the ways we currently organise ourselves in cities.

Throughout the 20th century and even today, the notion that cities are all about places which are reflected in their physical form is still a dominant paradigm. This is despite the focus on social processes that bring together people in cities to develop collective activities and despite the long line of urbanists from Jane Jacobs[1] to Edward Glaeser[2] who have argued that cities are essentially vehicles and instruments for enabling processes of interaction and connection that lead to prosperity, diversity, innovation, and welfare. Indeed Jacobs said: 'For cities, processes are of the essence ... they are always made up of unique combinations of the particulars...'. Contact systems and social networks which enable flows of everything material and ethereal (information) as we shown in define the city and, in this sense, change the focus from one of location to interaction, from form to function, and from place to people. Cities are therefore points where people cluster to interact and innovate and Glaeser sums all this up rather nicely when he says: 'Urban density creates a constant flow of new information that comes from observing others' successes and failures... '. From this it is clear that if we simply focus on the physical form of cities rather than their flux we miss their essence.

Yet physical form is still important. All the manifestations of urban processes find their ultimate expression in the form of cities. The way we attempt to

Figure 1 **Traditional London street showing the complex network of connections between public and private spaces – connections of movement, sight, sound, and smell. These connections are able to be controlled and modulated by the users of the spaces (with doors, windows, gates, blinds, etc.).**

manage and plan our cities is primarily by manipulating their physical form, as it is somewhat less controversial to attempt to influence behaviours in cities through their physical form than actually applying direct constraints that restrict human behaviours. In fact the form of cities has historically reflected their function in that when people cluster to interact, the density of the places they occupy increases, and as one becomes more central to the cluster, one is able to realise ever greater social and economic opportunities. In a market economy, such accessibility is increasingly valued, and the most central locations in cities show the highest land values and command the highest rental prices.

The question we will address here is the extent to which the form of the city might be altered if we were to move to a more sustainable economy where the various flows that define the city might be internalised or balanced in some sense. Currently cities generally function as processors of non-renewable energy and they grow by consuming ever more of such resources as they continue to sprawl outwards from their historic centres. If their economy were to become sustainable in that their resources could be fashioned in renewable cycles – in a circular economy for example – what would be their shape and composition? Would they still be of the form that dominates our current cities which are organised around points of high-density interaction, traditionally their market centres, or would they massively decentralise to make use of local production which tends to be more consistent with renewable technologies? These are key questions which, although we cannot answer here, we will pose as being crucial to the debate about the use of alternative sources of energy. But before we explore these implications, we will start with the simplest model of how a typical city is organised spatially, beginning in fact with the most basic of economic models first proposed some 200 years ago, which still dominates our understanding of the form and function of the contemporary city.

The shape of the contemporary city, its form and function

Over two hundred years ago, a German count by the name of Johann Heinrich von Thunen surveyed his estate in Lower Saxony and came to the conclusion that the way he and his tenants had organised the planting of crops seemed to follow an arrangement of roughly circular but concentric bands of similar cultivation around a central point which he had established to market his produce. If you could have flown up to 3,000 feet, you would have seen concentric rings of different crops. Closest to the market were those which were the most perishable and took the fastest time to grow, such as vegetables, while furthest away were the least perishable taking an extremely long time to grow such as forests. Between these extremes, his estate was organised into different types of crops cultivated on a seasonal basis but also cattle rearing and dairying which came in intermediate positions. Of course von Thunen was not merely intent on simply describing this pattern, he wanted to explain it, and so he figured out what ultimately has become the basis for how a spatial economy works: products that needed to get to market fastest would attempt to locate as close to the market as possible but would pay higher rents for this privilege while incurring lower transport costs. Those that took longer to grow and were less intensively produced would pay lower rents for their land further away from the market but would incur higher transport costs. In a perfect world, von Thunen theorised, the rent payable at the place of production plus the transport cost to market would always equal a constant.

Von Thunen did not design this regular arrangement. It was not planned as a collective effort from the top down but evolved over time from individual actions, its spatial organisation essentially evolving from many decisions made from the bottom up. The reason why the production of different agricultural products occupied space at different distances from the market was entirely due to the economics of that production, which reflected a trade-off between the cost of bringing the produce to market using transport and the extent to which each product competed with the others to determine how near the market it could be produced. A consequence of all this was that the density of production was higher the closer it was produced to the market; the yield was thus higher and if the producer was required to pay rent, this too would be higher the nearer the producer was located to the market. If the transportation routes to the market or the physical landscape for production were in some way distorted, then the circular patterns around the market would adjust. For example, if there was a much higher speed transport route in one direction than any other, this would lower transport costs from places adjacent to this route and the surface would adjust accordingly. The land uses, organised according to how much they could afford for occupying land at different distances from the market centre with a river or canal providing relatively lower transport costs to the market, are shown above in Figure 2.

Figure 2 **Von Thunen's Rings. Different agricultural land uses are arranged concentrically around their market centre determined by the trade-off between yield (rent) and transport cost. Note the way the land use zones are elongated by the existence of the river which acts as fast transport to the market**

- Centre
- Fresh produce
- Seasonal vegetables
- Milk production
- Dairying
- Sheep grazing
- Forestry

River

Von Thunen[3] did not consider how many market centres defining a system of central places would modify this pattern, nor did he speculate on how a real system might develop with all the noise and heterogeneity of the real world. But his ideas have remained intact and have become the basis for how we think the spatial form of entire cities are structured in the modern age. If we fast forward to contemporary times and ask the question 'how are our towns and cities now organised spatially?' they still approximate Von Thunen's rings. If you look at a large city, certainly those that have developed over the last 100 to 200 years anywhere in the world, their structure can also be seen as reflecting a strong market core – what the Americans call the 'Central Business District' (CBD) – and then circular rings of different land uses which reflect increasingly high rents as one approaches the centre. The classic example is Chicago[4] but many cities show similar patterns and, for a very long time during the last century, we thought that this concentricity, punctured by radial networks which enabled people to travel more quickly to the centre for work and shopping, represented an almost ideal type when it came to cities. It seemed to be the 'natural' way of things. It portrayed an equilibrium that went back well before the industrial revolution – to the medieval city certainly, and even to classical times, while the industrial era itself did not really upset the balance. It simply reinforced it with the central city getting bigger and more specialised and the suburbs growing less densely at ever greater distances from the core.

This model of city development, although assumed to represent a structure that is balanced in terms of the ability of urban activities to compete for space and pay an economic rent that reflects transport cost to the central business district, is by no means a perfect market. To an extent von Thunen's basic model, which now lies at the core of urban economics, was predicated on some sense of perfect competition but there are many missing pieces when it comes to modern-day cities where income differentials and inequalities are considerable. For example, although rents are higher near the centre of the city and one might assume that rich people are more likely to live there, outbidding the poor for such premium space, it turns out that in most western cities at least, the richer people live on the edge. There they can get more space and afford the transport costs as well while poorer people are crammed into more congested space nearer the centre. Poor people thus end up paying more for their housing per unit of space consumed than rich people and this is hardly perfect competition. To an extent, it makes the central and inner zones of modern cities poverty traps, zones where disadvantaged populations are forced to live, and where crime is often rife.

A linear urban economy with no limit and its transition to a circular economy
This model of the modern city with its radial transport routes to the centre tying the population together is entirely consistent with an economy that functions on the consumption of resources where there are no limits. Population growth is assumed to be continuous with ever wider rings of development at ever greater distances from the centre. In this model it is assumed that there are no limits on the energy resources used to make this kind of sprawling metropolis function, and that there are no limits on the financing of new development in high-rise office towers that are underpinned by an economy based on the manufacture of money and debt. The economy is one which simply produces inexorably for a growing population where new technologies are always adding to the products that are mass-produced for an ever-increasing consumption. This is a linear economy where resources are used to grow the system with a throughput that does not replenish the stock of resources input to the system. Energy and material resources, usually non-renewable, drive the system and waste is the ultimate product. There is little attention to renewing the resources used in any balanced way and thus the world which is created depends on an infinite supply of resources. In this sense, it is unsustainable, unless we find ways of generating such infinite supplies, which most people would consider to be akin to alchemy, the magic of turning metal into gold.

Cities which grow from a market centre into a wider space, which increases exponentially in area as one travels at linear distances away from the centre, are fashioned on the assumption that there is an infinite geometry. The only way a city's growth is limited in such a world is by the limits on transportation cost which in turn are related to transportation technologies. As we see in many North American cities, with sufficiently ingenious reorganisation of

Figure 3 **Ever-expanding concentric urban zones based on a linear economy**

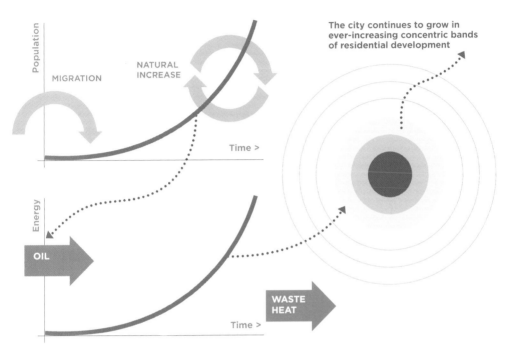

The city continues to grow in ever-increasing concentric bands of residential development

Unlimited growth in gasoline consumption leading to ever more travel as the city grows.

work, big cities appear to have an almost unlimited hinterland where there are few constraints posed by geometry. An increasing number of people are able to live many miles away from the city's core, implying almost unlimited growth potential. During much of the 19th and 20th centuries, cities have been growing in this unsustainable fashion. Their most likely physical form is concentric in the manner described and their economies are rarely self-sustaining in the sense of being balanced and renewable. Growing cities tend to pull resources from their wider hinterlands, rarely replacing these resources once they have been used and consumed. Typically their economies, which represent microcosms of the wider economy, tend to be focused on unsustainable consumption which is best illustrated by the fact that if cities continue to grow outwards as population continues to increase, they will continue to consume irreplaceable fossil fuels until the point where such resources give out. In this sense, the modern city's economy is essentially linear as we show diagrammatically above in Figure 3.

If the economy were balanced, its functions would embody a degree of circularity for it would replenish its resources via innovative flows of energy and materials. If we pose a thought experiment to idealise about our mid-20th-century city with its concentric physical form, it might be able to function as a circular economy if the city could give back to itself the resources it consumed and thus it could be replicable indefinitely. Imagine a city in a landscape or system of cities where each consumed each other's materials and products in such a way that demand and supply were balanced. The inputs to the production process might also be balanced across the cities with such inputs flowing in 'material cycles'. This might mean that transportation, so necessary for delivering products to market and people to work, must also be redesigned and this might be possible if electricity were generated from renewable energy sources to power these systems and enough surplus resources were devoted to replenishing the electricity used in a balanced way: solar power might be an obvious way although tidal and wind power and other alternative sources might be possible. In this way, one might envisage the city as growing ever bigger following its rings of growth outward from its centre but the way these rings are sustained through transport also embodies a functional circularity in that the means of transport is continually replenished. This idealisation of course might break down in that cities cannot grow indefinitely. In fact with the demographic transition now affecting all populations on earth, this model of a successively growing city is easily adaptable to one where its rings of growth are fixed once growth ends and a steady state ensues with the rings being successively redeveloped or replenished to cater for stable populations renewing themselves. One might almost imagine a concentrically zoned city with a circular economy providing the ultimate model for a stable economy composed of cities existing in a dynamic equilibrium.[5]

To an extent developing a circular economy probably depends on population growth stabilising. In fact the demographic transition suggests that this could well happen within the next 100 years. Moreover advances in medicine could well extend lifespans dramatically producing a world in balance in terms of its demography. Equally well, advances in medicine could lead to the opposite happening and of course if certain technologies are invented that enable great advances in sustainable resources engineering, then we might see population growing indefinitely. There are many open questions, and of course as our definition of dynamics implies, balance and equilibrium are forever evolving. However we might assume that if population does stabilise and growth in total levels out, there may well be the prospect for developing a regenerative economy that mirrors in various ways the ideas of the circular economy. A simple modification of our previous diagram showing cities in the linear economy illustrates how we might imagine this.

Figure 4 **Cities in a balanced circular economy**

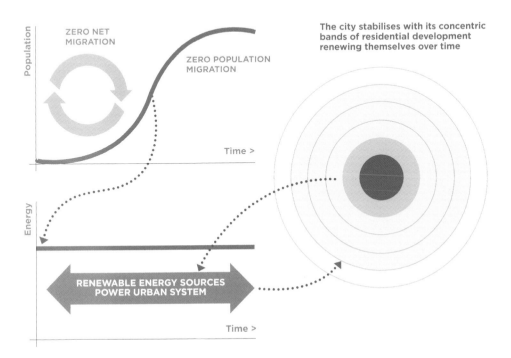

The complexity of the modern city: the disconnect between
form and function, places and people, locations and flows

Before we speculate in a little more detail on what cities might look like under
such a circular economy scenario, we should make a more detailed inquiry into
the nature of cities and how their forms and functions are changing in the 21st
century. Despite von Thunen's wonderful insights into why and how different
land uses cluster-like rings around a central market, his model is one that now
relates to a very different world from that of the contemporary 21st-century
city. In essence, the point in this chapter will be that the contemporary city
no longer ties form to function in the way that we have assumed it has done
since cities first emerged some 5 or more millennia ago. The single biggest
change over the last two centuries in the modern city has been its focus on
its central market – the core or CBD. As transportation systems have become
more efficient, the ties to the centre have weakened and many land uses and
economic activities that once needed to be close to the market no longer feel
this need. In fact as economies and their markets have globalised, the notion
of distributing one's product from a central point has changed dramatically.
From the mid 20th century on, the traditional centre began to lose its key
functions, manufacturing first and then retailing, to out-of-town centres, and

the emergence of the so-called 'edge city' became apparent: high-density clusters of economic functions that served to draw population from across the metropolis, often located at points of high accessibility in the suburbs that were becoming ever more specialised, segregated and heterogeneous. The CBDs in many major cities too began to fragment, with most large cities over 10 million population now sporting two or more.

To an extent this increasing disconnect between form and function is clearly determined by technological change. Material transport is being complemented and substituted for by information technologies. The telegraph and the telephone bound systems of cities together more closely in terms of their global reach but it needed the computer and its convergence with telecommunications to really loosen the cement that tied function to form, tied economic and social activities to particular places in the rather regimented and constrained fashion of the city of concentric zones. In the longer term, the physical manifestation of the city in its concentric or polar form now seems to be a phase transition between a world where there were no cities to a world where everything will be one kind of city or another. The industrial revolution is just the first transition to this world where information will be the key, where information is energy in another form, a world where atoms are bits, to coin Negroponte.[6] If you look at the modern city, it is highly diversified, much more so than von Thunen's simple model implies. Although von Thunen's original elements may always be intact, the development of an information society where the ways we communicate are no longer dominated by distance or geometry is sufficient to loosen the cement that binds the elements composing the traditional city together.

The world we have now joined is one where a dramatic disconnect between form and function is rapidly occurring. This does not mean that place and location are no longer significant – the 'death of distance' is a somewhat exaggerated hyperbole of this phenomenon.[7] Place and location still figure of course but the physical form of the modern city which is based on the concentric location of bands of land use around the centre no longer functions as von Thunen supposed. Land uses and activities have become much more footloose than ever before. This might be countered by the fact the cores of big cities continue to pull in the most profitable uses, namely financial services, but in many respects this is a residue from the past. Most money-making financial institutions now operate on the net and the fact that dense urban cores still attract such activities for reasons of economic profitability tends, in my view, to be a residual of a bygone world. There may be something in the notion of a need for face-to-face contact between the world's bankers in such places but in general, this is not where the action is. Electronic stock exchanges have decentralised. They no longer exist in the biggest cities. Moreover big city cores now contain prestige buildings that represent an asset class and the demand for such functions is as much due to being the best places to invest money in a volatile financial world as any focus on realising the highest returns by locating economic activity in such places. Much of what characterised such places over the last century is now diffusing to the net. Much of the contemporary city is moving to the cloud. What this will mean for the move to circular economy is unknown but it is part and parcel of the rise of new forms of communication which are providing new substitutes as well as complements for traditional, more unsustainable modes of transport and flow.

The city as a mosaic of fractal networks

In all of this, it is the city as a constellation of networks that marks the most fruitful way of thinking about urban structure and development in the 21st century. We already implied in von Thunen's model that there is a hierarchy of transport systems which serve the concentric city. This is a hierarchy composed of radial routes at the highest level and subsidiaries which branch off at successively lower levels serving the interstices of development between the radials. For example, cities need large roads to move critical goods over long distances, and small- to medium-sized roads to move goods throughout the city itself, but they also need small-scale pedestrian walkways and bicycle routes to help reduce energy usage and fuel costs, while increasing exercise, social exchanges and a sense of ownership of the urban space. In short, transport networks in cities where there is a very pronounced core tend to be treelike – they are dendritic, they are 'fractal', meaning that they are similar in form and function at smaller and smaller scales.[8] Such scale invariance is referred to as self-similarity: best seen as placing a microscope or telescope over an object and continuing to zoom in or out, thus displaying detail which is similar in appearance on every scale.

The only way you can build such networks is from the bottom up. They emerge as the product of countless decisions as to where people wish to work and live and the growing city can be seen much like a growing tree in the way its branches thicken to enable more materials and information as more and more energy is pumped into its source. These flows are essential to the city as a living organism and any move to a circular economy will reinforce their importance as fundamental to the way such a sustainable city operates. Traditionally that source of flows has been the market but as we have implied this is changing and now cities import energy in many places due to the functions that define our globally connected world. Analogies between the city and the body with respect to transportation – the glue that ties everything together – go back to Leonardo da Vinci and probably to the Greeks, with the heart, its arteries and vein structure providing one kind of delivery network to the lung and its components providing yet another. In fact, using insights from animal form and function, the human body is an excellent example of how one can build resilient cities as sustainable systems using notions about

Figure 5 **Concentric cities like London exhibit fractal properties**

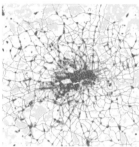 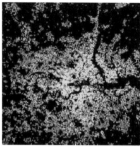 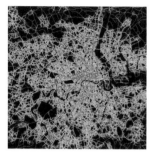

Retail centres of all sizes   Population density   Road transportation routes

© Michael Batty

order and networks which grow from the bottom up. In fact such networks in Figure 5 above display the idea that the city is fractal: break off a little bit of the network and magnify it up and the whole network appears in the magnification. This is evidence that cities build themselves using fractal patterns which ensure that they are robust and sustainable delivering energy to their most distant and deepest parts.

Urban networks and information flows

There are many other fractal hierarchies in cities. Information networks follow the same structure although we do not have very much data on what these information flows look like because they are largely invisible to our observations. Email networks, the way we use social media, mobile phone calls, the web itself and how we use it in terms of who and what we access, all of these imply hierarchical networks that are also connected together at various points. Add to this the energy networks and utilities as well as the plethora of production and distribution networks that characterise the city and you soon see how complex such a system is. There is no way such a system can be planned from the top down and it is hardly surprising that our best efforts in urban planning fall well short of the kinds of idealisation we seek. The complexity that the modern city portrays is mind-boggling and we are only beginning to try to make sense of it all.[9] A typical picture of the contemporary city as a constellation of fractal networks is shown above in Figure 5, revealing to an extent how von Thunen's rings are still evident but in much more muted fashion and more a consequence of the accessibility of each element within its urban network.[10]

What is encouraging to an extent, however, is that modern cities are increasingly resilient to disruption and disaster due to the proliferation of complex networks that betray a degree of redundancy in communications that enables populations to diversify when faced with difficult circumstances.

But in the same way, such a multitude of connections in cities can lead to dramatic and unanticipated repercussions which are unforeseen and often uncontrollable. In fact the move to the 'smart city' where many more things are connected to each other than ever before suggests the possibility of such problems, and there are many examples of how unwanted and undesirable effects diffuse across networks, diseases being the classic examples. Nevertheless, the fact that cities contain so many redundant pathways suggests that they are structures that might easily adapt to new forms of economy. Although we are a long way from the circular economy per se, there are elements in cities that might be exploited in the transition to such new forms of economic organisation.

Chief amongst these is the fact that populations in cities are increasingly in touch with one another. Until the advent of the new information technologies that are now all-pervasive, communication was restricted to a simpler model, where people were brought together in some central core or neighbourhood. This is changing very dramatically at present. The idea of involving wide populations in community action and in thinking about questions of resilience and socioeconomic development lies at the heart of crowd-sourcing, crowd-funding and the range of new forms of social interaction that new information technologies make possible. It is now not beyond our abilities to design and build cities which are powered in terms of their transport with much more sustainable technologies such as electric cars and trains. Even in a city like London whose weather is not ideally suited to the harvesting of solar power, it is not beyond our wit to mobilise a variety of alternative technologies that could provide all the energy a domestic household would require for its sustenance and transportation. The key to this is not the technology, for that is there already: it is being able to mobilise populations, and for this new information technologies provide the basis.

Cities, then, within the broader constraints defined by von Thunen, some of which still hold 200 years after he first laid them out, tend to grow naturally within these limits. The linear economy, which is dominated by high-value inputs and low-value outputs in terms of waste, provides a system in which cities naturally adjust to these constraints. The present situation is one of natural growth from the bottom up but within a straitjacket of an economic production process that is built around continuous consumption which is forced by increasing population growth and by a growing tendency for personal acquisition. If either one of these forces ends or even begins to stabilise, then it is very likely that the concentric city will change its shape. Suburbs will be less attractive and there will be increased densities near the cores which increasingly represent a polycentric landscape of specialised centres. The general principle that people cluster around some market centre trading off what they are prepared to pay in rent (or its investment equivalent) and transport cost is already beginning to blur as activities become more

Complex systems and complexity in cities

There is little doubt that as cities have evolved from the times they first appeared in the Fertile Crescent around 4000 BCE, they have become ever more complex. Indeed their size is a direct function of our innovations in technology and now with global communications, most cities cannot be understood without appealing to their function in the global economy. Complexity science seeks to explain their form and function on the basic premise that cities grow from the bottom up and in this sense evolve, providing new innovations which affect their structure through positive feedback. As there is no central control but a 'hidden hand', as Adam Smith so defined the social dynamic, cities are the product of historical accidents, where change is path-dependent and where new forms continue to emerge which are surprising. All this is consistent with the transition to a circular economy where connecting up the various parts of cities and societies to ensure balance and sustainability is the focal goal.

footloose and the locational nexus becomes more complex. The disconnect between form and function now dominates the contemporary city. In the past, when it comes to cities, what we saw is what we got: suburbs attracted young families needing more space than inner city dwellers, and retail and education functions adjusted to meet these spatial demands. Central cities became ever more concentrated in terms of financial and other services But the form that was developed to meet these functions is no longer appropriate. As populations become more footloose, as the nuclear family disappears, as life cycle effects become ever more varied, and as work, entertainment and health care drift to the web, the locational glue that kept all these things in place in the past is lessening. One of the key issues in this is that the fractal structure of cities built on multiplexing networks from the bottom up provides a structure which should be resilient enough onto which one can map a circular economy.

The future city and its many variants
In a world of circular economies, and doubtless there will be many different variants all interlocking with themselves in diverse ways, what will cities look like? Will their predominant spatial form in two dimensions be concentric in the same way they have been in the last five millennia? Is the notion of concentric cities around cores of specialised land uses reflecting accessibility and competition between one another a thing of the past? We began this essay with the notion that the predominant spatial form of the city is concentric

Figure 6 **Renewal and redevelopment already characterise the largest world cities**

© Sarah Kim- Flickr CC

but built on structures that reflected a linear economy. As we pointed out, it may still be possible to retain the advantages of this geometry if the economy shifts to circular forms based on continuous remanufacturing, recycling and replenishment. But this depends on population growth, and more particularly it depends on the way we will communicate in the future. It looks very much as though the world will be one where electronic flows begin to dominate physical or material flows, where the movement of information dominates most of the production and social cycles that define urban living. In such a world, the concentric city may still hold sway although it is more likely that its functions will be very different and the city itself will be something that continually renews itself and transforms to different functions without changing its physical form very much.

Our play here on the concentric city raises the question as to what our cities will look like in the medium-term future. The whole role of location is up for grabs, regardless of the nature of the circularity or otherwise of the economy, and the future of cities and their form is likely to be a heterogeneous mixture of centres of many types and structures that reflect different tenancies, ownerships and lifestyles. What we are likely to experience, however, in the move to a circular economy, is the decline of the homogeneous suburb, the proliferation of many different kinds of poly centre, and a cycle of renewal and redevelopment that complicates the clear concentricity of von Thunen's model, as we imply in Figure 6. Rent and transport costs will still be determinants of where we locate but these will be much influenced by capital markets, information technologies and a plethora of available information about the qualities of place.

What is very clear, however, with the passing of large-scale industrialisation and the demise of localised agriculture is that cities are becoming much more focused on the production of information and knowledge. These are the pursuits of an urban world. In this, networks of communications are critical in generating the conditions for new technologies, beyond those that we are now using to develop new modes of economic development. The key challenge will be on connecting up networks in new and diverse ways and avoiding the kind of polarisation that seems to be occurring in cities as ever more functions are being automated. At the start of this chapter, we referred to Jane Jacobs' focus on cities being all about processes of communication and interaction, and since she penned her prescient words, entirely new kinds of technologies have emerged that make her message ever more poignant. There is little doubt that coupling the myriad of networks that we now have at our disposal will enable us not only to invent new technologies but also implement and maintain them and provide the conditions for the behavioural change that is necessary to make circular economies a reality. It would be nice to be able to predict what this future of cities and their economies is going to be like in terms of their form and function but, as with all prediction, we can merely speculate, informing the debate over the future in the way we have attempted here. There is much work to do on linking the physical shapes and forms of cities to the nature of their economies and organisations, and this represents a formidable challenge. Here we have but pointed to future directions but it requires continued effort on new theories, methods, and models to enrich our understanding.

Notes

1 J. Jacobs, *The Death and Life of Great American Cities* (New York: Random House, 1961).

2 E. Glaeser, *Triumph of the City* (London: Macmillan, 2011).

3 J. H. Von Thunen, *Der Isolierte Staat*, Volume I, *Perthes* (Hamburg, Germany, 1826), and P. Hall (ed.), *Von Thünen's Isolated State*, trans. by Carla M. Wartenberg (Oxford: Pergamon Press, 1966).

4 If you go to Google Maps and click on the Earth View, and key in CHICAGO, you can zoom in and out of the map which implies that the city has developed concentrically with rings of different densities of development around its urban core, the Central Business District (CBD); see https://www.google.com/maps/@41.9053632,-87.8036544,68575m/data=!3m1!1e3

5 Cities like most human systems are never in equilibrium. Complexity theory tells us that such organised and self-organising structures are far from equilibrium in that they continually import energy and defy entropy. But there are many levels of equilibria in cities, and, in a routine sense, we can consider cities which are sustainable in energetic terms as being in a dynamic equilibrium which is a steady state. This dynamic can be disturbed with it returning to its past equilibrium but it is more likely that this dynamic is continually evolving. Linear economies are more likely to explode in that there are no limits whereas circular economies tend to be balanced by negative feedback; but all this motion is set within the wider context that cities and economies are continually evolving and, in this sense, are always far-from-equilibrium.

6 N. Negroponte, *Being Digital* (New York: A. A. Knopf and Company, 1995).

7 F. Cairncross, *The Death of Distance: How the Communications Revolution Is Changing Our Lives* (Cambridge, MA: Harvard Business School Press, 2001).

8 M. Batty and P. A. Longley, *Fractal Cities: A Geometry of Form and Function* (San Diego, CA and London: Academic Press, 1994, www.fractalcities.org).

9 M. Batty, *The New Science of Cities* (Cambridge, MA: MIT Press, 2013).

10 P. A. Krugman, *The Self-Organizing Economy* (Boston, MA: Blackwells, 1996).

See also:
Park, R. E., Burgess, E. W., and McKenzie, R. D. *The City* (Chicago, IL: The University of Chicago Press, 1925)

20

Manufacture

G.E.BELLISS

BIRMINGHAM

PRESSURE

10

E. BOURD

Inven.ⁱⁿ & Man

0

PARIS

CIRCULARITY INDICATORS
Chris Tuppen

11

Since the 1970s, businesses have used measurement tools to assess some of their critical environmental impacts. From Life Cycle Analysis to carbon footprint metrics, these measurements have been widely adopted and embedded in standards. However, until now, no such tool existed for assessing the effectiveness of material flows for either products or companies. For businesses that are shifting towards a regenerative economy the Circularity Indicators will help track performance and prioritise actions, whereas for investors or customers its specification can stimulate adoption of circular economy business models. In this chapter, one of the leading experts who worked alongside the Ellen MacArthur Foundation on the Circularity Indicators Project, gives an account of the developments and benefits of this tool.

Chris Tuppen
Chris has been involved in sustainability for more than 20 years. He runs Advancing Sustainability LLP and he is an Honorary Professor at Keele University. He was previously BT's Chief Sustainability Officer.

If we believe the old adage that we 'manage what we measure' then surely the corollary must also be true, that we should 'measure what we manage'?

Any organisation intending to embed a circular economy approach into their strategy will at some point want to have a measure of progress. Until 2015 no such metric existed – at least not in any open, standardised way. This chapter describes an approach to product- and company- level metrics developed by the Ellen MacArthur Foundation in collaboration with Granta Design.

The metrics are expected to have a number of benefits and uses including product design for circularity, internal performance metrics, inclusion in procurement specifications, external reporting, and investor analysis. The chapter includes a brief introduction into the derivation of the metrics along with a worked example.

A historic perspective

Spurred on by an increasing consumer consciousness of environmental issues in the 1960s and 1970s, people began asking the question 'which product is the most eco-friendly?' For example, is it better to use a disposable cup or wash up a china cup, or, is a disposable nappy (diaper) better than a cloth one?

In 1969 the Coca-Cola Company funded a study[1] to compare resource consumption and environmental releases associated with beverage containers. Meanwhile, in Europe, a similar approach was being developed by Ian Boustead of the UK's Open University.[2] He calculated the total energy used in the production of various types of beverage containers, including glass, plastic, steel, and aluminium. These early approaches eventually led to the scientific field of Life Cycle Analysis (LCA) that is today defined in the international standards ISO 14040 and 14044.

LCAs, whilst informative, are generally time consuming and complex and have largely remained in professional circles. They have been used mostly at a product level and, compared to the massive number of products on the market, are really quite rare. When LCA results are published they sometimes take the form of an Environmental Product Declaration (EPD).

An LCA will cover the full life cycle of a product and consider a comprehensive range of environmental impacts, typically covering items such as:

• global warming/energy
• ozone depletion
• eutrophication
• photochemical smog
• toxicity
• resource depletion
• land and water use

In parallel with the developing field of LCA, the early 1990s saw a widespread realisation that increasing emissions of greenhouse gases would lead to dangerous levels of global climate change. This led to a strong focus on carbon footprint metrics, first at country level, then at organisational level, and to a lesser extent at product level. A partnership between the World Resources Institute and World Business Council for Sustainable Development led the charge for a standardised approach to company-level carbon metrics. The resulting set of Greenhouse Gas Protocols[3] has since been embedded in ISO and many other standards.

Initially a company's disclosure of its carbon footprint was voluntary, but today it has essentially become a *de facto* necessity for all large businesses. This has been in part led by disclosure requirements from investors, particularly from CDP,[4] and in part by marketplace pressure such as customer procurement specifications and the natural inclination for companies to be at the top of sustainability league tables. The UK government has gone a step further and made carbon reporting mandatory for all UK quoted companies.[5] The net result of these actions has meant that companies have placed significant focus on reducing their carbon footprint and have developed a number of related internal management tools.

Measuring circularity

In some respects LCA and GHG accounting already cover a number of attributes associated with the circular economy such as low carbon energy and waste minimisation. However, neither offers a straightforward measure of the restorative nature of material flows associated with the circular economy. It was the identification of this gap that resulted in the Circular Indicators project led by the Ellen MacArthur Foundation in collaboration with Granta Design.

The project ran from August 2013 to July 2015 and was part-funded by the EU LIFE+ programme. Its primary objective was to develop an open-source methodology to assess the restorative material flows for both products and companies.

Stakeholders from about 30 organisations attended a sequence of workshops during the course of the project. They represented investors, regulators, consultancies and universities. At an early workshop stakeholders confirmed the view that there was no existing metric of restorative material flows, even though a number of related, but not always open, methodologies were identified.

Based on the Circularity Indicator methodology developed during the project Granta Design has also produced a comprehensive online tool for product-level assessments.

The benefits of circularity indicators

The system-level benefit of developing circularity indicators is to help drive companies to adopt the circular economy approach. If they are already on that path then standardised indicators can help them track performance and prioritise actions. Alternatively, if others, such as investors or customers begin to require disclosure from their respective investees and suppliers, then this can further incentivise adoption, just as has happened over the past two decades with carbon accounting.

Overall, companies see opportunity in following the circular economy model. It allows them to capture additional value from their products and materials once they have reached the end of their current use phase. Those economic opportunities are significant, totalling, for example, USD 630 billion of savings for medium-lived complex goods in the EU[6] and USD 706 billion for fast-moving consumer goods globally.[7] Such detailed analysis found that more economic value can often be captured in the end-of-use strategies corresponding to the inner, shorter, circles illustrated in Figure 1. Indeed, reusing a product preserves more of its integrity, embedded energy, and complexity than recycling it, which consists of only recovering its basic materials.

At a more granular level the anticipated applications of product-level circularity metrics are:

• To enable the design of new products to take circularity into account as criteria and input for design decisions. The metrics should allow designers to compare different versions ('what if?' scenarios) of a product regarding its circularity at the design stage. It could also be used to set designers' minimum circularity criteria. This can apply to new products as well as the further development of products, in particular with the aim to make those more circular. Aspects of a product design that can be influenced by the circularity scores go from material choices to business and service models for the product.

• To be used for internal reporting purposes. Companies are able to compare different products. This also allows stakeholders from different departments to learn from each other regarding circular product design.

• To allow organisations across private and public sectors to use circularity indicators as part of their procurement process, for example by defining a minimum threshold for the products they buy.

And the anticipated applications of company-level indicators are:

• Used internally to compare the circularity of different departments and product ranges. They can also allow tracking of progress on a product range, department or at the whole company level.
• Reported publicly by the company to illustrate its overall progress towards a circular business model.
• Used by company rating organisations to compare the circularity of different companies that make their scores available to them.
• Used by investors to inform their investment decisions, particularly with respect to minimising longer-term risks to volatile and increasing raw material costs.
• Used to benchmark different companies within a given sector.

The Material Circularity Indicator

The Material Circularity Indicator developed under the Circular Indicators Project measures the extent to which the material flows associated with a product or company have shifted from a linear to a restorative model. It is based on the following four principles:
i)   using feedstock from recycled or reused sources,
ii) reusing or recycling materials or components at end of a use phase,
iii) keeping products in use longer, and
iv) making more intensive use of products.

The current version of the methodology focuses exclusively on the technical cycle as the circularity strategies and associated business benefits are better understood than those relating to the biological cycle. The technical cycle is illustrated on the right-hand side of Figure 1.

The question arises whether a *product is more circular because it has a longer serviceable life, even if at end of use it is being landfilled?* as covered by principles iii) and iv). These are considered appropriate as case studies have shown that an increased serviceable life or a higher usage intensity leads to substantial materials savings – see for example the analysis of reusable bottles in *Towards the Circular Economy* (2013). In addition, longer serviceable lives often enable the creation of repair, reuse and/or resale (e.g. refillable products or second-hand shops) and are therefore well suited to the idea of increased circularity.

Figure 1 **Circular economy systems diagram**

PRINCIPLES

1

Preserve and enhance natural capital by controlling finite stocks and balancing renewable resource flows – for example, replacing fossil fuels with renewable energy or using the maximum sustainable yield method to preserve fish stocks.

2

Optimise resource yields by circulating products, components and materials at the highest utility at all times in both technical and biological cycles – for example, sharing or looping products and extending product use cycles.

3

Foster system effectiveness by revealing and designing out negative externalities, such as water, air, soil, and noise pollution; climate change; toxins; congestion; and negative health effects related to resource use.

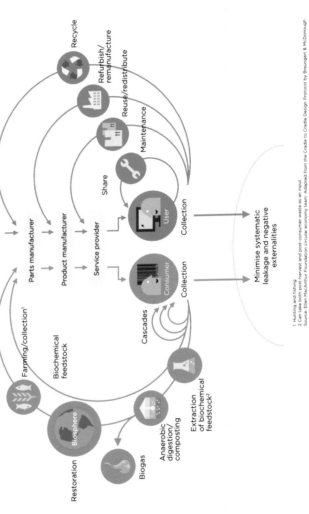

1 Hunting and fishing
2 Can take both post-harvest and post-consumer waste as an input.
Source: Ellen MacArthur Foundation circular economy team. Adapted from the Cradle to Cradle Design Protocol by Braungart & McDonough

In the development of the Material Circularity Indicator the proportion of the product being restored – through reuse and recycling – and coming from restored sources (i.e. principles i) and ii)) is described as the restorative part of the flow. Principles iii) and iv) are treated as improvements on the linear part of the flow, that is, the part that comes from virgin materials and ends up as landfill or energy recovery.

The product-level Material Circularity Indicator then measures the extent to which a product has minimised the linear and maximised the restorative flow of its component materials. It is essentially constructed from a combination of three product characteristics: the mass of virgin raw material used in manufacture, the mass of unrecoverable waste,[8] and a utility factor that accounts for the length and intensity of the use phase. The associated material flows are summarised in Figure 2.

Figure 2 **Representation of material flows**

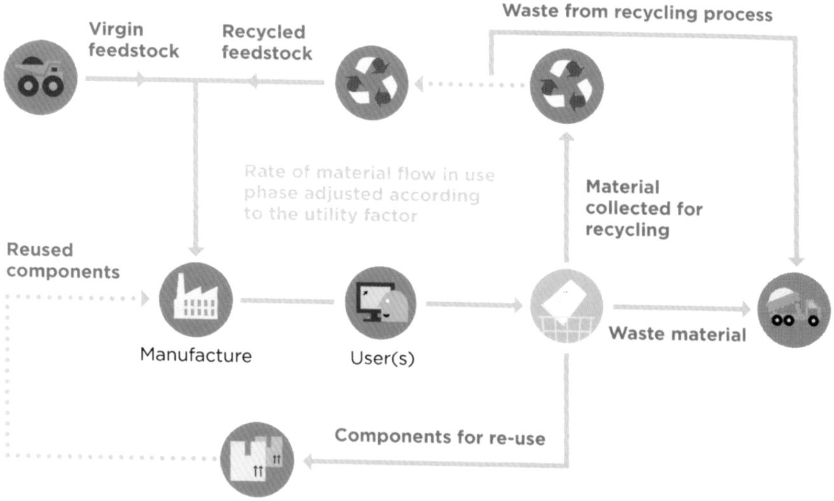

Any product that is manufactured only using virgin feedstock and ends up in landfill at the end of its use phase can be considered a fully 'linear' product. On the other hand, any product that contains no virgin feedstock and is completely collected for recycling or reuse at the end of its use phase can be considered a fully 'circular' product. In practice, most products sit somewhere between these two extremes and the Material Circularity Indicator (MCI) measures the level of circularity in the range 0 to 1 (fully circular).

The dashed lines in Figure 2 indicate that the methodology does not require a perfectly closed loop. That is to say, for example, that recycled feedstock does not have to be sourced from the same product but can be sourced on the open market.

The full methodology complete with its derivation from first principles is available for public download from the Ellen MacArthur Foundation's website.[9] It went through two detailed peer reviews by an expert panel of reviewers and was tested by a group of companies using real product data. Testing was an iterative process running through five test phases and including in-person and virtual workshops. Each iteration used data from existing, in-market products to test the validity of the methodology. A number of potential re-designs were also assessed to evaluate the effect of more circular products on the MCI. After each test cycle the full methodology was reviewed and improvements incorporated.

In addition to the product-level indicator, the development of a company Material Circularity Indicator[10] was based on the working hypothesis that the material circularity of a company can be built up from a summation of the company's products. As such the Material Circularity Indicator for a company follows the same general approach as the Material Circularity Indicator for a product.

For many businesses it would not be practical to undertake a Material Circularity Indicator assessment for every single product it places on the market. The company methodology therefore takes a reference product approach where each reference product represents a range of similar products.

On the one hand, the greater the number of reference products the more accurate the company assessment is likely to be. On the other hand, the lower the number of reference products the more practical the process becomes. Therefore, it is not possible to give a general rule on how many reference products should be chosen. This is up to the user of the methodology. However, the user is asked to describe the process undertaken for reference product selection and the criteria used to draw an appropriate balance between accuracy and practicality.

For a product to be part of a product range represented by a reference product, it should be sufficiently similar to the reference product. In particular it should exhibit:

• similar material composition in terms of the types of materials and their relative masses;

* similar levels of recycled and reused content in the feedstock;
* similar levels of recycling and reuse at the end of the use phase; and
* similar levels of length and intensity of use.

When a company has one or more ranges of products that together constitute a small amount of the company's overall business activities then these can be omitted from the assessment according to a *de minimis* rule. The methodology specifically requires that:

* the total of the mass of all *de minimis* products is not greater than 5% of the total mass of shipped product, and
* the total revenue arising from *de minimis* products is not greater than 5% of the total revenue arising from shipped product.

If either of these criteria is not satisfied then further reference products need to be created.

The Material Circularity Indicator for each reference product can now be determined using the standard product approach. This Material Circularity Indicator is then applied to all products in the reference product range.

In order to combine the Material Circularity Indicators for a number of reference products representing different product ranges, there needs to be a normalising factor that is used to determine a weighted average value for a company's material circularity.

In the Circular Indicators project, a number of candidates were considered for the normalising factor. All have advantages and disadvantages and at present the user is asked to choose between product mass and sales revenue as defined below:

Table 1 **Normalising factor options**

Factor	Definition	Comments
Product mass	The mass of the final manufactured product. Equal to the parameter M used in the product-level methodology.	• Mass is the option most consistent with the product-level MCI. • Heavy products can dominate the final result. • Input data is easily available
Sales revenue	Revenue (turnover) generated from the sale of the product.	• Input data is easily obtainable from company accounting systems

The Material Circularity Indicator is not a silver bullet

While the Material Circularity Indicator provides an indication of how much a product's materials circulate, it neither takes into account what these materials are, nor does it provide information on other impacts of the product. It would therefore be extremely risky to make business decisions on the basis of the Material Circularity Indicator alone. As additional support to decision-making, the Material Circularity Indicator methodology recommends an approach to prioritise product and company improvements by using the Material Circularity Indicator in combination with two types of complementary indicators that identify associated risks and impacts:

• Complementary risk indicators give an indication on the urgency of implementing circular practices. These are related to the drivers for change from the current linear model. These include, for example, measures of material scarcity, which has a substantial impact on the value of recovering them, and a measure of toxicity, which impacts the risks and costs of manufacture, reverse logistics, and public safety liabilities.

• Complementary impact indicators giving an indication of some of the benefits of circular models. They include energy and water impacts as well as assessing the impact on profitability of moving to more circular business models.

In this respect the Material Circularity Indicator (MCI) presents the following differences and common points with Life-Cycle Assessment (LCA) methodologies:

• LCA focuses on assessing a range of environmental impacts throughout the life cycle of a product for different scenarios, whereas the MCI concentrates on the flow of materials through the product life cycle. The MCI specifically encourages the use of recycled or reused material and recycling or reusing it at the end of use, while recognising increased utility of a product (e.g. durability or usage intensity).

• Many of the input data required for an LCA are the same as for the MCI and many complementary impact indicators may indeed be derived from an LCA approach (e.g. using the ISO standard to assess the carbon footprint of a product). Additionally, in the future, the MCI could be one of the environmental parameters considered as an output from an LCA or eco-design approach, alongside those already typically used.

The Widget Store case study[11]

Due to the commercial sensitivity of the data it is not possible to disclose results for actual products assessed during the development of the methodology. However, an indicative case study for the fictitious company *Widget Store* has been developed to illustrate how the Circularity Indicators can be used. It has been inspired by actual examples and real world cases of companies adopting circular economy principles.

The Widget Store has an annual turnover of EUR 30.7m and ships 3,600 tonnes of product every year.

The current product range

The head designer of Widget Store wants to compare the circularity of Widget Store's products. The company produces a predominantly ABS plastic standard widget and a predominantly aluminium premium widget. The plastic is from virgin sources and the aluminium supplier uses half recycled, half virgin input. Collection data for Widget Store's main markets show that three quarters of the aluminium and one quarter of the ABS are usually recycled. However, the ABS is mixed in with other plastics during the collection process resulting in a much lower recycling efficiency compared to the aluminium. The latest customer survey that shows Widget Store's standard widgets are usually used for 8 years and premium widgets for 12 years, while the industry average is 10 years.

Table 2 **Evaluation of materials used in widgets**

Material	Feedstock		End of Use Collection Rates		Recycling Process Efficiency
	Reused	Recycled	For Reuse	For Recycling	
Aluminium	0%	50%	0%	75%	90%
ABS plastic	0%	0%	0%	25%	40%

Using a tool based on the Circularity Indicators methodology, the head designer computes the Material Circularity Indicator of the standard widget to be 0.06 and that of the premium widget to be 0.61. The large difference reflects the much higher levels of recycled feedstock and of after-use recycling, along with the higher recycling efficiency, for aluminium compared to ABS.

Improving the design

After learning more about the circular economy and circular products and business models, the head designer convinces the CEO of Widget Store to trial a new widget better leveraging circular economy opportunities.

The Circularity Indicators tool is used to test the circularity of possible designs. The newly selected product weighs less than the current widget range. It is still made of aluminium and ABS but only uses material feedstock from recycled sources. Working with their suppliers and customers, Widget Store also introduces a closed-loop return system, meaning that it collects all old widgets after their use. Experience shows that 83% of the aluminium components can be reused while the rest of the product goes into two mono-material recycling streams which also allows for an increase in the ABS recycling efficiency. The lifetime of the new widget is found to be similar to the existing premium products.

Table 3 **Bill of materials for a circular widget**

Material	Feedstock		End of use collection rates		Recycling process efficiency
	Reused	Recycled	For Reuse	For Recycling	
Aluminium	83%	17%	83%	17%	90%
ABS plastic	0%	100%	0%	100%	80%

The Material Circularity Indicator of the newly designed circular widget is a near perfect 0.98.

Improving the widget's carbon footprint

The head designer wanted to see if the changed design not only improved the Material Circularity Indicator but also reduced a widget's carbon footprint – an example of a complementary impact indicator.

Using industry standard carbon intensities for aluminium and ABS, the carbon footprints have been calculated.

Table 4 **Widget carbon footprints**

	Mass (kg)	CO_2e (kg)
Standard widget	10	42.1
Premium widget	10	58.1
Circular widget	7	3.9

The premium widget has a somewhat higher carbon footprint than the standard widget due to the higher carbon intensity of aluminium compared to ABS. The much improved carbon footprint for the circular widget is due to the very significant reductions in virgin raw material use.

Profitability and business models
The Widget Store's finance team produces a business case for the new circular widget. They identify significant manufacturing cost savings through component reuse and furthermore increased customer loyalty due to the take-back process. Additionally, Widget Store offers a rental model whereby the customer can pay a service charge rather than buying the widget outright attracting some new customers.

Overall, the business case for the new circular product is very attractive, not only demonstrating higher margins but also increasing customer loyalty.

Company-level circularity
The Widget Store's Board is so impressed by the commercial success of the new circular widget that it makes circularity an important part of the company's business strategy and decides to compute the company's overall Material Circularity Indicator.

Widget Store produces a wide range of standard, premium and circular widgets, and the specific products considered earlier serve as reference products for these ranges. Using the revenue numbers for the different widgets a weighted average Material Circularity Indicator of 0.60 is calculated for the Widget Store company as shown in Figure 3.

Figure 3 **Consolidating three product ranges into a company-level score**

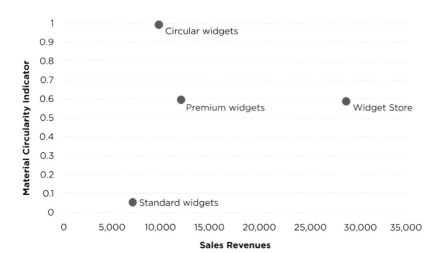

Figure 4 shows the improvement in various Widget Store KPIs as a result of moving towards a more circular business model. Scenario A was the position before introduction of the circular widget. Scenario B represents the situation described above and scenario C an extrapolated company target. The aluminium material cost saving represents the savings associated with the reduced purchase of aluminium due to the reuse of components.

Widget Store also incorporates this analysis in its annual report to shareholders, highlighting the commercial success of its circular widget range. A number of industry analysts were struck by these insights and asked other companies in the sector to disclose similar information. This led to circularity becoming an important competitive issue in the industry.

Figure 4 **Improving KPIs as company circularity increases**

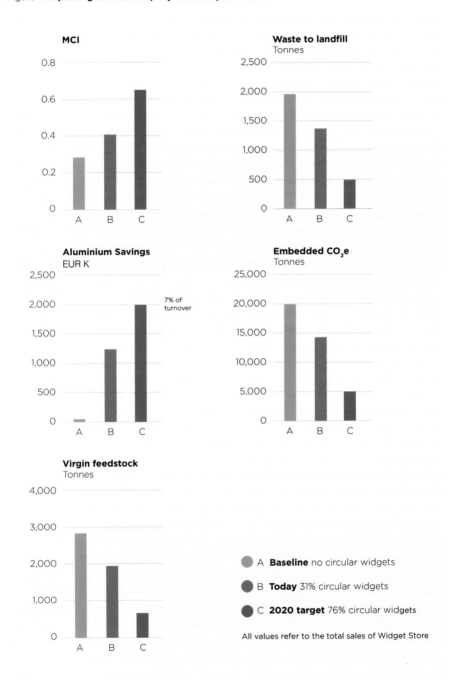

MCI

Waste to landfill
Tonnes

Aluminium Savings
EUR K

7% of turnover

Embedded CO$_2$e
Tonnes

Virgin feedstock
Tonnes

A **Baseline** no circular widgets

B **Today** 31% circular widgets

C **2020 target** 76% circular widgets

All values refer to the total sales of Widget Store

Future developments

The current Material Circularity Indicator methodology has focused on the technical cycle and materials from technical sources. An important next step would be to extend it to embrace biological cycles and materials from biological sources, including consumables like food. This might also include a proper consideration of conversion of end-of-use materials into energy, for example via producing biofuels from food waste or burning wood.

The formulation of the Material Circularity Indicator could also be further refined, for example by:

• Developing a more comprehensive approach on downcycling, taking into account the level of material quality loss in the recycling process;
• Introducing a consideration for more granular levels of recovery beyond recycling and reuse, such as remanufacturing or refurbishment.

While the current methodology allows one to consider the influence of leasing or hiring business models via improvements to the product's utility, the product-level methodology could further be extended to cover a wide range of business models, for example pure services and reselling via secondary markets. This would also allow an extension of the company-level methodology to include and allow comparisons between all kinds of companies.

Further developments could also extend the technique to consider Material Circularity Indicators for major projects, such as building a railway line, as well as Material Circularity Indicators for geographic regions, such as a city or state.

Finally, the methodology could be developed into an official standard such as an ISO standard. Such a standard could then also be used for the certification of products or companies.

Notes

1 European Environmental Agency, *Environmental Issues Series No 6: Life Cycle Assessment – a guide to approaches, experiences and information* (1997).
2 Ibid.
3 Greenhouse Gas Protocol, www.ghgprotocol.org
4 CDP website, www.cdp.net
5 The UK Companies Act 2006 (Strategic Report and Directors' Report) Regulations 2013 (S.I. 2008/393).
6 Ellen MacArthur Foundation, *Towards the Circular Economy 1* (2012).
7 Ellen MacArthur Foundation, *Towards the Circular Economy 2* (2013).
8 The term 'unrecoverable waste' covers landfill, waste to energy and any other type of process at end of use phase where the materials are no longer recoverable.
9 For Circularity Indicators see http://www.ellenmacarthurfoundation.org/programmes/insight/circularity-indicators
10 The pilot companies included CHEP, Cisco Systems, Desso, Dorel, Hewlett-Packard, Kingfisher, Nespresso and Rolls Royce.
11 This Widget Store case study is a simplified version of the one given in the full methodology which covers a wider span of product ranges.

CPSIA information can be obtained at www.ICGtesting.com
Printed in the USA
LVIW01n0218190118
563170LV00007B/61